Tolley's Commercial Contracts Checklists

Rex O Nwakodo
LLB (Hons), LLM
Barrister (SCN), Solicitor
Wallace LLP, Solicitors

Members of the LexisNexis Group worldwide

United Kingdom	LexisNexis UK, a Division of Reed Elsevier (UK) Ltd, 2 Addiscombe Road, CROYDON CR9 5AF
Argentina	LexisNexis Argentina, BUENOS AIRES
Australia	LexisNexis Butterworths, CHATSWOOD, New South Wales
Austria	LexisNexis Verlag ARD Orac GmbH & Co KG, VIENNA
Canada	LexisNexis Butterworths, MARKHAM, Ontario
Chile	LexisNexis Chile Ltda, SANTIAGO DE CHILE
Czech Republic	Nakladatelství Orac sro, PRAGUE
France	Editions du Juris-Classeur SA, PARIS
Germany	LexisNexis Deutschland GmbH, FRANKFURT AND MUNSTER
Hong Kong	LexisNexis Butterworths, HONG KONG
Hungary	HVG-Orac, BUDAPEST
India	LexisNexis Butterworths, NEW DELHI
Ireland	Butterworths (Ireland) Ltd, DUBLIN
Italy	Giuffrè Editore, MILAN
Malaysia	Malayan Law Journal Sdn Bhd, KUALA LUMPUR
New Zealand	LexisNexis Butterworths, WELLINGTON
Poland	Wydawnictwo Prawnicze LexisNexis, WARSAW
Singapore	LexisNexis Butterworths, SINGAPORE
South Africa	LexisNexis Butterworths, DURBAN
Switzerland	Stämpfli Verlag AG, BERNE
USA	LexisNexis, DAYTON, Ohio

© Reed Elsevier (UK) Ltd 2004

All rights reserved. No part of this publication may be reproduced in any material form (including photocopying or storing it in any medium by electronic means and whether or not transiently or incidentally to some other use of this publication) without the written permission of the copyright owner except in accordance with the provisions of the Copyright, Designs and Patents Act 1988 or under the terms of a licence issued by the Copyright Licensing Agency Ltd, 90 Tottenham Court Road, London, England W1T 4LP. Applications for the copyright owner's written permission to reproduce any part of this publication should be addressed to the publisher.

Warning: The doing of an unauthorised act in relation to a copyright work may result in both a civil claim for damages and criminal prosecution.

Crown copyright material is reproduced with the permission of the Controller of HMSO and the Queen's Printer for Scotland. Any European material in this work which has been reproduced from EUR-lex, the official European Communities legislation website, is European Communities copyright.

Whilst every care has been taken to ensure the accuracy of the contents of this work, no responsibility for loss occasioned to any person acting or refraining from action as a result of any statement in it can be accepted by any of the authors, editors or the publishers.

A CIP Catalogue record for this book is available from the British Library.

ISBN 0406979545

Typeset by Letterpart Ltd, Reigate, Surrey

Printed and bound in Great Britain by Hobbs the Printers Ltd, Totton, Hampshire

Visit LexisNexis UK at www.lexisnexis.co.uk

Dedication

For Sir Rex and Lady Felly Nwakodo
  'Always ... '

To Nnena, Chi-Chi and Zee
  'It's done ...   now!'

Acknowledgements

Let me take this opportunity to thank a number of people. I would like to first thank Cara Annett of LexisNexis for all her hard work in progressing and completing this project.

I must also mention my partners and colleagues at Wallace LLP, in particular Claire Davies and Melanie Costello for all their hard work. I also thank Chiji, Obi, Ola and Anayo for their guidance and support at all times. There are also others deserving of thanks whom I have not acknowledged personally.

Finally, as with all matters, my family are most deserving of thanks for their patience, love, encouragement and support. NneChiZee, I told you 'it's done'.

Rex Nwakodo

Preface

This book has been prepared to provide practical guidance in general terms in relation to various commercial agreements and transactions. It is not a legal textbook but a practical guidance tool for business. The general commentary provides an overview of the relevant contract or transaction, sets out the practical guidance, main issues to consider, sample provisions and definitions, in addition to a contract/transaction checklist with precedent.

The book is designed as a useful and practical ready desk reference tool for reviewing, understanding, negotiating or preparing a wide range of commercial agreements or documents. The checklists, precedents and practical guidance contained in this book are intended as guides only as to matters to consider. They should not be treated as a comprehensive guide on all subjects or matters to consider.

The checklists and precedents contain an extensive range of specimen draft contracts, matters and documents which most businesses will find useful, may require or could get involved with in the course of business. The precedents are all drafted under English law and should not be used blindly but as a mere starting point. Each precedent must be used with caution and always be amended to reflect the particular circumstances. All errors or omissions are mine. Any feedback or comments on this work may be addressed to me or the publisher.

I hope the users of this work find it practical and very useful. The book is not to be taken as a substitute for legal advice and such advice should always be sought. My firm, Wallace LLP will always be happy to provide such advice.

Rex Nwakodo

London, September 2004

About the Author

Rex Nwakodo is a Partner and Head of Commercial Technology and Media at Wallace LLP. His practice areas are corporate, commercial, technology, intellectual property and international.

Rex advises on business sales and purchases, re-organisations, joint ventures, MBOs and other corporate transactions. He leads the firm's technology/media practice and has extensive experience of outsourcing and commercial agreements. He specialises in technology, media, IP, information practice matters, the internet, e-commerce and on-line trading issues. Rex also advises on international commercial contracts and arrangements. He acts for a number of commercial organisations including media, entertainment and technology businesses.

Rex speaks regularly at seminars in the UK and abroad on various commercial law subjects. He writes articles for several publications and is the author of *Commercial Contracts and Transactions*, a regular and major contributor to *E-Contracts* (LexisNexis) and has also contributed to *Business Client Handbook*.

rex.nwakodo@wallace.co.uk
www.wallace.co.uk
One Portland Place
London
W1B 1PN
Tel: +44 (0) 20 7636 4422
Fax: +44 (0) 20 7636 3736

Contents

1	General Contracts and Arrangements		
	1.1	Confidentiality and Non-Disclosure Agreement	3
	1.2	Heads of Terms/Letter of Intent	11
	1.3	Exclusivity and Lock Out Agreement	20
	1.4	Commission Agreement	26
	1.5	Finder's Fee Agreement	32
	1.6	Memorandum of Understanding Agreement	35
	1.7	Non-Circumvention and Fee Protection Agreement	39
	1.8	Test and Evaluation Licence Agreement	42
2	General Commercial Agreements		
	2.1	Manufacturing Agreement	51
	2.2	Venue Hire Agreement	61
	2.3	Terms and Conditions Agreement	72
	2.4	Representation/Agency Agreement	86
	2.5	Marketing Agreement	97
	2.6	Franchising Agreement	105
	2.7	Provision of Services Agreement	120
	2.8	Distribution Contract	128
	2.9	Consultancy Agreement	140
	2.10	Management Agreement	149
3	Computer/Technology Agreements		
	3.1	Software/Hardware Sale and Purchase Agreement	165
	3.2	Licensing Agreement	177
	3.3	Maintenance and Support Agreement	192
	3.4	Escrow Agreement	201
	3.5	Information Technology Procurement and Turnkey Contract	211
	3.6	Outsourcing/Application Service Provision Agreement	223
4	Lending and Security Documents		
	4.1	Loan Agreement	241
	4.2	Security Document (Legal Charge/Debenture)	251
	4.3	Guarantee	261
5	Intellectual Property and Media-Related Agreements		
	5.1	Sponsorship Agreement	271
	5.2	Technical Services/Know-How Agreement	282
	5.3	Data Processor Agreement	292
	5.4	Presenter's Agreement	303
	5.5	Contributor's Agreement	312
	5.6	Research and Development Agreement	319
6	Corporate Contracts		
	6.1	Acquisition Due Diligence Questionnaire	331
	6.2	Employment/Service Agreement	337
	6.3	Share/Asst Sale and Purchase Agreements	348
	6.4	Joint Venture/Shareholders Agreement	360

Contents

	6.5	Partnership Agreement	371
7	Internet and E-Commerce Contracts		
	7.1	Web Development/Hosting	385
	7.2	Website Materials	396
	7.3	Advertising Terms and Conditions/Agreements	404
	7.4	Affiliate Program Services Agreement	412
	7.5	Promotion Agreement	422

Table of Statutes

Business Names Act 1985   6.5

Companies act 1985   2.6, 4.1, 4.2, 6.3, 6.4, 6.5
     s 395   2.3
     s 736   2.5, 6.3
     s 744   6.4

Companies Act 1989   2.5

Competition Act 1998   2.6, 2.8, 5.6, 6.3, 6.4

Compliance with Business Names Act 1985   6.5

Consumer Protection Act 1987   2.3, 2.8

Contracts (Rights of Third Parties) Act 1999   6.3

Copyright, Designs and Patents Act 1988   1.8, 3.1, 3.2, 5.5
     Part II   5.4

Data Protection Act 1998   2.4, 2.6, 3.3, 3.6, 5.3, 6.2, 6.4, 7.1, 7.2

Employment Rights Act 1996   6.2

Finance Act 2000   5.5, 5.6

Finance Act 2003   6.3

Financial Services and Markets Act 2000   1.5

Income and Corporation Tax Act 1988   6.3

Insolvency Act 1986   4.2
     s 123   3.2

Landlord and Tenant Act 1954   2.10

Late Payments of Commercial Debts (Interest) Act 1998   2.3

Law of Property Act 1925   4.2

Law of Property (Miscellaneous Provisions) Act 1994   6.3

Limitation Act 1980   6.3

Limited Liability Partnership Act 2000   6.5

Occupiers' Liability Act 1957   2.2

Partnership Act 1890   6.5

Sale of Goods Act 1979   2.8, 3.1

Sale and Supply of Goods and Services Act 1982   2.8, 3.1, 3.3

Supply of Goods and Services Act 1982   3.1

Taxes Act 1988   6.2

Trade Marks Act 1994   1.8, 2.6

Taxation of Chargeable Gains Act 1992   6.3

Unfair Contract Terms Act 1977   1.4, 2.1, 2.2, 2.3, 2.8, 2.9, 3.1, 3.2

Table of Statutory Instruments

Commercial Agents (Council Directive) Regulations 1993 SI 1993/3053	2.4	Copyright and Rights in Databases Regulations 1997 SI 1997/3032	3.1
Control of Misleading Advertisements Regulations 1988 SI 1988/915	2.6	Transfer of Undertakings (Protection of Employment Regulations) 1981 SI 1981/1794	2.10, 3.6, 6.3
Control of Misleading Advertisements (Amendment) Regulations 2000 SI 2000/914	7.5	Unfair Terms in Consumer Contracts Regulations 1999 SI 1999/2083	2.3, 2.8, 3.1, 3.2, 3.3
Consumer Protection (Distance Selling) Regulations 2000 SI 2000/2334	2.3, 7.2	Working Time Regulations 1988 SI 1998/1833	6.2

1 General Contracts and Arrangements

1.1 Confidentiality and Non-Disclosure Agreement

1.2 Heads of Terms/Letter of Intent

1.3 Exclusivity and Lock Out Agreement

1.4 Commission Agreement

1.5 Finder's Fee Agreement

1.6 Memorandum of Understanding Agreement

1.7 Non-Circumvention and Fee Protection Agreement

1.8 Test and Evaluation Licence Agreement

General Contracts and Arrangements

1.1 Confidentiality and Non-Disclosure Agreement

Overview

Description of Agreement/Document

A confidentiality agreement, or non-disclosure agreement, is a standard document in many commercial transactions. The agreement relates to the disclosure and protection of confidential information and confirms the relationship of confidence between the parties. It sets out in detail the expectations of the discloser of information and the obligations undertaken by the recipient of such information. The principal obligations relate to the use of information for a specific purpose and prohibition of unauthorised disclosures.

Practical Guidance/Issues List

It is essential that owners of confidential business information seek appropriate practical methods of protecting such information. The following practical steps may be of assistance to any business or person seeking to protect their information and/or provide evidence of ownership:
- Record the manner in which they obtained or hold information.
- Mark or stamp such documents containing relevant information with the usual "secret and confidential".
- Set up a confidentiality procedure or process (involving storage, monitoring of disclosure and destruction of confidential documents).
- Disclose confidential documents on the basis of a sealed envelope marked "secret and confidential" attached to a confidentiality letter indicating that it is not to be opened until the accompanying confidentiality letter is read, accepted and signed.
- Produce a record indicating dates or periods when the information was produced and the manner of creation of the confidential information.
- Restrict access to persons under obligations or confidentiality.
- Ensure that any recipient of information understands and acknowledges that the information is regarded as confidential.
- Make sure that prior to any disclosure, the recipient enters into a written confidentiality letter or agreement expressly dealing with the relevant rights and obligations.
- Produce and maintain records of costs and expenses involved in the creation and maintenance of the information together with the time spent in such creation so as to provide, if required, an indication of value, loss or damages.
- Deposit a copy of a confidential report setting out the information to a solicitor or other professional for safekeeping and to assert copyright with all rights reserved.
- Maintain a list of recipients of the confidential information or reports containing the business intelligence together with a record of when, how and to whom it is disclosed. Provide a sealed copy duly stamped and post a copy to oneself by recorded or registered delivery to be kept unopened with the date stamp as evidence of the confidentiality and possession at the relevant time by the owner.
- Seek legal advice and guidance from an experienced lawyer as to the best form of protection and relevant or additional steps.

Law/Compliance Requirement

The law of confidence can be found in case law and breach of confidence is recognised as an equitable wrong. The cases establish the relevant elements of confidential information, identify relationships or situations importing obligations of confidence and set out the position in respect of liability and available remedies. The remedies for breach of a confidentiality agreement vary and may in relevant circumstances include damages, accounting for profits, injunction, specific performance, disposal or delivery up of the discloser's property.

Confidentiality and non-disclosure agreements are used as a standard in business to protect information which a party considers particularly sensitive and which that party wishes to limit the use of following disclosure to a third party. This is usually pursuant to a transaction or other arrangement.

It is always worthwhile to review and consider practical measures as to how best to protect such information.

Commercial Contracts Checklists

Advice should be taken in specific or relevant situations as the position may differ in relation to employees, investors, business partners, consultants or inventors.

Some Key Definitions

'Authorised Person' means [specify as relevant or general as follows] any employee, director, consultant or agent of the [Recipient] and any other named firm, individual or company engaged in providing services directly to the [Recipient] [and/or] who has been previously approved in writing by the [Discloser].

'Confidential Information' means [specifically defined information or general as follows] such information as the [Discloser] may from time to time provide to the [Recipient] (in whatever form including without limitation orally, written, electronic, tape, disk, physical or visual form), relating to the [Project], and all know-how, trade secrets, tactical, scientific, statistical, financial, commercial or technical information of any kind [directly or indirectly] disclosed [before or after the date of this Agreement] by the [Discloser] to the [Recipient or any Authorised Person] whether in existence at the date of this Agreement or which subsequently comes into existence including any copies, reproductions, duplicates or notes in any form whatsoever.

'Project' means [details of project, engagement or otherwise].

'Purpose' means the permitted purpose of review and evaluation of the Confidential Information in connection with [the proposed transaction].

Specific Provisions

Acknowledgement
The Recipient acknowledges that the rights which are sought to be protected by this Agreement are unique and that any breach by it or by an Authorised Person of these terms would cause the Discloser irreparable and unquantifiable damage and that the Discloser shall be entitled to apply for and obtain (but without prejudice to any such rights as the Discloser may have to obtain damages in any such respect) interlocutory and/or final injunctive or other equitable relief against or in respect of any actual or threatened breach hereof by the Recipient or any Authorised Person.

Indemnity
The Recipient agrees that it shall be responsible for any breach of any of the terms of this Agreement by it (including its directors, officers, agents and employees) or by any Authorised Person and the Recipient will indemnify the Discloser from and against all loss or damage (including but not limited to legal costs) which may arise from the unauthorised disclosure or use of any of the Confidential Information by the Recipient or its directors, officers, agents or employees, or by any Authorised Person.

General Contracts and Arrangements

Appendix 1.1 Confidentiality Agreement Checklist

In preparing a heads of terms/letters of intent/heads of agreement, individuals or businesses should consider the following non-exhaustive matters.

Actions/Issues:	Comments:	✎

1. Consider relevant parties, details and information to be covered, the permitted purpose together with relevant exclusions to the non-disclosure obligations. In particular: ☐

    1.1 consider the purpose of the agreement; ☐

    1.2 consider whether the agreement should be unilateral or reciprocal; ☐

    1.3 consider the correct parties to the agreement; ☐

    1.4 consider whether to specify a sole contact for each party to be responsible for handling the information and disclosures; ☐

    1.5 consider whether the agreement should be unilateral or reciprocal; ☐

    1.6 verify the correct contracting party's name, correspondence, service or business address together with other contact details (email and fax); ☐

    1.7 state the extent of confidential information and provide details of the product or business process to which it relates (if applicable); ☐

    1.8 state how and in what form the information will be disclosed (orally, written, tape, disk or other form). ☐

2. Consider specific undertakings from the recipient including: ☐

    2.1 an obligation to use of the confidential information for the permitted purpose only; ☐

    2.2 a non-competition restriction on the recipient for a specified time from disclosure of the information, termination of agreement or return of the information; ☐

    2.3 a non-solicitation restriction on the recipient in respect of the discloser's business, customers and employees; ☐

    2.4 a lock-out period during which the discloser will not be able to contract with another party following supply and disclosure of information to the recipient (or otherwise allow third parties access to the confidential information in connection with the proposed transaction); ☐

Commercial Contracts Checklists

2.5 an exclusivity period during which the recipient has exclusive access to the information for evaluation purposes in connection with a negotiation, product review and analysis or proposed transaction; ☐

2.6 restrictions on the recipient copying the information in whole or in part or otherwise adapting the information without prior written consent of the discloser; ☐

2.7 indemnifying the discloser for any costs in implementing or enforcing the agreement; ☐

2.8 an express obligation by the recipient not to directly or indirectly seek or procure a commercial advantage over the discloser through use or disclosure of the information; ☐

2.9 an obligation to inform the discloser of any unauthorised or inadvertent disclosures by the recipient; ☐

2.10 use of the confidential information and disclosure on any other transaction specific terms as agreed between the parties. ☐

3 What is the term of the agreement and for how long will the obligations subsist? Consider: ☐

3.1 exactly how long the specific obligations are required to last; ☐

3.2 commencement date of the agreement; ☐

3.3 the appropriate period of the agreement; ☐

3.4 any general or specific termination rights; ☐

3.5 any required procedure for dealing with destruction or return of information at the end of the term; ☐

3.6 whether the agreement and its obligations will be ongoing or subject to an end date; ☐

3.7 any provisions which will or are intended to survive termination of the agreement or expiration of the term. ☐

4 Consider whether there will be: ☐

4.1 a payment to the discloser; ☐

4.2 reference to other form of value or consideration (including exchange of information); ☐

4.3 execution of the agreement by deed as is necessary if there is no consideration. ☐

General Contracts and Arrangements

5 Consider the permitted use(s) of the confidential information. Will the information be used for: ☐

    5.1 evaluation in connection with an acquisition or other commercial transaction? ☐

    5.2 intellectual property research and development? ☐

    5.3 review and evaluation in connection with the manufacture or distribution of a product? ☐

    5.4 ascertaining the viability of a process, product or transaction? ☐

    5.5 any other specific purpose? ☐

6 Are there any authorised disclosures? Can the information be disclosed to: ☐

    6.1 any employee? ☐

    6.2 selected employees only (on a need to know basis or those forming part of the project team)? ☐

    6.3 directors or officers of the recipient? ☐

    6.4 agents and representatives of the recipient? ☐

    6.5 bankers, financiers and investors? ☐

    6.6 professional advisors of the recipient? ☐

    6.7 any other person? ☐

7 Should there be an obligation: ☐

    7.1 that information disclosed by the recipient be disclosed only to those bound by confidentiality obligations to the recipient? ☐

    7.2 on the recipient to procure compliance with the agreement by those to whom it discloses the information? ☐

    7.3 for subsequent recipients of the information from the recipient to sign an acknowledgement or express agreement? (Will this be practicable?) ☐

    7.4 to maintain a list of recipients of the confidential information together with relevant records? ☐

Commercial Contracts Checklists

8   Exclude the right or ability of the recipient to acquire any rights in the disclosed information. ☐

9   What is the status of the information supplied to the recipient by the discloser? Can the document or information be copied? Are there any notification or further record keeping requirements? ☐

10   Consider the specific purpose of disclosing the information and whether sufficient restrictions have been imposed on the recipient as to use and to whose benefit? Are there any transaction specific restrictions required? ☐

11   Consider what the consequences of unauthorised disclosure will be for the business and review available legal remedies including: ☐

     11.1   damages; ☐

     11.2   injunction; ☐

     11.3   account for profits; ☐

     11.4   destruction or return of property; ☐

     11.5   specific performance; ☐

     11.6   any indemnities for loss or enforcement of the agreement by the discloser. ☐

12   Specify or consider agreed terms as to: ☐

     12.1   storage and security of the information; ☐

     12.2   delivery of information; ☐

     12.3   contribution to or payment of legal costs for the preparation, negotiation and implementation of the agreement; ☐

     12.4   confirmation that the recipient does not already have the confidential information or similar information. ☐

13   Review and consider the circumstances in which the discloser can be forced to disclose the information to third parties? ☐

14   Consider disclosure of information by the recipient to relevant bodies including regulatory authorities or agencies such as the Inland Revenue and Customs & Excise in connection with the payment of tax. ☐

15   Consider the effect and consequences of breach of the agreement or publication of the information by the recipient or its representatives. ☐

16 Review relevant arrangements as to termination, return or destruction of the information and the basis upon which such a request can be made. ☐

17 How will the confidential information be delivered? Consider use of a sealed envelope attached to the non-disclosure letter. ☐

18 Consider the authority of the signatory proposed on behalf of the recipient. ☐

19 Are there any other specific requirements in relation to maintaining the information? ☐

20 Exclude liability for errors in the information, its completeness, currency or accuracy. Consider excluding any commitment to proceed with further transaction as a result of the supply of information. ☐

21 Include acknowledgements by the recipient that no representations, expressions or opinions are made in relation to the information. ☐

22 Provide that the discloser can decline to provide further information and reserves the right to require the return of all information at anytime. ☐

23 Consider whether the rights under the agreement will be assignable. ☐

24 Consider: ☐

    24.1 restrictions on announcements; ☐

    24.2 entire agreement provision setting out that document contains the whole agreement between the parties and supersedes prior agreements; ☐

    24.3 notice provision setting out manner of and address for service of notices; ☐

    24.4 which clause or provision will survive termination if incorporated into another agreement; ☐

    24.5 further assurance provision requiring a party to sign further documents or do other things to further implement the agreement; ☐

    24.6 governing law and jurisdiction clause; ☐

    24.7 a provision relating to consent (where required, can it be unreasonably withheld or delayed?); ☐

    24.8 waiver, variation and severance provisions. ☐

25 Where forced disclosure is required by law, court or appropriate body: ☐

Commercial Contracts Checklists

    25.1   can the information be disclosed without further reference to the discloser or will there be an obligation on the recipient to notify the discloser? ☐

    25.2   will there be an undertaking by the recipient to assist the discloser (if required) to resist disclosure? ☐

26   Include an acknowledgement of the importance of the information and that breach of the agreement will cause irreparable and unquantifiable harm. ☐

27   Include acknowledgement that the discloser may obtain injunctive or other relief. ☐

28   Is a guarantee required or necessary? ☐

29   Are there any obligations on the discloser? Is the discloser subject to an obligation to keep the confidential information a secret? ☐

30   Seek confirmation of the authority of person signing on behalf of the recipient or any other party. ☐

31   Consider whether there are any applicable legal requirements in any jurisdiction where the agreement may need to be enforced. ☐

See Precedent 1.1 on accompanying CD.

1.2 Heads of Terms/Letter of Intent

Overview

Description of Agreement/Document

Heads of terms and letters of intent are documents used in commercial transactions by parties to set out in brief detail the proposed terms of their agreement, undertaking or arrangement. In certain cases, the document is more than a pre-contractual statement of terms and preliminary agreement and instead sets out the basic legal agreement. The legal status of such a document normally depends on the parties' intention as to whether or not the provisions are legally binding or non-binding. In most cases, the document is drafted as non-binding but with specific provisions having legal effect.

Practical Guidance/Issues List

The document should contain the important provisions as well as the 'understanding' or 'deal' rather than drafting points. Either party to a commercial arrangement or proposed transaction may require or prepare a set of heads of terms for different reasons.

Some practical guidance as to the relevant issues in relation to the document follows:
- Use of the phrase 'subject to contract' will assist with interpretation and should be enough to create a presumption against a binding contract.
- Avoid uses of phrases such as 'subject to terms', 'subject to definite documents', 'subject to approval', 'conditional agreement'; and 'subject to more complete documentation' as they may create ambiguity and may not be interpreted as intended.
- Avoid conflicting provisions to reduce uncertainty or difficulties of interpretation. The *contra proferentem* rule and other rules of construction can not always be relied upon to produce the anticipated effect. Clarity and plain English is always best.
- The document may be labelled or referred to by other terms including 'letter of intent', 'memorandum of understanding', 'heads of agreement', 'statement of terms' or simply 'heads' but it is the substance of the provisions that matters.
- It should be made clear whether the document relates to pre-contract matters or represents the agreement of the parties.
- The legal status of the document should be stated on the document to reflect the parties' intention and for the avoidance of doubt, as the various terms are meaningless in law. Again, it is the substance of the terms set out in the document that is important.
- Parties to such a document should be careful in the preparation of a draft heads of terms to avoid any misunderstanding and to properly reflect the intention.
- Care needs to be taken in drafting the document where the intention is not to be legally bound but yet all the main terms are agreed and set out in the document without any express exclusion of the intention to create a binding contract.
- Mostly, parties do not intend for the letter of intent to have legal effect but find it useful for detailing or outlining the proposed terms or transaction. In effect, they believe it makes it difficult for the other party to seek to change the basis or main terms agreed in principle prior to agreement.
- Regardless of what the document contains, there is always a risk where the parties have 'agreed' all relevant terms during their discussions that an agreement will be deemed to have been entered into between them. In effect, the agreed terms may constitute a sufficiently certain and enforceable agreement.
- Even if not legally binding as a whole, certain provisions of the heads can be made to have contractual force or effect and become legally enforceable. These usually relate to obligations of confidentiality, or an agreement to grant an exclusive period for consideration of the proposed transaction or evaluation of information prior to entry into the definitive agreement.
- Many such documents require a more detailed document or agreement to be prepared. In effect, a lot of time can be spent discussing, preparing or negotiating such a heads of terms document instead of the main or definitive agreement itself.
- In many cases, it will be better to simply proceed to the main or definitive agreements rather than negotiating a set of heads.
- It is always advisable to ensure that the relevant term (such as 'good faith') used in relation to the document does not impose any unintended obligation on a party especially with regard to other jurisdictions.

Law/Compliance Requirement

The basic law applicable to heads of terms or letters of intent is contract law. In particular, contract formation principles will apply. If the elements are complete for a legally binding agreement to come into existence, then a contract will be held to have come into force. If not, the provisions are simply for guidance and impose no contractual obligation on the parties.

The courts apply the laws of contact with reference to the parties' intentions. Case law has shown the importance of the parties' intentions and actions as well as certainty of provisions. In effect, the intention to exclude formation of a legally binding contract must be clear.

Use of heads of terms in certain sectors may be subject to legal restrictions or require compliance with specific industry regulations.

Misrepresentation may also be relevant in the event that provisions or terms in a letter of intent, or statements made during contract negotiations, may amount to misrepresentation.

Some Key Definitions

'Proposed Transaction' means the proposed [entry into a commercial arrangement in respect of [specify]] [acquisition of the business and assets of [Party X] in respect of which the principal terms and conditions are set out in this letter].

'Definitive Documentation' means the agreements [or the following agreements] to be prepared (incorporating the principal terms set out in this letter), negotiated and entered into by the parties with the intention of creating binding legal relations.

'Exclusivity Period' means the period starting on the date of this agreement and ending on [200[ ]] (or such earlier date on which both parties agree that the Proposed Transaction shall not proceed) granted to [Party B] for the purpose of [reviewing the documents/due diligence/negotiating the transaction/assessing or evaluating the viability of the Proposed Transaction].

Specific Provisions

Documentation
The parties agree to [negotiate in good faith and] enter into the Definitive Documentation in relation to the Proposed Transaction. Accordingly, each party shall instruct their respective solicitors to proceed with preparation of the Definitive Documents and to seek to agree the terms within the specified timetable.

Legal Force and Effect
The provisions of clauses [ ] to [ ] inclusive as set out in this letter are and shall remain wholly the parties' current intentions relating to the Proposed Transaction and are not intended to be legally binding or have legal force or create enforceable rights.

Offer
Notwithstanding any provision to the contrary, nothing in this [letter] shall be taken to constitute an irrevocable offer to contract or an agreement to execute the Proposed Transaction.

Binding Obligations
Paragraphs [ ] to [ ] inclusive of this letter are legally binding and will become enforceable by the parties upon execution or counter signature of this letter.

Appendix 1.2 Heads of Terms/Agreement Checklist

In preparing a heads of terms/letters of intent/heads of agreement, individuals or businesses should consider the following non-exhaustive matters.

Actions/Issues:		Comments:	✍

1. Consider:

    1.1 relevant parties to the document;

    1.2 transaction details;

    1.3 proposed principal terms;

    1.4 legal status of document;

    1.5 any agreed assumptions;

    1.6 purpose of document;

    1.7 need for such a pre-agreement or formal 'heads' (obtain commitment from other party);

    1.8 effect on future negotiations and drafting of definitive agreements;

    1.9 whether best to proceed to main agreement if straightforward transaction.

2. Review proposed provisions and in particular consider:

    2.1 taking advice on specific issues;

    2.2 consequences of document;

    2.3 whether it should be legally binding, partially binding or non-binding;

    2.4 in general any required approvals or consents;

    2.5 advice on any risk of adverse tax consequences;

    2.6 responsibilities for drafting definitive agreements;

Commercial Contracts Checklists

    2.7   proposed timetable. ☐

3   Specify or consider: ☐

    3.1   any provisions intended to be legally binding (if generally non-binding heads of terms); ☐

    3.2   making it clear that the document is subject to contract and not legally binding except as expressly and specifically provided; ☐

    3.3   main transaction terms or agreed points and if relevant; ☐

    3.4   parties involved; ☐

    3.5   agreed transaction or intention; ☐

    3.6   mechanism or process; ☐

    3.7   applicable timetable; ☐

    3.8   charges, fees or payment structure; ☐

    3.9   main agreed or variable terms of deal. ☐

4   Do you require any approval or consents? Consider: ☐

    4.1   board approval; ☐

    4.2   regulatory consent or approval; ☐

    4.3   shareholder approval or consent; ☐

    4.4   relevant tax clearance, if applicable; ☐

    4.5   third parties; ☐

    4.6   licences; ☐

    4.7   approvals under relevant existing agreements. ☐

5   Should there be any conditions and an agreed long stop date? If relevant, consider: ☐

General Contracts and Arrangements

    5.1   satisfactory due diligence; ☐

    5.2   satisfactory documentation; ☐

    5.3   related agreements or ancillary transactions; ☐

    5.4   time limits; ☐

    5.5   provision of information or documents. ☐

6   In preparing to draft the documents, consider: ☐

    6.1   who has initial responsibility or continued control of the drafting; ☐

    6.2   specifying the nature of the transaction and any obligation to negotiate; ☐

    6.3   whether there will be third party involvement; ☐

    6.4   mainly covering transactional issues (and drafting points only where critical) in the document; ☐

    6.5   avoiding the provisions which amount to 'agreement to agree'; ☐

    6.6   setting out issues related to the transaction which may be the subject of dispute; ☐

    6.7   which provisions (if not wholly binding) should have legal effect, such as exclusivity, governing law or jurisdiction, public announcements and confidentiality); ☐

    6.8   clearly stating the 'legal' nature of the document at the top or end of the document. ☐

7   If a non-binding document is intended, the document could: ☐

    7.1   provide that the parties will enter into further or formal documents; ☐

    7.2   be made 'subject to contract'; ☐

    7.3   expressly state that the arrangements do *not* have any legal force or effect. ☐

8   If intended to be legally binding, the document could: ☐

    8.1   be headed 'legally binding heads of terms/letter of agreement' or other clear provision in the body of the document; ☐

Commercial Contracts Checklists

    8.2   set out the relevant consideration in addition to the intention to enter into legal relations; ☐

    8.3   be executed as a Deed. ☐

9   If intended to be partly binding, the document should specifically state the provisions which have legal effect and are binding on the parties. ☐

10   Consider the following in preparation of the draft document: ☐

    10.1   introductory paragraph setting out the history and proposed transaction; ☐

    10.2   parties; ☐

        10.2.1   correct representatives of each party or parties together with the relevant business or service address; ☐

        10.2.2   inserting other relevant contact details (email, mobile and fax) or identification (company or business registration number); ☐

    10.3   review and confirm in the document the nature of the transaction (e.g. acquisition of assets or commercial trading arrangement transaction); ☐

    10.4   in relation to charges or price, consider:

        10.4.1   price payable; ☐

        10.4.2   price calculation; ☐

        10.4.3   satisfaction of price; ☐

        10.4.4   expenses and costs; ☐

        10.4.5   any other payments; ☐

    10.5   with regard to conditions and timetable:

        10.5.1   specify any applicable conditions; ☐

        10.5.2   indicate manner of satisfaction of conditions; ☐

        10.5.3   indicate manner of disposal, acquisition or arrangements timetable; ☐

General Contracts and Arrangements

    10.5.4   specify approvals and consents; ☐

    10.5.5   set out required licences required (if any); ☐

10.6   specify undertakings and obligations in the document. Consider (if applicable): ☐

    10.6.1   who, what, when and where; ☐

    10.6.2   provision of services; ☐

    10.6.3   specific payment obligations or responsibilities; ☐

    10.6.4   costs and expenses; ☐

    10.6.5   action required to be taken; ☐

    10.6.6   provision of information; ☐

10.7   confidentiality. Consider (if relevant): ☐

    10.7.1   stating nature of transaction and purpose of intention; ☐

    10.7.2   agreed use by recipient in connection with document or proposed deal; ☐

    10.7.3   provision for documents to be marked 'confidential'; ☐

    10.7.4   basis of disclosure and authorised disclosures; ☐

    10.7.5   definition of 'Confidential Information'; ☐

    10.7.6   mutuality of confidentiality obligations; ☐

    10.7.7   required acknowledgements; ☐

    10.7.8   providing for an indemnity for costs and losses resulting from breach of confidentiality obligations; ☐

10.8   in relation to the final or definitive agreement, consider making provision: ☐

    10.8.1   for negotiation, preparation and execution of final documents; ☐

10.8.2 for lawyers responsible for preparing and negotiating the initial draft definitive agreement; ☐

10.8.3 specifying governing law for definitive documents; or ☐

10.8.4 for reference to specific required content or provision; ☐

10.9 exclusivity and lock out provisions. If applicable, consider: ☐

    10.9.1 relevant period of exclusivity or lock out; ☐

    10.9.2 state time commencing and ending (5.30 p.m. on specified date); and ☐

    10.9.3 state effect of expiry of the fixed period; and ☐

    10.9.4 specify obligations of each party during the exclusivity period including: ☐

- no further dealings with third parties; ☐

- no supply of information or solicitation of proposals; ☐

- any restrictions on certain business transactions; ☐

- other specific agreed obligations. ☐

    10.9.5 what happens upon receipt of unsolicited enquiry during the period; ☐

    10.9.6 effect of breach of exclusivity undertaking (reimbursement of fee up to agreed cap); ☐

10.10 General/miscellaneous. Consider provisions relating to:

    10.10.1 restricting announcements without consent; ☐

    10.10.2 restricting third party rights of enforcement; ☐

    10.10.3 payment of costs of document or its implementation by the parties; ☐

    10.10.4 signing of the document in a number of counterparts; ☐

    10.10.5 assigning the agreement, if legally binding; ☐

General Contracts and Arrangements

10.10.6 legal effect of the document either in whole or by reference to specified paragraphs; ☐

10.10.7 matters beyond reasonable control of the parties; ☐

10.10.8 clarity on the parties' commitment to proceed with the proposed deal or otherwise; ☐

10.10.9 compliance with specific or general legal requirements (data protection, licensing or law generally); ☐

10.10.10 the term of the arrangements (if applicable); ☐

10.10.11 acknowledgement of certain matters by the parties and exclusion of liability; ☐

10.10.12 illegality, entire agreement, notices, interpretation, etc if legally binding; ☐

10.10.13 governing law and jurisdiction provision; ☐

10.10.14 need for guarantor in definitive agreements or in the document if legally binding; ☐

10.10.15 consent (where required, can it be unreasonably withheld or delayed?); and ☐

10.10.16 other boiler plate provisions including severance, further assurance, variation and waiver. ☐

See Precedent 1.2 on accompanying CD.

1.3 Exclusivity and Lock Out Agreement

Overview

Description of Agreement/Document

The term 'exclusivity agreement' is interchangeable with 'lock out agreement'. This is a mechanism for ensuring a fixed period during which a party can review, evaluate, consider, negotiate, arrange financing or complete a commercial transaction. During the relevant agreed fixed period, the parties agree that one party (usually the seller) will undertake not to deal with nor provide information to any other third party.

Practical Guidance/Issues List

Exclusivity and lock out agreements are useful because they seek to secure an exclusive period during which a party may carry out its due diligence, negotiate the deal or consider matters without the fear of losing the deal to a third party.

Note that an exclusivity letter:
- can be prepared as a letter or short form agreement;
- is useful as it saves time, management effort, expense of due diligence and relieves the commercial pressure on the parties;
- may be of great assistance but of little effect in certain circumstances;
- cannot force a party to negotiate the agreement effectively during the exclusivity period.

The consideration for entering such agreement is often the supply of confidential information for evaluation, the incurring of costs and expenses in investigation/due diligence or the payment of an exclusivity fee. Where there is no consideration, the document should be executed as a deed.

Avoid obligations to negotiate in good faith as the enforceability of such requirements under English law are neither established nor certain. In certain European jurisdictions the obligation is enforceable with potential liability.

Care should be taken to ensure that the parties are not unintentionally bound to proceed with a transaction. The documents and exchange of correspondence should be 'subject to contract'. Any offer to purchase assets or enter into relevant commercial transactions should be conditional on satisfactory due diligence or other matters.

Other points to be aware of are as follows:
- The exclusivity period (together with other provisions of the exclusivity agreement) should be clear and avoid uncertainty.
- You should ensure that the agreement is terminable (if necessary) during the period for material or specified breach.
- The agreed period of lock out and exclusivity should be reasonable having regard to the relevant requirements of the parties.
- In an acquisition, the buyer may wish to factor in time for third parties to assist with due diligence or produce reports together with financing delays.
- The use of liquidated damages provisions can be an effective means of enforcement.
- Any such sum representing a liquidated damages amount should be a genuine pre-estimate of loss and supportable by costs. In certain cases, a party may wish to seek specific performance, damages for breach or an injunction.

Law/Compliance Requirement

Contract law is applicable to exclusivity agreements. Any such agreement will need to comply with the rules of contract to be binding legal obligations. Contracts require certain elements including offer and acceptance, consideration, intention to create legal relations and certainty. In effect, the exclusivity period must be a set fixed period and not open.

An exclusivity or lock out agreement should be in writing. This will ensure that there are no difficulties in establishing the parties' agreement or intention. There is no specified legal form for such an agreement. Such an agreement is often set out in a letter but must still comply with contract law to be effective.

Such agreements are usually enforceable if properly drafted and entered into by the parties. The applicable remedies include specific performance, injunction, damages and liquidated damages.

In *Walford and Others v Miles [1992] 2 AC 128*, the court held that an 'obligation to negotiate in good faith' within a fixed time was not enforceable. Such a lock in agreement was uncertain. However, a lock out agreement with sufficient certainty remains enforceable.

Some Key Definitions

'Exclusivity Period' means the period starting from the date of this agreement and ending at 5 p.m. on [   ] 200[ ] (or such earlier date upon which the parties agree that the proposed transaction shall not proceed).

'Payment' means the sum of [   ] pounds (£[   ]) paid by [Party X] to [Party Y] in consideration of [Party Y] entering into this Agreement.

'Proposed Acquisition' means the proposed acquisition by [Party A] of [the business and assets of [Party B/the entire issued share capital of [Target Company A2ZEE Limited]].

Specific Provisions

Exclusivity

In consideration of your payment today to us of the sum of [   ] pounds (£[   ]) ('the Payment'), we agree for the period starting on the date of this agreement and ending at 5 p.m. on [   ] 200[ ] (the 'Exclusivity Period') (or such earlier date upon which we all agree that the proposed acquisition shall not proceed), we shall not:

(a) advertise the Business for sale through any medium;
(b) sell or otherwise dispose of the whole of the Business to any third party;
(c) continue or enter into any or further discussions or negotiations with any third party potential buyer (other than your professional advisers) relating to the disposal of the Business; or
(d) grant to any third party (other than pursuant to this agreement) access to the Confidential Information, books, accounts, records and other information relating to the Business for the purpose of making an offer to buy the Business.
(e) withdraw and shall procure that none of our employees, agents, directors or representatives shall carry out any of the foregoing.

Termination

If at any time you are in breach of any of your obligations contained in this agreement or you indicate that you wish to reduce the price offered by you for the Business or defer the basis on which it is to be paid or propose any material change in the terms of your subject to contract offer for the Business, we reserve the right to terminate the Exclusivity Period referred to in this agreement by notice in writing with immediate effect.

Principal

We acknowledge that you [have incurred costs and will continue to incur costs/will be incurring costs and expenses from the date of this letter agreement] in connection with the proposed acquisition of the Business in reliance on our representatives and obligations set out in this agreement.

Appendix 1.3 Exclusivity and Lock Out Agreement Checklist

In preparing an exclusivity and lock out agreement or letter, individuals or businesses should consider the following non-exhaustive matters.

Actions/Issues:	Comments:	✎

1   Consider relevant parties to the agreement, details and information to be covered. ☐

2   Are there any restrictions on the parties entering into such arrangements? ☐

3   In particular, consider provisions: ☐

    3.1   to ensure appropriate consideration for entering into the agreement as indicated; ☐

    3.2   granting one party a period of exclusivity; ☐

    3.3   providing for relevant restrictions on one party during the exclusivity period; ☐

    3.4   for executing the agreement as a deed if not supported by relevant consideration; ☐

    3.5   setting out the purpose of the exclusivity agreement and the specific requirements of each party; ☐

    3.6   confirming the legally binding nature of the exclusivity arrangements; ☐

    3.7   setting out the appropriate remedy in the event of breach of the agreement; ☐

    3.8   dealing with liquidated damages, appropriately and reasonably drafted to avoid being considered a penalty; ☐

    3.9   imposing a relevant timetable for review, evaluation, due diligence or otherwise in relation to the proposed transaction; ☐

    3.10   specifically dealing with the enforcement of the agreement. ☐

4   With reference to the exclusivity obligations or restrictions, consider undertakings during the exclusivity period not to: ☐

    4.1   provide corporate and business information to third parties for the purpose of an offer or evaluation of the business; ☐

    4.2   continue discussions or negotiations with third parties; ☐

General Contracts and Arrangements

4.3 sell or agree to sell the asset in question to any other party; ☐

4.4 enter into any transaction during the period; ☐

4.5 advertise the business for sale or otherwise solicit buyers; ☐

4.6 procure or allow employees or others to do any of the restricted acts; ☐

4.7 refuse to negotiate in accordance with the timetable. ☐

5 Consider setting out the position in respect of attempts by a party to: ☐

5.1 reduce the original price offer for the business; ☐

5.2 change the agreed basis of payment or calculation of the price; ☐

5.3 alter the transaction or any of its main terms. ☐

6 Set out the circumstances in which the agreement or exclusivity period may be terminated. ☐

7 Consider the effect and consequences of termination. Are there any required actions or obligation on a party. ☐

8 Consider the need for: ☐

8.1 non-solicitation restriction for a specified period after termination; ☐

8.2 non-competition restriction for a specified period after termination. ☐

9 Require or consider indemnity provisions in respect of costs or losses flowing from breach of agreement. Is a guarantor necessary or required? ☐

10 Consider provisions confirming that no party is bound to acquire or sell the business. ☐

11 Consider a separate non-disclosure agreement or insert confidentiality obligations including: ☐

11.1 specific and general non-disclosure obligations; ☐

11.2 circumstances of permitted disclosure; ☐

11.3 consultation requirement prior to disclosure; ☐

11.4 involuntary or legally required disclosure; ☐

11.5 appointing sole representatives responsible for information handling; ☐

11.6 not to copy the information; ☐

11.7 on obligations to return or destroy the information following termination. ☐

12 Define 'confidentiality' to reflect the business and information provided or to be provided. Consider including: ☐

    12.1 a wide definition of confidentiality; ☐

    12.2 specific information or class of information; ☐

    12.3 requirement for information to be marked 'confidential'; ☐

    12.4 extending definition to include information however disclosed from time to time. ☐

13 Consider: ☐

    13.1 any required or specific acknowledgements; ☐

    13.2 enforcement rights of third parties or exclude such third party rights; ☐

    13.3 restrictions on announcements; ☐

    13.4 making time of the essence in respect of the obligations or certain obligations; ☐

    13.5 setting out the agreed position on costs and liability for payment; ☐

    13.6 provisions intended to survive termination of the agreement and specify accordingly or provide general statement; ☐

    13.7 governing law and jurisdiction; ☐

    13.8 various boilerplate provisions which assist legal and construction efficacy including: counterparts, waiver, severance, entire agreement provisions. ☐

14 Ensure (or consider): ☐

    14.1 correct details of parties including service address and other contact details; ☐

General Contracts and Arrangements

    14.2   appropriate signatories to the agreement have authority; ☐

    14.3   that the agreement is dated appropriately; ☐

    14.4   appointment of process agent (if necessary); ☐

    14.5   that the agreement is exchanged if signed as counterparts. ☐

15   Review drafts and consider taking advice or whether there are any applicable legal requirements where the agreement is to be enforced. ☐

See Precedent 1.3 on accompanying CD.

1.4 Commission Agreement

Overview

Description of Agreement/Document

A percentage fee commission agreement is used in many commercial transactions. The agreement formalises an arrangement for one party to pay the other party a commission fee. The fee is normally in consideration of a party introducing transactions, clients or third parties to the other party. The agreement sets out the percentage fee commission or amount agreed together with the obligations of each party. The principal obligations relate to payment of the commission fee, responsibility for compliance with laws, confidentiality, non-circumvention undertakings, liquidated damages and liability.

Practical Guidance/Issues List

It is essential that the arrangements between parties for the payment of commission are documented. In any event any party involved in such a commercial arrangement should consider the following steps:
- Obtain acknowledgement that the introduction is made by the relevant party.
- Sign a short form or letter of agreement to reflect the main terms or arrangement.
- Ensure a non-disclosure and confidentiality agreement is signed to protect information or contacts disclosed.
- Maintain records of introductions and referrals.
- Ensure the recipient party acknowledges each introduction.
- Confirm each introduction in writing.
- Ensure that the contract is supported by relevant consideration or signed as a deed.
- Seek legal advice with regard to regulated areas, sectors or matters.
- Ensure the agreement is signed by an authorised person.
- Ensure the agreement is properly signed in duplicate or counterparts and exchanged.
- Date the agreement appropriately following signature but before any introductions.
- Ensure that any calculation of proposed liquidated damages is reasonable. Such a provision is subject to interpretation as a penalty if exclusive and unenforceable.
- Seek a guarantee where the likely payer is an entity without apparent substance.
- Agree payments into escrow accounts where commission is dependent on third party payments.

Law/Compliance Requirement

Any compliance requirements relate to regulations governing certain activities or fields. Many professional bodies prohibit payment of commission in return for referrals in certain circumstances.

Depending on the area, it may be that a licence or relevant approval is required. The law applicable to such an arrangement is the law of contract, found in statute and case law. The agreement needs to be sufficiently certain and fulfil the requirements of all contracts including the existence of consideration.

Relevant provisions such as any liquidated damages clause, non-compete or non-solicitation clauses will be subject to the Unfair Contract Terms Act 1977.

A liquidated damages provision has to amount to a genuine pre-estimate of loss to avoid being a penalty. The non-compete and non-solicitation undertakings will only be enforceable to the extent considered reasonable by the courts.

Note that money laundering regulations will be applicable to any arrangements for the payment of funds in circumstances where there is no proper commercial arrangement.

Some Key Definitions

'Subsidiary' in this Agreement (and particularly in relation to the non-circumvention obligations) shall (unless the context otherwise forbids) be deemed to include and refer to not only the Company (named in this Agreement) but also to each and every subsidiary or holding company of the Company and any company affiliated or associated with the Company in any way during the period of this Agreement and the Company shall be deemed to be contracting for itself and each and every such other company.

'Term' means the period from the date of this Agreement and continuing thereafter unless and until terminated in accordance with the provisions of this Agreement or as agreed between the parties in writing.

'Non-Circumvention' means any act or omission in any manner directly or indirectly intended to circumvent the operation of this Agreement and deprive [Party X] of any of the benefits intended under or pursuant to this Agreement.

Specific Provisions

Exclusivity
Nothing in this Agreement shall constitute an exclusive arrangement or appointment as between the Introducer and the Company and, for the avoidance of doubt, the Introducer shall continue in connection with its business carried on at the date of this Agreement to introduce clients and organisations to other finance brokers, banks, arrangers, investors or entities.

Licences
The Company shall be responsible for obtaining all licences, permits and approvals which are necessary, requested or advisable in connection with [the fund raising, investment or otherwise] in respect of its business or the performance of its obligations.

Compliance
[The Company shall comply with all applicable laws and regulations.]

Records
The Company shall keep separate, reasonably detailed, true and accurate books and records of all transactions and funds procured, introduced or raised together with any amounts received by it in connection with the transactions or projects and the Introducer (together with its agents, advisers and representatives) shall be entitled at its expense to inspect the same on reasonable notice during normal business hours and to take copies of all extracts from such books and records.

Non-Circumvention
The Company shall not in any manner, directly or indirectly attempt to circumvent the operation of this Agreement so as to otherwise deprive the Introducer of any of the benefits intended under or pursuant to this Agreement.

Compensation
In the event of circumvention, directly or indirectly by the Company or on its behalf, the parties agree and acknowledge that the Introducer shall be entitled to legal monetary compensation as liquidated damages for loss of bargain equal to [   ] per cent ([   ]%)] of all sums due or payable to the Company or in respect of such transaction plus any and all expenses incurred by the Company, including all legal fees involved in the recovery of such compensation.

Further Assurance
At any time after the date of this Agreement the Company shall, at the request of the Introducer, execute or procure the execution of such documents and do or procure the doing of such acts and things as the Introducer may require for the purpose of giving to the Introducer the full benefit of all the provisions of this Agreement.

Appendix 1.4 Percentage Fee Commission Agreement Checklist

In preparing a commission agreement or letter, the following non-exhaustive matters should be considered.

Actions/Issues:	Comments:	✎

1 Consider: ☐

    1.1 relevant parties; ☐

    1.2 need for a guarantor; ☐

    1.3 introductory paragraph reciting the transaction and history. ☐

2 Detail: ☐

    2.1 the proposed transaction and agreed terms; ☐

    2.2 any assumptions; ☐

    2.3 any acknowledgments; ☐

    2.4 previous introductions or commercial arrangement. ☐

3 Consider: ☐

    3.1 the proposed term of the agreement; ☐

    3.2 any ad hoc arrangement; ☐

    3.3 use of a simple form contract or letter. ☐

4 Will the arrangements include: ☐

    4.1 any exclusivity; ☐

    4.2 a right of first refusal; ☐

    4.3 an obligation to investigate third parties prior to introduction. ☐

General Contracts and Arrangements

5   What are the agreed fees? ☐

6   Will the fees be a percentage or straight fee? ☐

7   Are the fees: ☐

      7.1   dependant on third party payment or performance; ☐

      7.2   payable upon contract with third party or receipt of payment; ☐

      7.3   payable by cheque, cash or telegraphic transfer; ☐

      7.4   subject to interest for late payment (if so, at what rate?); ☐

      7.5   subject to a guarantor from a bank, individual or third party. ☐

8   What are the obligations in relation to: ☐

      8.1   confidentiality? ☐

      8.2   record keeping? ☐

      8.3   auditing contractual and financial records? ☐

      8.4   non-circumvention? ☐

      8.5   licences and legal compliance? ☐

9   What is the proposed duration or agreed term of the agreement? ☐

10   Upon what basis can the arrangements be terminated? Consider: ☐

      10.1   material breach; ☐

      10.2   insolvency; ☐

      10.3   non-payment; ☐

      10.4   circumvention; ☐

10.5 notice. ☐

11 What happens after termination? Are there any post-termination obligations. Consider: ☐

    11.1 return or destruction of information; ☐

    11.2 non-solicitation or non-compete provisions; ☐

    11.3 certification of compliance with obligations. ☐

12 Will there be liability for all delays? Consider force majeure provisions for matters beyond the parties' reasonable control. ☐

13 Consider: ☐

    13.1 specific provisions and obligations in relation to data protection; ☐

    13.2 guarantor obligations; ☐

    13.3 dispute resolution; ☐

    13.4 alternative dispute resolution; ☐

    13.5 arbitration; ☐

    13.6 proceedings. ☐

14 Review and detail relevant boilerplate provisions including: ☐

    14.1 notices; ☐

    14.2 status of parties as non-partners; ☐

    14.3 entire agreement clause; ☐

    14.4 third party rights; ☐

    14.5 assignment or non-assignment; ☐

    14.6 further assurance; ☐

14.7   exclusion of parties as agents or employees;   ☐

14.8   governing law and jurisdiction.   ☐

See Precedent 1.4 on accompanying CD.

Commercial Contracts Checklists

1.5 Finder's Fee Agreement

Overview

Description of Agreement/Document

This type of agreement is used in a variety of commercial transactions. It relates to the payment of a finder's fee in consideration of the introduction of a third party or specific deal. It is a simpler or shorter form of the percentage fee commission type agreement. This agreement relates to finding an investor who may be willing to provide or procure investment or loans to an entity. The principal obligations relate to the introduction of an investor and the payment of an agreed fee.

Practical Guidance/Issues List

A written agreement greatly assists the argument in a dispute. A properly prepared and enforceable agreement avoids a dispute in relation to what the parties intended or agreed. An agreement in writing is always more certain than unwritten and unrecorded arrangements. In this instance, as the arrangement is simple, the parties can keep the contract simple.

Parties should seek to:
- Keep records of instructions.
- Obtain acknowledgment of each introduction.
- Enter into such contracts by deed if no relevant consideration.
- Make specific arrangements for payment (especially where payment is subject to third party payment).
- Obtain a guarantee in respect of relevant payment.
- Argue and specifically define the term of the contract.
- Agree and reflect the position in respect of future transactions.

Law/Compliance Requirement

The party seeking to introduce a company to an investor should take advice to ensure compliance with applicable laws. Depending on the relevant circumstances, the Financial Services and Markets Act 2000 may apply to such activities. Advice should always be taken.

Some Key Definitions

'Investor' means a company, firm, person, entity or entities introduced or to be introduced by the Finder to the Company who will be willing to consider making an investment in the Company.

'Fee' means the sum equal to [ ] per cent of the total loans and/or equity investment made by the Investor in and/or to the Company and payable in pounds sterling to the Finder.

Specific Provisions

For the purposes of this Agreement (and for the avoidance of doubt) the Finder shall not be entitled to any fee or other monies until the Company has entered into a binding arrangement with the Investor resulting primarily from the efforts of the Finder.

Any arrangements made by the Finder with any other persons or third party entities with whom the Finder is involved shall be the Finder's total responsibility.

In the event that the Company enters into an agreement with an Investor introduced by the Finder during the term of this Agreement or within [ ] months after the expiration of this Agreement, the Company shall pay to the Finder the Fee.

Appendix 1.5 Finder's Fee Agreement Checklist

In preparing a finder's fee agreement or letter, individuals or businesses should consider the following non-exhaustive matters.

Actions/Issues:	Comments:	✎
1 Consider:		☐
1.1 recital paragraph and background issues;		☐
1.2 details of proposed transaction;		☐
1.3 fee payment arrangements.		☐
2 Are there any:		☐
2.1 guarantee arrangements;		☐
2.2 exclusivity arrangements;		☐
2.3 related transactions or arrangements;		☐
2.4 non-circumvention obligations;		☐
2.5 good faith undertakings.		☐
3 Set out:		☐
3.1 the agreed fee payment date;		☐
3.2 any conditions;		☐
3.3 any obligations on either party;		☐
3.4 any confidentiality terms;		☐
3.5 pre-contract representation of either party;		☐
3.6 documents to be incorporated into the agreement;		☐

Commercial Contracts Checklists

3.7 position of third parties or agents of either party; ☐

3.8 responsibility for investigating the financial viability of any transaction or prospective investor's finances; ☐

3.9 what happens if investment is made after the term of the agreement; ☐

3.10 responsibility of legal costs for the preparation of the document; ☐

3.11 obligations relating to: ☐

    3.11.1 record keeping; ☐

    3.11.2 dispute resolution; ☐

    3.11.3 notices and service; ☐

    3.11.4 provision of information; ☐

    3.11.5 further assurance; ☐

    3.11.6 assignment; ☐

    3.11.7 appointment of process agent (if party outside the UK); ☐

3.12 relevant boilerplate clauses for legal efficacy; ☐

3.13 governing law and jurisdiction submission (provide exclusive or non-exclusive jurisdiction submission); ☐

3.14 any terms which need to survive termination? Consider: ☐

    3.14.1 confidentiality; ☐

    3.14.2 Indemnity provisions; ☐

    3.14.3 further assurance provisions; ☐

3.15 whether the agreement for a fixed term or terminable on agreed terms. ☐

See Precedent 1.5 on accompanying CD.

General Contracts and Arrangements

1.6 Memorandum of Understanding Agreement

Overview

Description of Agreement/Document

Parties to a commercial transaction may often commence negotiations on a plain sheet of paper prior to agreeing terms. The final agreement, as with non-binding heads of agreement, is based on the parties' memorandum setting out their understanding of the proposed transaction. The memorandum of understanding (MOU) sets out their expectations, understanding and specific requirements without being legally bound but as a plain language aide-memoire. The parties usually acknowledge that neither party will be bound until the final agreement is settled and executed on the given date.

Practical Guidance/Issues List

Parties may wish to consider the following:
- MOU provisions are best when short and to the point.
- The terms should be expressed in simple but clear and plain English to avoid any dispute or misunderstanding.
- No extensive drafting should be attempted but the MOU should be prepared in a manner that the document adequately sets out the proposed deal.
- A plain and clearly drafted document enables the transaction to be 'sold' to third parties, where relevant, as it should provide a concise and useful explanation or statement of the main or material terms of the proposed deal.
- Even if the MOU will not be binding in its entirety or specifically in relation to the proposed arrangements, the document should contain some certainty.
- The relationship of the parties other than the basic outline of the proposed arrangements can be made certain and legally binding.
- The practical guidance and issues list relating to Heads of Agreement and letters of intent may contain useful information.
- The document should ideally set out in outline the agreed proposed transaction subject to contract. The parties should avoid spending time negotiating a detailed document. Negotiations should be reserved for the main legal agreements incorporating the terms set out in the MOU.
- It should be noted that the MOU is regarded as creating a moral commercial commitment between the parties even if not legally binding.
- Once a matter is set out as provisionally agreed in the MOU, it can be difficult to change during negotiations or in the final documents.

Law/Compliance Requirement

The document is intended to be non-binding and non-contractual. To avoid any dispute, the document should clearly state its legal status and be marked 'subject to contract'.

Even where not legally binding, a memorandum of understanding can evidence the existence of an 'arrangement' affecting tax matters.

Some Key Definitions

'Final Agreements' means the formal final legal agreements to be negotiated [in good faith], approved by the parties and entered into between the parties to this Memorandum of Understanding in respect of the proposed transaction as set out in the Memorandum of Understanding [being/including] the following:

'Main Agreement' means the agreement for [specify the relevant transaction agreement (i.e. Share Sale Agreements, Business Asset Sale Agreement)] in relation to which [Party X] shall [insert details of aim of main transaction agreement] in connection with the Proposed Transaction.

Specific Provisions

This Memorandum sets out in basic outline the main principles that the parties have provisionally agreed, subject to contract, for Party A and Party B to enter the proposed arrangements as further set out in detail in the Schedule.

The Final Agreements following approval and execution by the parties shall supersede this Memorandum.

Either party may withdraw from time to time from the negotiations at any time prior to signature and entry into the Final Agreement without incurring any liability to the other party.

General Contracts and Arrangements

Appendix 1.6 Memorandum of Understanding Agreement Checklist

In preparing a memorandum of understanding agreement or letter, individuals or businesses should consider the following non-exhaustive matters.

Actions/Issues:	Comments:	✎
1 Consider:		☐
1.1 keeping it simple;		☐
1.2 setting out the proposed arrangements in outline and full description in a schedule;		☐
1.3 proposed legal status of the provisions of the memorandum of understanding;		☐
2 Consider setting out:		☐
2.1 the list of the proposed final agreements;		☐
2.2 the agreed timetable (and making time of the essence);		☐
3 What is the position in respect of:		☐
3.1 period of exclusivity for negotiations?		☐
3.2 change of control during the agreed exclusive negotiations period?		☐
3.3 non-disclosure and confidentiality undertakings?		☐
4 Can the memorandum be terminated on:		☐
4.1 insolvency of either party?		☐
4.2 unremedied material breach by the other?		☐
4.3 excessive delay following a force majeure event?		☐
4.4 inability to agree final legally binding documents (within an agreed period)?		☐

Commercial Contracts Checklists

5   Consider: ☐

    5.1   relevant post termination obligations; ☐

    5.2   boilerplate provisions, as appropriate; ☐

    5.3   governing law and jurisdiction; ☐

6   Review the guidance and checklist provided in relation to Heads of Terms Agreement (Appendix 1.2). ☐

See Precedent 1.6 on accompanying CD.

1.7 Non-Circumvention and Fee Protection Agreement

Overview

Description of Agreement/Document

This type of agreement often surfaces in international contracts between buyers and sellers of products. Its intention is to ensure non-circumvention and protect the relevant fee by reference to a bank. It is not always entirely effective and the desired result can be achieved by a simple form bank guarantee or instruction to a bank to make a relevant payment. Parties can also consider entering into an escrow agreement as an alternative.

Practical Guidance/Issues List

The arrangements between the parties must be clear and certain. If the agreement relates to the cooperation of the parties in respect of a commercial endeavour, then it should be documented.

The parties can always enter into a similar but simpler form contract by means of a letter setting out the agreed terms.

Parties should beware of entering into legal documentation which is not expressly clear as to effect or enforceability.

Depending on the exact nature of the commercial transaction, relevant arrangements can be entered into for the protection of the fee including guarantee or escrow arrangements.

Law/Compliance Requirement

The agreement is a matter of contract law. Therefore, certainty and consideration will be required to ensure that an enforceable contract is in existence.

Some Key Definitions

'Transaction' means each transaction pursuant to the contract for the sale, purchase and supply of products specified in the Contract and as agreed between the parties from time to time (whether or not as part of the Services and Additional Services).

'Circumvention' means any act or omission directly or indirectly calculated to deprive [Party X] of any benefit intended by this Contract.

Specific Provisions

Guarantee
We further guarantee that no details relating to any fees, retainer or guaranteed private remunerations will be disclosed to any persons (other than to agreed banks or as required by law or pursuant to an order from a court (or regulatory body)) including other intermediaries, consultants and agents of the Seller or Buyer without your prior written consent.

Fax Exchange
This agreement shall be signed and exchanged via facsimile transmission. Each copy shall be accepted as legal and binding as an original.

Appendix 1.7 Non-Circumvention and Fee Protection Agreement Checklist

In preparing a fee protection agreement or letter, individuals or businesses should consider the following non-exhaustive matters.

Actions/Issues: **Comments:**

1   Consider:

    1.1   necessity for agreement;

    1.2   what agreement seeks to protect;

    1.3   relevant parties to the agreement;

    1.4   other forms of protection or arrangement;

    1.5   signing a non-disclosure letter depending on exchange or provision of information.

2   In preparing a short form letter, review the terms of the proposed transaction and consider:

    2.1   the relevant fee payment and arrangement;

    2.2   definition of underlying contract;

    2.3   method of fee payment;

    2.4   required guarantee;

    2.5   specifying additional obligations.

3   Insert obligations:

    3.1   not to directly or indirectly circumvent each other;

    3.2   to make the payment within an agreed period or date or upon occurrence of an event;

    3.3   to indemnify for loss, costs and expenses;

    3.4   to assign rights under the letter and contractual arrangements;

3.5 relating to confidentiality and non-disclosure of information; ☐

3.6 requiring express written consent; ☐

3.7 relating to signature and acceptance of fax copies (where necessary, relevant and verifiable); ☐

3.8 to irrevocably instruct bank to pay. ☐

4 Consider relevant boilerplate provisions. ☐

5 Consider alternative dispute resolution provisions including mediation. ☐

6 Insert governing law with submission to jurisdiction clause. ☐

See Precedent 1.7 on accompanying CD.

Commercial Contracts Checklists

1.8 Test and Evaluation Agreement

Overview

Description of Agreement/Document

This agreement for the testing and evaluation of materials, products or software is commonly used in commercial transactions. The parties agree the basis for testing and evaluating the product, together with the agreed obligations following successful testing. In many cases, successful testing leads to the entering into licensing arrangements for the commercial exploitation or use of such materials, products or software.

Practical Guidance/Issues List

The methods of testing the materials should be agreed and set out. The allocation of responsibilities and assessment of results (if intended) may be detailed and a draft licence agreement (or other relevant agreement) can be attached and required to be entered into following a successful or specified result after the evaluation period. An option may not be sufficient in certain circumstances.

In intellectual property related matters, arrangements should be made with respect to ownership of initial and developed intellectual property.

If it is likely that the test and evaluation will be successful, then it would be best to have an agreed form licence with suitable warranties or provisions attached to the document.

Law/Compliance Requirement

Intellectual property rights, licences and arrangements are covered by various pieces of legislation including the Copyright, Designs and Patents Act 1988 and the Trade Marks Act 1994. An agreement for the evaluation of certain materials or compounds which includes obligations to carry out research and development may be subject to R & D Block Exemption Regulation (EC Commission Regulation 2659/2000 of 29 November 2000), Official Journal L304, 05.12.2000. In effect, such an agreement should be drafted taking into account the provisions of the regulations.

It should be noted that an obligation in an agreement which amount to a bare obligation to negotiate an good faith is not legally binding as it is regarded as uncertain. See *Walford v Miles [1992] 2 AC All ER; [1992] 2 WLR 174 (HL)*.

Some Key Definitions

'Evaluation' means the testing and evaluation of the [software/materials] by the Licensee prior to commercial lease in accordance with the test criteria and guidelines set out in the Schedule.

'Test or Evaluation Period' means the period for the testing and evaluation of the product commencing on the [   ] 200[ ] and ending on [   ] 200[ ] unless reviewed by the parties in accordance with the provisions of this Agreement.

Specific Provisions

The Licensee shall, pursuant to the Licence granted under this Agreement, use the Software upon the terms and subject to the conditions of this Agreement for the Evaluation Period for the sole purpose of reviewing and evaluating whether or not the Software meets the requirements of the Licensee ('the Requirements') specified in Schedule [2] to this Agreement.

In the event that the Software does not meet the Requirements, the Licensee shall within [(   )] days after the expiry of the Evaluation Period return (or, if the Owner shall instruct, destroy) the Software and all copies in whole and in part in any form including partial copies or modifications of the Software received from the Owner or made in connection with this Agreement and all documentation relating thereto.

The Licensee has agreed to test the Product free of charge by using the Product in the Licensee's [office environment] ('Specified Location') and using the approved hardware ('Specified Hardware' as indicated in Schedule [1]) by the Licensee's employee(s) skilled in the business sector which would normally use such a product. Such employees will be capable of evaluating the quality, content and functionality of the Product as well as its marketability ('the Test').

Upon expiry of the Test Period, the Licensee hereby undertakes to return all copies of the Product together with all software, documentation and other data relating thereto whether prepared by the Licensee or the Owner and return or permit the Owner to collect the Equipment (if any) provided by the Owner in accordance with the foregoing clause.

The Licensee agrees not to cause or permit anything which may damage or endanger the Intellectual Property or other intellectual property rights of the Owner or the Owner's title to it or assist or allow others to do so.

Commercial Contracts Checklists

Appendix 1.8 Test and Evaluation Agreement Checklist

In preparing an evaluation agreement or letter, individuals or businesses should consider the following non-exhaustive matters.

Actions/Issues: **Comments:**

1 Consider setting out:

    1.1 the background to the evaluation;

    1.2 relevant details of the parties;

    1.3 the purpose of the evaluation;

    1.4 the effect of a successful outcome or evaluation:

        1.4.1 entry into licence;

        1.4.2 grant of option to enter into licence;

    1.5 the basis for testing and evaluating the material or software to be tested.

2 Review confidentiality prior to commercial release.

3 Set out provisions relating to:

    3.1 the relevant consideration;

    3.2 the grant of licence for the limited purpose;

    3.3 whether the licence to be granted is:

        3.3.1 exclusive or non-exclusive;

        3.3.2 transferable or non-transferable;

        3.3.3 subject to fee or royalty free;

    3.4 delivery of the materials and/or software for evaluation;

General Contracts and Arrangements

    3.5   any restrictions on copying or use of the products and materials; ☐

4   Consider detailing: ☐

    4.1   the specified requirements which the material or product is to be evaluated against; ☐

    4.2   the obligation for the licensee to enter into a full licence agreement in the event of a successful evaluation; ☐

    4.3   the applicable licence fee payable upon execution and entry into the full licence; ☐

    4.4   the effect of the materials failing the test. ☐

5   Will there be any obligations to: ☐

    5.1   provide details and reports of the evaluation? ☐

    5.2   keep information confidential? ☐

    5.3   discuss the test results at a meeting? ☐

    5.4   destroy or return the materials upon failure of the test? ☐

6   Consider how the test will be carried out. Is there need for specific equipment? Any required conditions? ☐

7   What is the period of evaluation? ☐

8   What happens to improvements? What about other intellectual property? ☐

9   Will the:

    9.1   agreement terminate on the expiry of the Evaluation Period? ☐

    9.2   agreement terminate forthwith upon service of notice in writing by either party? ☐

    9.3   agreement require termination upon service of written notice giving a specified period? ☐

    9.4   agreement be terminable upon material breach or insolvency of either party? ☐

    9.5   licensee be required to comply with any post-termination obligations? ☐

Commercial Contracts Checklists

    9.6   agreement set out the agreed remedy for breach of its terms? ☐

10   Consider intellectual property provisions including: ☐

    10.1   setting out ownership of intellectual property; ☐

    10.2   making provision for modifications and improvements; ☐

    10.3   relevant warranties (if any); ☐

    10.4   relevant indemnity for breach of third party intellectual property rights; ☐

    10.5   acknowledgement of ownership and undertaking not to assert any claim on the intellectual property; ☐

    10.6   further assurance provisions or obligations to assist in specific ways including carrying out requested act or signing further documents to implement the agreement or ensure benefit of its terms; ☐

    10.7   restrictions relating to exploitation and circumvention; ☐

    10.8   disclaimers of liabilities and limitation of liability provisions; ☐

    10.9   an exclusion of liability for indirect and consequential loss; ☐

    10.10 force majeure acknowledgements including termination for long delays; ☐

    10.11 notices/service of notice; ☐

    10.12 relevant boilerplate provisions and details as necessary; ☐

11   Are any approvals or consents required? ☐

12   Consider relevant schedules setting out details of: ☐

    12.1   the products, materials or software; ☐

    12.2   required equipment; ☐

    12.3   test criteria; ☐

    12.4   specific requirements; ☐

12.5 the evaluation process; ☐

12.6 the evaluation period; ☐

12.7 specific reporting requirements; ☐

12.8 the proposed licence agreement in agreed form. ☐

See Precedent 1.8 on accompanying CD.

2 General Commercial Agreements

2.1 Manufacturing Agreement

2.2 Venue Hire Agreement

2.3 Terms and Conditions Agreement

2.4 Representation/Agency Agreement

2.5 Marketing Agreement

2.6 Franchising Agreement

2.7 Provision of Services Agreement

2.8 Distribution Contract

2.9 Consultancy Agreement

2.10 Management Agreement

2.1 Manufacturing Agreement

Overview

Description of Agreement/Document

A manufacturing agreement represents a contract between a manufacturer and a business for the manufacture of specified products. The agreement sets out the manufacturing and supply arrangements and details the fees, timetable, specification and the respective obligations of the parties.

Practical Guidance/Issues List

It is important that the manufacturing agreement contains quality control mechanisms in respect of the products.

In addition, it would be useful to ensure that an alternative manufacturer can be used in the event of non-performance.

Insurance is an important part of the arrangements especially prior to delivery of the products to the owner.

The parties should:

- Take legal advice in relation to any restrictions.
- Consider liquidated damages provisions.
- Agree reasonable procedures for checking and acceptance of deliveries.
- Ensure adequate insurance remains in place during the term.
- Review liability limitation provisions in respect of reasonableness under the Unfair Contract Terms Act 1977.
- Take advice on product liability and consumer protection.
- Avoid incorporation of standard terms of trading and simply insert relevant provisions.

Law/Compliance Requirement

A manufacturing agreement may be subject to the application of various regulations and laws. The restrictions (such as against manufacturing for third parties or competitors) will be subject specifically to competition law.

The limitation of liability provisions will be subject to legislation such as the Unfair Contract Terms Act 1977 and only enforceable to the extent considered reasonable by the courts.

Product liability legislation will apply to the arrangements together with various consumer protection statutes. There are various national and international regulations which may apply including with respect to marking, packaging and labelling.

Some Key Definitions

'Quality Control Tests' means the quality control and procedures set out in [the Schedule] as amended from time to time by [the parties/Party A] and required to be carried out by [Party B] in accordance with the provisions of [specify relevant document].

'Cost Price' means in relation to a Product the sum of (a) the cost price of the parts of such Product, (b) the direct labour costs of manufacturing the Product, and (c) the cost price of packaging, transportation and insurance charges on shipments or deliveries of the Product; save that where the manufacture of a Product is sub-contracted by the Manufacturer, the 'Cost Price' means the price paid to the sub-contractor for each Product manufactured together with the cost price of packaging, transportation and insurance charges on shipments or deliveries of the Product.

Specific Provisions

Application and Grant
The Owner appoints the Manufacturer, its manufacturer in the Territory of the Products and grants to the Manufacturer (and the Manufacturer accepts) the non-exclusive right to manufacture the Products for the Term on the terms but subject to the conditions contained in the Agreement.

Storage
The Manufacturer agrees to store the Products in safe conditions complying with any requirements of the Owner together with any applicable insurance policy.

Stock Count
Immediately on the request of the Owner (to be made not more than once in every *[3]* months of the Term) the Manufacturer shall arrange for a physical stock count of the Products and representatives of the Owner shall be entitled to attend the stock count for the purpose of verification.

General Commercial Agreements

Appendix 2.1 Manufacturing Agreement Checklist

In preparing a manufacturing agreement or letter, individuals or businesses should consider the following non-exhaustive matters.

Actions/Issues:	Comments:	✎

1   General and preliminary matters: ☐

    1.1   ascertain and review: ☐

        1.1.1   the nature of the business; ☐

        1.1.2   existing arrangements; ☐

        1.1.3   present terms and conditions; ☐

        1.1.4   extent of service required; ☐

    1.2   consider proposed parties to the agreement and detail: ☐

        1.2.1   full name and address together with all other contact details; ☐

        1.2.2   legal status of the company together with registered office; ☐

        1.2.3   partnership details and partners' names, trading name and principal place of business (or company number if relevant); ☐

        1.2.4   responsible legal entity. ☐

2   Definitions. Consider principal terms to be defined: ☐

    2.1   product or goods; ☐

    2.2   order; ☐

    2.3   instructions; ☐

    2.4   client or owner; ☐

    2.5   quality control; ☐

2.6 manufacturer; ☐

2.7 delivery date; ☐

2.8 package or packaging case; ☐

2.9 specification; ☐

2.10 quantity. ☐

3 Grant and appointment. Consider provisions setting out: ☐

    3.1 appointment of manufacturer; ☐

    3.2 exclusive or non-exclusive appointment; ☐

    3.3 the grant of right to manufacture the products. ☐

4 Duration: ☐

    4.1 what is the proposed term of the manufacturing agreement? ☐

    4.2 is the term fixed or terminable on notice? ☐

    4.3 consider initial fixed period with option for either party to terminate; ☐

    4.4 specify reasonable notice period; ☐

    4.5 consider relevant commencement date: ☐

        4.5.1 date of agreement; ☐

        4.5.2 specified date; ☐

        4.5.3 following first order. ☐

5 Parties' obligations. Consider and set out agreed duties and obligations of each party including: ☐

    5.1 in relation to the owner: ☐

General Commercial Agreements

	5.1.1	provision of instructions;	☐
	5.12	delivery of product information;	☐
	5.13	provision of requested information;	☐
	5.1.4	confirmation of specification and order;	☐
	5.1.5	approval of samples and changes;	☐
	5.1.6	making relevant payment;	☐
	5.1.7	confirmation of required delivery date;	☐
	5.1.8	compliance with specified legal requirements;	☐
	5.1.9	arranging time and place for delivery;	☐
	5.1.10	inspection of goods upon delivery;	☐
	5.1.11	acceptance of delivered manufactured goods;	☐
	5.1.12	indemnifying manufacturer, where relevant, in respect of breach of third party intellectual property;	☐
5.2		in relation to the manufacturer, consider undertakings in relation to:	
	5.2.1	confidentiality obligations;	☐
	5.2.2	non-circumvention of the owner;	☐
	5.2.3	manufacture of the products;	☐
	5.2.4	performance and compliance with quality control tests;	☐
	5.2.5	compliance with specifications;	☐
	5.2.6	delivery of products within time scale;	☐
	5.2.7	packaging;	☐

5.2.8 accurate record keeping of products manufactured (including list of defective goods); ☐

5.2.9 allow owner access to manufacturing premises (or manufacturer's premises); ☐

5.2.10 allow owner access to records and grant of audit rights; ☐

5.2.11 provide periodic reports and statements; ☐

5.2.12 maintenance of insurance. Consider: ☐

- all risks; ☐

- full replacement value; ☐

- owner as additional insured; ☐

- naming owner or noting owner's interest on policy; ☐

- policy inspection and copying right. ☐

6 Price. Specify what the price includes. Consider whether price will: ☐

6.1 include VAT for all time or quoted for a specific period; ☐

6.2 be valid for all time or quoted for a specified period; ☐

6.3 be subject to variation and on what terms; ☐

6.4 include interest for late payment; ☐

6.5 include any discounts or early payment provisions; ☐

6.6 include further amounts. ☐

7 Payment terms Consider payment terms and specify: ☐

7.1 any rights of set off; ☐

7.2 deposit or advance payment required; ☐

General Commercial Agreements

7.3 agreed method of payment; ☐

7.4 required security for payment; ☐

7.5 guarantee; ☐

7.6 escrow arrangements; ☐

7.7 third party payment; ☐

7.8 bank payment; ☐

7.9 letter of credit; ☐

7.10 currency of payment; ☐

7.11 exchange rate variation provisions. ☐

8 Supply and trading conditions. Consider provisions relating to: ☐

8.1 packaging and labelling; ☐

8.2 specification and order changes; ☐

8.3 delivery of products; ☐

8.4 right to reject goods on delivery, inspection of goods and acceptance (including deemed acceptance); ☐

8.5 effect of deviation from order; ☐

8.6 passing of risk and title generally; ☐

8.7 any retention of title provisions (where applicable); ☐

8.8 quality and quantity of products; ☐

8.9 marking of goods and storage/warehousing; ☐

8.10 responsibility for obtaining relevant licences; ☐

8.11 product liability insurance responsibility; ☐

8.12 method of instruction, order generation and specification confirmation. ☐

9 Undertakings of the manufacturer: ☐

 9.1 to provide relevant or required assistance; ☐

 9.2 not to copy or otherwise infringe any relevant intellectual property; ☐

 9.3 not to assign the contract or sub-contract the manufacturing; ☐

 9.4 not to manufacture products of the same description for agreed third parties; ☐

10 Review owner's warranties and consider provisions relating to: ☐

 10.1 compliance with relevant licensing requirements; ☐

 10.2 obtaining all necessary consents and approvals; ☐

 10.3 ownership of the products and related intellectual property. ☐

11 Termination and expiry. Consider termination of agreement: ☐

 11.1 upon service of written notice; ☐

 11.2 following expiry of initial period; ☐

 11.3 upon occurrence of extended force majeure event; ☐

 11.4 in the event of non-performance by manufacturer; ☐

 11.5 in the event of unremedied material breach; ☐

 11.6 for non-payment on due date; ☐

 11.7 upon insolvency of either party; ☐

 11.8 following occurrence of specified events of default; ☐

11.9 for conflict of interest, bad faith or prejudicial conduct; ☐

11.10 effect or post-termination consequences and obligations including: ☐

    11.10.1 return owner's material; ☐

    11.10.2 cease manufacturing; ☐

    11.10.3 cessation of all rights. ☐

12 Specify provisions relating to quality control and any relevant tests. Consider: ☐

  12.1 third party testing; ☐

  12.2 random sample testing; ☐

  12.3 full and proper examination; ☐

13 Liability. Consider extent of liability including: ☐

  13.1 product liability insurance; ☐

  13.2 setting out excluded liability; ☐

  13.3 setting out liability limitation provisions; ☐

  13.4 effect of Unfair Contract Terms Act 1977; ☐

  13.5 conditions to be satisfied prior to acceptance of liability; ☐

  13.6 applicable time limits; ☐

  13.7 provisions relating to indemnity: ☐

    13.7.1 to be given by the manufacturer regarding loss resulting from manufacturing defects or faults and manufacturing acts; ☐

    13.7.2 to be given by the owner regarding intellectual property and the products. ☐

14 Consider miscellaneous provisions including; ☐

Commercial Contracts Checklists

    14.1   force majeure; ☐

    14.2   waiver; ☐

    14.3   third party rights; ☐

    14.4   severance; ☐

    14.5   notices; ☐

    14.6   costs liability; ☐

    14.7   entire agreement; ☐

    14.8   status of the parties; ☐

    14.9   survival of provisions; ☐

    14.10 cumulative remedies; ☐

    14.11 set off; ☐

    14.12 further assurance. ☐

15   Specify or consider dispute resolution procedure. Review and consider: ☐

    15.1   alternative dispute resolution procedure; ☐

    15.2   arbitration; ☐

    15.3   proceedings; ☐

    15.4   governing law; ☐

    15.5   jurisdiction. ☐

See Precedent 2.1 on accompanying CD.

General Commercial Agreements

2.2 Venue Hire Agreement

Overview

Description of Agreement/Document

The venue hire agreement relates to the hire of premises for a function or event. The agreement can be prepared in short form depending on the nature of hire, hirer and premises. The agreement sets out the respective obligations of the parties. It is based on a front single sheet agreement with general and special conditions of contract incorporated. The venue hire contract normally grants the hirer a licence to use the premises for an agreed period or for a one-off event.

Practical Guidance/Issues List

The owner of premises may wish to let out its premises for use on an informal basis for a function, event or period. A written agreement in respect of the hire of the venue is essential and informal arrangements should be avoided. A written agreement sets out the obligations and liabilities of each party in addition to evidencing the terms applicable to the arrangement.

The owner and hirer of the premises should consider their requirements in respect of:
- insurance and any additional cover that may be required;
- the fee structure, terms of any deposit payment arrangements;
- age restrictions, minors and parental responsibility;
- specific purpose of the hiring (i.e. public entertainment, plays, party or sports events);
- legal and statutory requirements.
- The position should be made clear in terms of each party's obligations and responsibilities;
- liabilities.

Other practical matters include provision of information by the owner of the premises to the hirer regarding:
- the premises;
- any special rules;
- safety and security instructions;
- health and hygiene matters;
- fire precautions.

Consider what happens if the premises are for whatever reason no longer available.

The relevant special conditions may refer to agreed provisions between the parties. This may include conditions regarding:
- removal of equipment;
- special requirements of either party;
- obligations to terminate;
- cancellation;
- sale of alcohol;
- licensing compliance and consents.

The owner should confirm the legal authority and status of the proposed hirer. Is there a need for a guarantor or is the deposit sum sufficient in the relevant circumstances?

It is important that the purpose of the hiring is declared. In addition, to avoid difficulties the owner should also reserve certain rights for its protection. Such rights can include refusal of entry, cancellation for illegality and approval of content or materials.

As the likelihood of loss or damage will be subject to the type of event, it is advisable to obtain an indemnity from the hirer, but note that an indemnity is only of any value if the giver is able to stand by the undertaking.

It may be useful to produce a guide and information sheet for hirers of premises where the owner regularly hires out the premises.

Commercial Contracts Checklists

The special conditions of hire contracts can be used to deal with issues not covered in the general conditions. The provisions may reflect variations of the general conditions. A conflict provision can be added, although it is best to avoid any conflicting provisions.

Always take advice in respect of the agreement or specific events or regulations applicable to such events.

Law/Compliance Requirement

An agreement of this type will be subject to various laws and applicable regulations. Apart from the law of contract, a venue hire contract may attract certain property or town and planning legislation, intellectual property laws of copyright, advertising law and licensing obligations.

The Unfair Contract Terms Act 1977 may apply to certain restrictions contained in the venue hire contract. Such restrictions may include cancellation provisions and liability limitations.

There are many statutes applicable to venues with reference to the venue, circumstances and activity intended. The Occupiers' Liability Act 1957 may apply.

Some Key Definitions

'Club' means the club being the venue at [address] and the term 'Venue' shall have the same meaning

'Hire Period' means [date] between the hours of [ ] a.m./p.m. and [ ] a.m./p.m.

'Rules' means the rules of the Club relating to [details].

['Services' means the services (if any) agreed to be provided by the Club in respect of the Event as specified in Schedule [1].]

Specific Provisions

Club Hire
In consideration of the Fee, the Owner agrees and permits the Hirer to use the Club for the Event during the Hire Period and the Hirer agrees to hire the Club on the terms of and subject to the General Conditions and the Special Conditions of this Agreement.

Obligations of the Hirer
The Hirer agrees with the Owner to observe and perform the General Conditions and the Special Conditions of the Hire Contract.

Deposit
Upon execution of the Agreement the sum representing the Deposit shall be paid or sent to the Owner by the Hirer so that it is received [by the close of business on [date]/the date of this Agreement]. [In the absence of written extensions, if the above deadline is not met, then this Agreement shall lapse and be of no further effect.]

Fee
Subject always to the other provisions of this Agreement, the Hirer will pay to the Club without set off or deduction the Fee [on date/within seven days of the Hire Date].

Cancellation
[Subject as expressly provided, if the Event is cancelled at least [ ] calendar months before the Event is due to take place then the Deposit (less any expenses/costs already incurred by the Club in connection with the Event) is fully refundable. If the Event is cancelled within [ ] calendar months of the Event taking place then the Deposit is non-refundable and a cancellation fee (being that sum representing the balance of the Fee) plus any expenses/costs already incurred by the Club in connection with the Event shall be payable to the Club by the Hirer which cancellation fee shall be payable on demand.]

Compliance
The Hirer is responsible for all advertising of the Event at the Hirer's own cost and will ensure that no advertising/promotional material shall infringe or violate any copyright, trademark or other proprietary right of any other person or render the Club liable to any proceedings whatsoever and that all such material will comply with the requirements of all the relevant codes relating to advertising or marketing regulations and legislation for the time being in force (from time to time) including but not limited to that relating to incitement of racial prejudice and/or obscenity;

Commercial Contracts Checklists

Appendix 2.2 Venue Hire Agreement Checklist

In preparing a manufacturing agreement or letter, individuals or businesses should consider the following non-exhaustive matters.

Actions/Issues:	Comments:	✎

1   Preliminary matters: □

     1.1   review: □

         1.1.1   requirements of hirer (for example catering, music or gaming); □

         1.1.2   nature and purpose of venue hire; □

         1.1.3   extent of service and facilities required; □

         1.1.4   any special licences required and if alcohol is to be provided; □

         1.1.5   required insurance cover; □

     1.2   consider: □

         1.2.1   proposed hirer and relevant details; □

         1.2.2   status of hirer (corporate partnership, minors or other individual); □

         1.2.3   contract and representative details; □

         1.2.4   requirement for a guarantors or other form of security; □

         1.2.5   deposit payment requirement; □

         1.2.6   the responsible legal entity; □

         1.2.7   whether any minors are involved and any required or necessary arrangements; □

     1.3   are there any specific terms that require definition. Consider: □

         1.3.1   capacity; □

1.3.2 event or purpose; ☐

1.3.3 venue rules; ☐

1.3.4 proceeds, fee or deposit; ☐

1.3.5 facilities, permissible special effects and standard security; ☐

1.3.6 unlawful use; ☐

1.3.7 club or venue; ☐

1.3.8 licences; ☐

1.3.9 de-rigging; ☐

1.3.10 hirer, hirer entourage staff or security. ☐

2 Hire. Specify: ☐

2.1 permission to hire venue; ☐

2.2 agreed hire period; ☐

2.3 hiring subject to terms and conditions of agreement. ☐

3 Charges: ☐

3.1 how much will the hirer pay? ☐

3.2 is a deposit payable and is the deposit returnable? On what terms? ☐

3.3 are there arrangements in relation to any gate receipts or proceeds; ☐

3.4 who will be responsible for any additional costs and expenses: ☐

3.4.1 telephone and fax? ☐

3.4.2 additional key? ☐

Commercial Contracts Checklists

3.5 is a cancellation fee or penalty payable? ☐

3.6 what about licence fees? ☐

3.7 is a fee chargeable in respect of insurance? ☐

3.8 when are the fees payable? ☐

3.9 what about any shortfall? ☐

3.10 specify payment of VAT at prevailing rate and consider a default interest payment liability for late payment. ☐

4 Obligations of hirer. Consider: ☐

4.1 payment of deposit, hire charge and hire expenses including damage (on due date or upon demand); ☐

4.2 an obligation to seek consent for use of equipment or any alteration; ☐

4.3 undertaking to indemnify the owner of premises: ☐

    4.3.1 for breach of agreement; ☐

    4.3.2 negligence; ☐

    4.3.3 death or personal injury; ☐

    4.3.4 damages, theft and loss of equipment; ☐

4.4 compliance with laws and applicable regulations; ☐

4.5 obtaining required consents, licences and approvals; ☐

4.6 restrictions on: ☐

    4.6.1 advertising; ☐

    4.6.2 intoxicants, food or tobacco; ☐

    4.6.3 animals without consent; ☐

General Commercial Agreements

    4.6.4   children; ☐

    4.6.5   certain activities; ☐

    4.6.6   gaming and betting; ☐

    4.6.7   sale of goods; ☐

4.7   responsibility for all agreed or specified costs (including at end of hire period); ☐

4.8   use of venue for specified purpose only; ☐

4.9   not to use for dangerous or illegal activities; ☐

4.10   not to obstruct access to venue; ☐

4.11   to keep the venue's capacity and monitor admissions; ☐

4.12   obtain prior approval of publicity material; ☐

4.13   not to alter venue or any approved arrangements; ☐

4.14   comply with house or venue rules including opening and closing times; ☐

4.15   obtaining and maintaining agreed insurance. ☐

5   In relation to the owner's obligations. Consider: ☐

    5.1   provision of access to venue; ☐

    5.2   compliance with applicable laws; ☐

    5.3   provision of agreed service; ☐

    5.4   provision of agreed facilities; ☐

    5.5   provide responsible representative (or venue manager) and contact details; ☐

    5.6   ensuring adequate and experienced staff; ☐

Commercial Contracts Checklists

    5.7   agree to rescheduling subject to availability and agreed cancellation fee; ☐

    5.8   agreed insurance obligations; ☐

    5.9   providing relevant information relating to the premises; ☐

    5.10   co-operating with the hirer with respect to event. ☐

6   Set out specific provisions relating to cancellation and closure. ☐

7   Reserve relevant rights for owner (as necessary) including:

    7.1   force majeure (matters beyond its control) event forcing cancellation or rescheduling; ☐

    7.2   termination in the event of breach of licensing regulations; ☐

    7.3   provision of in-house facilities; ☐

    7.4   provision of staff and security; ☐

    7.5   reduction of capacity for safety or legal reasons. ☐

8   Specify the capacity of the venue and the maximum number to be admitted. ☐

9   Who is responsible for compliance with relevant or specified statutory requirements? ☐

10   Are there any specific obligations in respect of decorations or advertising? ☐

11   Consider restrictions on broadcasting, photographs or filming without prior consent. ☐

12   Consider required obligations and responsibilities at the end of the hire period. Is the hirer required to:

    12.1   remove any equipment? ☐

    12.2   clear any premises? ☐

    12.3   leave premises in an orderly state? ☐

    12.4   report all accidents or dangerous occurrences? ☐

12.5 carry out any specific cleaning? ☐

13 What is the position regarding damage to property? ☐

14 Consider use of a signed inventory. ☐

15 Will the owner reserve the right to refuse entry? ☐

16 Liability: ☐

16.1 are there any specific exclusions of liability required by the owner in relation to: ☐

16.1.1 consequential loss or loss of profit? ☐

16.1.2 loss due to machinery or equipment breakdown? ☐

16.1.3 cancellation by council or regulatory authority for whatever reason? ☐

16.1.4 cancellation by hirer? ☐

16.2 injury to attendees caused by third parties. ☐

17 How are complaints to be handled? ☐

18 What is the agreed dispute resolution procedure? ☐

19 Insert guarantor/guarantee provision and obligations if applicable. ☐

20 Consider setting out the force majeure provisions. Review requirements and consider: ☐

20.1 effect of force majeure event; ☐

20.2 obligations upon occurrence; ☐

20.3 notice to other party and provision of information; ☐

20.4 any right to terminate if event continues for specified period. ☐

21 Is insurance cover in place? Whose responsibility is it to obtain cover? Consider what insurance is required: ☐

Commercial Contracts Checklists

    21.1   public liability; ☐

    21.2   normal commercial risks; ☐

    21.3   indemnity limit; ☐

    21.4   loss or damage; ☐

    21.5   third party risks. ☐

22   Specify the rights of the hirer granted in addition to the licence to use the premises. These may include the right to: ☐

    22.1   supervise ticket sales and collection; ☐

    22.2   use specified or all facilities; ☐

    22.3   erect advertising; ☐

    22.4   take photographs; ☐

    22.5   arrange the event; ☐

    22.6   provide its own staff and security. ☐

23   What are the termination provisions? Is the agreement terminable: ☐

    23.1   on notice with immediate effect? ☐

    23.2   on specified notice? ☐

    23.3   upon non-payment of deposit or fees? ☐

    23.4   upon expiry of hire period? ☐

    23.5   non-performance of obligations? ☐

    23.6   insolvency or bankruptcy of hirer? ☐

24   Consider usual provisions relating to: ☐

24.1 notices; ☐

24.2 entire agreement; ☐

24.3 third party rights; ☐

24.4 severance; ☐

24.5 waiver; ☐

24.6 assignment; ☐

24.7 governing law; ☐

24.8 jurisdiction; ☐

24.9 other relevant boilerplate provisions. ☐

See Precedent 2.2 on accompanying CD.

Commercial Contracts Checklists

2.3 Terms and Conditions Agreement

Overview

Description of Agreement/Document

Standard conditions of trading are used by many businesses in relation to the supply of goods and/or services. Many businesses insist on supplying goods only on their terms and conditions of business. Such standard terms will depend on the nature of the goods or services to be supplied. In general, a terms and conditions agreement will set out the exclusive application of the terms, limit the supplier's liability and set out the arrangements in relation to delivery, price and payment, warranties and indemnities together with the usual boilerplate provisions.

Practical Guidance/Issues List

Use of standard terms and conditions is relatively common in business. Suppliers and buyers use them to set out the relevant terms of the contract between them. In using such terms, the following should be considered.

- Standard terms are usually one sided and may contain onerous provisions.
- Many of the provisions will be subject to challenge if applied against a consumer having regard to consumer protection law.
- The terms and conditions must be properly incorporated into the contract.
- The party seeking to rely on the standard terms should avoid the 'battle of forms' which may arise in exchange of correspondence with the other party.
- It may be of assistance to include a reference to the terms ('subject to our terms and conditions') or print the terms on relevant brochures, catalogues and business contracting material including invoices. It should be noted that invoices are post-contractual documents and do not incorporate terms (other than by way of course of dealing) into a contract.
- The provisions seeking to limit liability or exclude certain obligations will be subject to the test of reasonableness or challenge under relevant statute.
- Any exclusion clause should be properly but reasonably drafted to be effective.
- It may be sensible to obtain a written confirmation from the other party that they accept the terms of trading.
- Care should be taken that terms are not accepted or allowed to be introduced by way of course of dealing (if not intended).
- The effectiveness of retention of title clauses in practical terms may be debatable, and other protective mechanisms may be better.
- It may be more effective to consider and take contractual quality or supply precautions to reduce any risk.
- Protection may also be sought through a guarantor or suitable security arrangements.
- The delivery terms and arrangements (including any testing, inspection or deemed acceptance or right of rejection) are always subject to dispute. The parties should ensure that the terms are very clear.
- International contracts may require further attention including specifying responsibility for obtaining required licences.
- Account should be taken of the nature of the goods and whether they are high value goods.
- Insurance is a very important part of the trading arrangements and offers the relevant protection required in certain circumstances.
- Useful to ensure sales or contracting staff are properly instructed with regard to contract formation. Relevant contracting procedures should be put in place to incorporate standard terms to any contract.
- To reduce mistakes, valuable contracts may be subject to senior directors' or legal approval.
- It is good practice to use acknowledgement of order and/or confirmation of order forms with reference to incorporation of the standard conditions.
- Many large organisations or properly advised businesses may seek to negotiate the conditions.
- Establish a procedure for amending the contract or conditions and notifying customers as provided in the accompanying precedent (Precedent 2.3, see CD).
- Local legal advice may be useful with regard to export contracts and should be considered where appropriate.
- Buyers should consider resisting any right of the seller to increase prices without a corresponding cancellation right for the buyer.
- Buyers may wish to retain the right to reject delivery if incomplete or instalmental.

- Care should be taken in preparing workable specifications with relevant tolerances/allowable quantity discrepancies.
- Statements made on behalf of a seller may result in potential liability. Instruct staff not to deal 'outside' the standard conditions and make any representations or promises to customers.

The conditions will not normally be binding unless, before the contract was made, the other party (client/buyer) has signed a document incorporating them into the contract. They will be binding if reasonable steps are taken to bring the conditions to the attention of the other party and the contract has been expressly stated to be subject to those conditions.

If a party writes to the other stating that it is prepared to accept business on its own conditions and the other party replies indicating that they are writing to accept the work but on their own conditions, it is likely that the latter conditions will prevail.

Law/Compliance Requirement

Standard conditions of trading are subject to contract law, common law and various statutes. With respect to standard conditions and contracts, there are numerous statutes which imply terms into the contract and regulate the obligations under the relevant agreement. Some of these are:
- Unfair Contract Terms Act 1977;
- Unfair Terms in Consumer Contracts Regulations 1999;
- Consumer Protection Act 1987;
- Consumer Protection (Distance Selling) Regulations 2000;
- Relevant European Directives.

There are numerous cases which have interpreted various provisions of standard terms and conditions of trading, including sale of goods and services.
- *McCutcheon v David Macbrayne Limited [1964] All ER 430; [1964] 1 WLR 125 (HL)* on course of dealing.
- *Clough Mill Limited v Marlin [1984] 3 All ER 982; [1985] 1 WLR 111* confirming that no registrable change is created by a simple retention of title provision.
- *Photo Production Limited v Securicor Transport Limited [1980] All ER 556* on equal bargaining power and apportionment of risk.

Many of these cases have been referred to and re-interpreted in other cases.

Some Key Definitions

'Contract' means the contract between [the Company or Supplier] and the [Purchaser or Customer/the Parties] for the [sale and purchase of the Goods/provision of the Services].

'Goods' means any goods or items agreed to be supplied by the Supplier to the Purchaser under or pursuant to the Contract.

'Order' means a written order on the prescribed form attached to Schedule [1] given in accordance with the provisions of clause [4].

'The Purchaser' means the person(s), firm, company whose details are set out at clause [ ] or who purchases the [Products] from the [Supplier] pursuant to the Contract.

'Specification' means the description of the [Goods/Products/Services] set out in Schedule [1] or any other description of the [Goods/Products] agreed between the Parties in writing from time to time.

Specific Provisions

Acknowledgement
The Company acknowledges, agrees and accepts that:
(i) It has satisfied itself following inspection or examination of and as to the condition of the [items supplied].

(ii) No warranty whatsoever is given by the Supplier to the Company as to the satisfactory quality, fitness for any purpose of the [Goods] [and any items supplied] and all terms, conditions or warranties (whether implied or express) are expressly excluded to the fullest extent permissible by law.

(iii) The absence of a ['Notice of Rejection'] within [ ] days of delivery of the [Goods] shall be conclusive evidence that the [Company] has examined them and accepts them to be in accordance with the Contract (including as to description, specification, quality and condition), in good order and condition, of satisfactory quality and fit for any required purpose.

Warranty
The Supplier agrees to and warrants that it will at its option (following notice from the buyer) either replace or repair any goods found to be defective within [ ] months of the date of delivery of the Goods.

Exclusion
All warranties and conditions (whether implied by statute or otherwise) are excluded from this agreement but nothing in this agreement shall be taken to exclude or restrict liability for fraudulent misrepresentation or for death or personal injury resulting from the negligence of the [Supplier].

Nothing in this agreement shall affect the statutory rights of any individual dealing as a consumer notwithstanding any provision to the contrary.

Exclusive Application
These standard conditions shall apply to all [sale of Goods/supply of Services] by the Supplier to the Customer to the exclusion of any other conditions including without limitation any terms on which the Customer may seek to or purport to apply pursuant to any purchase or confirmation order and similar documents.

Liability
The liability of the Company under this Agreement shall in no circumstances exceed the sum paid by the Client to the Company for the Goods [or Services] under this Agreement.

Default
Neither party shall be entitled to repudiate this agreement as a result of the failure of the Supplier to deliver or the failure of the Company to make payment for any one or more instalments of the goods.

General Commercial Agreements

Appendix 2.3 Standard Conditions of Trading/Supply or Purchase Contract Agreement Checklist

In preparing a standard conditions of trading or supply agreement should consider the following non-exhaustive matters.

Actions/Issues:		Comments:	✎

1 What is the nature of the business? ☐

2 Have the main terms of the proposed contract been agreed? Will there be certainty in relation to: ☐

    2.1 the price of the goods or services? ☐

    2.2 the subject matter of the agreement (goods, services, supply, purchase)? ☐

    2.3 the agreed discounts or rebates? ☐

    2.4 payment terms? ☐

    2.5 period of contract? ☐

    2.6 time scales? ☐

    2.7 delivery instructions? ☐

    2.8 cancellation rights? ☐

3 Definitions: ☐

    3.1 ensure all relevant terms are defined. Consider defining: ☐

        3.1.1 products, goods, item, bespoke goods; ☐

        3.1.2 seller, buyer, parties, customer, supplier; ☐

        3.1.3 services, additional services; ☐

        3.1.4 specification, order; ☐

Commercial Contracts Checklists

      3.1.5   conditions, contracts; ☐

      3.1.6   quantity, shipment; ☐

      3.1.7   delivery, FOB, CIF; ☐

      3.1.8   proposal, quotation; ☐

      3.1.9   intellectual property. ☐

4   Charges, price and payment. State: ☐

    4.1   price: ☐

    4.2   whether price includes VAT and any other items; ☐

    4.3   consider additional charges including: ☐

      4.3.1   interest; ☐

      4.3.2   delivery; ☐

      4.3.3   insurance; ☐

      4.3.4   packaging; ☐

      4.3.5   offloading/loading; ☐

      4.3.6   credit charges; ☐

      4.3.7   other duties; ☐

    4.4   if price is guaranteed or period for which price remains valid; ☐

    4.5   default interest provisions for overdue payments; ☐

    4.6   bulk purchase reductions or early payment rebates; ☐

    4.7   provision for changing prices set out in brochure/sales literature. ☐

5　　Payment terms. What is the: ☐

　　5.1　currency of payment (if relevant, export sales)? ☐

　　5.2　required obligation to notify the other party of price changes and any cancellation rights as a result of price changes? ☐

　　5.3　payment date? ☐

　　5.4　relevant times and dates? Will time be of the essence of the contract? ☐

　　5.5　instalment default penalty with all sums becoming due immediately? ☐

　　5.6　basis for payment? Is it to be made in clear funds, without deduction, withholding or set off? ☐

　　5.7　method of payment (cash, telegraphic transfer, cheque or other agreed method)? ☐

　　5.8　requirement for payment? Consider: ☐

　　　　5.8.1　guarantee; ☐

　　　　5.8.2　bond; ☐

　　　　5.8.3　deposit; ☐

　　　　5.8.4　escrow; or ☐

　　　　5.8.5　credit insurance arrangement; ☐

　　5.9　relevant arrangements in respect of credit and payments? ☐

　　5.10　penalty for late payment? Consider the Late Payments of Commercial Debts (Interest) Act 1998 ☐

6　　Delivery arrangements (goods): ☐

　　6.1　consider and specify: ☐

　　　　6.1.1　place of delivery; ☐

　　　　6.1.2　time of delivery; ☐

Commercial Contracts Checklists

      6.1.3   at whose risk the goods are in transit; ☐

      6.1.4   details of inspection of goods; ☐

      6.1.5   details relating to acceptance of a delivery; ☐

      6.1.6   whether delivery of instalments is permitted; ☐

6.2   are the goods subject to import or export licences? ☐

6.3   whose responsibility is it to obtain all licences, approvals and consents? ☐

6.4   Who: ☐

      6.4.1   is liable for the payment of applicable duties? ☐

      6.4.2   who bears costs of delivery? ☐

6.5   can delivery be by instalment or for more or less than the ordered quantity? ☐

6.6   is it an international contract? ☐

6.7   are the INCOTERMS applicable? Will delivery be: ☐

      6.7.1   FOB? ☐

      6.7.2   CIF? ☐

6.8   are goods to be delivered to the buyer by: ☐

      6.8.1   delivery to the buyer's carrier? ☐

      6.8.2   delivery to the seller's carrier? ☐

      6.8.3   collection from the seller's premises? ☐

      6.8.4   collection from the seller's carrier? ☐

      6.8.5   delivery to any other place designated by the buyer? ☐

6.9 is time of delivery to be of the essence or will time be as estimated only? ☐

6.10 will force majeure apply to delivery obligations (resolve conflict with time being of the essence)? ☐

6.11 what happens in the event of failure to accept delivery? Should goods be put in storage at buyer's expense or sold?. ☐

7 Risk and property: ☐

7.1 specify when risk in goods will pass; ☐

7.2 state when property in good passes; ☐

7.3 will rights against any third party carrier or entity be included in respect of damage in transit? ☐

7.4 is a retention of title provision appropriate? ☐

7.5 can title to goods pass to the buyer at any time before payment in full? ☐

8 Retention of title: ☐

8.1 are the goods to be subject to retention of titles? Where a retention of title provision is appropriate, consider relevant terms; ☐

8.2 provide for title to pass only on payment of all outstanding charges or monies; ☐

8.3 make provision for identification, marking and storage of goods; ☐

8.4 consider provision permitting entry into premises to repossess; ☐

8.5 what about right to trace proceeds of sale? ☐

8.6 does the buyer have a right to sell or resell the goods pending payment? ☐

8.7 specify any other obligations on the buyer relating to restrictions on the goods including: ☐

8.7.1 storage; ☐

8.7.2 insurance; ☐

8.8 are all (including previously supplied and identifiable) goods covered by the provisions? ☐

8.9 consider whether charge requiring registration under companies act 1985 (section 395) has been created; ☐

8.10 it is an 'all monies' clause? ☐

8.11 consider the position of goods such as heavy equipment, plant and machinery. Could such goods become attached or annexed to property? ☐

8.12 what about events of default/triggering payment and repossession right? ☐

8.13 consider right to inspect goods periodically to ensure compliance. ☐

9 Liability matters: ☐

9.1 consider potential exposure to liability and basis of liability; ☐

9.2 specify what liability the seller is willing to accept; ☐

9.3 state the conditions to be fulfilled prior to acceptance of liability by supplier: ☐

    9.3.1 notification within specified period; ☐

    9.3.2 compliance with agreed reasonable steps; ☐

    9.3.3 retention of goods; ☐

    9.3.4 proof of fault arising solely as a result of faulty design or workmanship; ☐

    9.3.5 proof of proper use; ☐

    9.3.6 fault within warranty period; ☐

9.4 consider product liability and product liability insurance; ☐

9.5 review exposure to and compliance with consumer protection legislation; ☐

9.6 what liability is to be excluded; ☐

    9.6.1 indirect liability? ☐

    9.6.2 consequential loss? ☐

	9.6.3	loss of data/data corruption?	☐
	9.6.4	loss of profits or business and events?	☐
	9.6.5	third party claims?	☐
	9.6.6	misrepresentation?	☐
	9.6.7	business interruption?	☐
	9.6.8	loss of goodwill?	☐
	9.6.9	waste of staff or management time?	☐

9.7 consider basis for limitation of liability: ☐

    9.7.1 agreed and specified sum; ☐

    9.7.2 purchase price or service fee; ☐

    9.7.3 insurance sum or limit; ☐

    9.7.4 percentage of amount; ☐

9.8 ensure liability for personal injury or death due to negligence, fraud, fraudulent misrepresentation and other non-excludable liability are *not* excluded; ☐

9.9 require insurance cover; ☐

9.10 consider reasonableness of liability and exclusion provisions; ☐

10 Warranties: ☐

    10.1 specify that the supplier has the right to sell and title to the goods; ☐

    10.2 will the goods be free from any charge or encumbrance? ☐

    10.3 will the buyer enjoy quiet possession of the goods? ☐

    10.4 consider need for 'limited title' provision; ☐

Commercial Contracts Checklists

    10.5   consider warranties in respect of: ☐

        10.5.1   no infringement of third party rights; ☐

        10.5.2   description of product; ☐

        10.5.3   performance of product or service; ☐

        10.5.4   suitability or fitness for purpose; ☐

        10.5.5   quality of goods or services; ☐

        10.5.6   bulk to correspond with sample goods; ☐

        10.5.7   goods being free from defect; ☐

        10.5.8   time period (within [12] months from supply); ☐

    10.6   seller's warranty to repair or replace defective goods or re-perform defective services (at its option); ☐

11   Indemnity:

    11.1   consider indemnities from the seller in respect of: ☐

        11.1.1   the use of goods and services; ☐

        11.1.2   the defects or faults in goods/services; ☐

        11.1.3   infringement of third party rights; ☐

    11.2   consider indemnities from the buyer in respect of: ☐

        11.2.1   expenses incurred as a result of instructions; ☐

        11.2.2   third party claims; ☐

        11.2.3   infringement of third party intellectual property; ☐

    11.3   is there a need for a cap on indemnity liability? ☐

General Commercial Agreements

12 Trading terms. In addition to the foregoing trading terms, the parties (or a business) should consider : ☐

    12.1 excluding any other terms and conditions; ☐

    12.2 whether the terms apply to the exclusion of other party's or any other terms and conditions; ☐

    12.3 do the terms include all agreed terms? ☐

    12.4 is the specification (where applicable) for the goods/services agreed? ☐

    12.5 consider provisions relating to the specification and required levels of compliance. Indicate: ☐

        12.5.1 who prepares the specification; ☐

        12.5.2 if it can be updated; ☐

        12.5.3 where it can be departed from; ☐

        12.5.4 allowed and accepted tolerances; ☐

    12.6 how will the terms be varied from time to time? What about unilateral variation and a party's right to cancel the contract? ☐

    12.7 when and on what terms can the contract be cancelled by either party or both parties? ☐

    12.8 what are the agreed termination provisions? ☐

    12.9 consider the relevant post termination obligations and consequences of termination; ☐

    12.10 will director's approval be required for any orders or contract changes? ☐

    12.11 consider exclusion of all pre-contract representations; ☐

    12.12 can the contract be terminated upon the insolvency of either party? ☐

    12.13 will there be a dispute resolution mechanism or reference provision? ☐

    12.14 are there any specific requirements or formalities in connection with service of notice? ☐

    12.15 will the buyer get an assignment of the manufacturer's warranties? ☐

Commercial Contracts Checklists

12.16 what are the agreed arrangements in respect of pre-payments and deposits? ☐

12.17 will there be any right of set off? ☐

12.18 taking care not to extend the obligations of either party; ☐

12.19 are there applicable confidentiality obligations in relation to either party's confidential information? ☐

12.20 export contract provisions including: ☐

    12.20.1 basis and method of payment; ☐

    12.20.2 currency of payment; ☐

    12.20.3 specific export/import licence required; ☐

    12.20.4 INCOTERMS provisions (if appropriate); ☐

    12.20.5 consider specific meanings and relevant duties in respect of standard international expressions or corrections such as DDP (delivery duty paid), FOB (free on board), ex works and CIF (costs, insurance and freight); ☐

12.21 what are the agreed provisions or obligations in relation to deemed acceptance of goods and services, packaging and labelling? ☐

13 General. Consider the following boilerplate provisions: ☐

    13.1 assignment or non-assignment; ☐

    13.2 notices and service; ☐

    13.3 waiver; ☐

    13.4 illegality and severance; ☐

    13.5 arbitration, mediation or alternative dispute resolution; ☐

    13.6 Contracts (Rights of Third Parties Act; ☐

    13.7 distance selling regulations; ☐

General Commercial Agreements

    13.8   force majeure; ☐

    13.9   amendments and variations; ☐

    13.10 entire agreement provision. ☐

14   Law. Specify governing law and exclusive or non-exclusive jurisdiction. ☐

15   Review. Ascertain and review any existing terms or arrangements between the parties in relation to the subject matter (goods and services). Ensure such terms and arrangements are properly terminated or acknowledged as substituted. ☐

See Precedent 2.3 on accompanying CD.

2.4 Representation/Agency Agreement

Overview

Description of Agreement/Document

The representation or agency agreement governs the commercial and legal relationship between two parties where one party instructs the other to act on its behalf.

The agreement sets out the type of agency, the extent of the representation or agency required and also details the specific agreed terms in relation to the parties' duties, rights and obligations. It is normal for the agreement to deal with issues relating to exclusivity, extent of activities and authority of the agent, application of relevant agency regulations, relevant sales targets and commission payment arrangements. It also details the duration and termination provisions applicable to the appointment.

Practical Guidance/Issues List

The representation or agency appointment terms can easily be set out in a less formal way and is often so set out between the parties in a detailed letter.

Where an organisation appoints several agents, it may find it useful to have a standard form contract prepared in respect of each type of agent, including the marketing, sales, exclusive or non-exclusive agents and with regard to relevant territories.

The principal:
- will wish to ensure that it is free to appoint the agent and is not still bound by any previous exclusive appointment;
- should consider the enforceability of any restrictions as they will still need to be considered in the light of reasonableness;
- will reserve the right to vary the price or list of products;
- should consider imposing minimum targets and reserving the right to terminate for failure to meet targets.

The agent:
- may wish to secure exclusivity of a relevant territory;
- resist and avoid obligations to use its best endeavours to do anything as this will be onerous;
- should be aware of the protection provided to agents during the agency and upon termination pursuant to the Commercial Agents Regulations 1993 (see below)
- should secure written guarantees of support required in respect of the agency;
- should seek to reserve the right to object to the principal's alteration of the product range as this may have a direct impact on the agent's earnings;
- should secure an obligation to be provided with relevant marketing budget, expenses and materials for use in the territory;
- should review definitions carefully as some (such as net sales, net profits or net price) may directly impact on how much commission the agent gets paid;
- should reserve the right to accept unsolicited orders from outside the territory;
- may wish to resist any minimum sales targets as this may have a direct impact on remuneration, exclusivity or appointment;
- should resist restrictive covenants that deprive it of its ability to continue earning following termination of the representation or agency agreement.

The parties should:
- aim for an agreement that provides adequate protection for both the agent and principal;
- clearly detail the extent of the agent's authority to act on behalf of the principal including marketing, sales, negotiation and conclusion of contracts;
- secure relevant arrangements in respect of insurance required in connection with the products, services or parties' agreement;
- should provide a set of written terms of representation or agency as this limits the potential disputes;

- decide on who will be responsible for compliance with applicable laws generally or in the relevant location;
- detail how product liability and other claims will be handled;
- should provide responsible handover arrangements;
- detail whether the principal can make direct sales into the agent's territory;
- review the application and effect of the Commercial Agents Regulations and make appropriate provision in the representation or agency contract;
- set out expressly what is intended in terms of the appointment and avoid reliance on any perceived terms of art such as 'sole or exclusive'.

Law/Compliance Requirement

The relationship governed under the agreement is a matter of general contract law. However, relevant statutes and regulations apply to the relationship and the agreement.

Since 1 January 1994, the Commercial Agents (Council Directive) Regulations 1993 (SI 1993/3053) has provided protection for commercial agents in their dealings with principals.

The main effect of the Regulations is that the agent will be entitled to compensation following termination of the agency contract in addition to the relevant protection provided during and after the agency agreement. The parties will need to comply with the provisions of the Regulations.

Some Key Definitions

'Customer' means any person firm or company who is contracted or in the process of contracting with the Principal or any Group Company at any time during [specify period] for the supply of any Restricted [Matters/Products/Services].

'Restricted Area' means the [specify relevant geographical area] and any territory in which the Principal carries on business or is able to demonstrate that it has substantive and developed plans to commence doing business in relation to supply of [the Products and Services].

'Term' means the period from the Commencement Date and continuing in full force and effect until the Expiry Date unless and until terminated in accordance with the provisions of this Agreement.

Specific Provisions

Introduction
The Principal designs and manufactures a range of [specify relevant products] under the Principal's range of products and it wishes to appoint the Agent as its local marketing and sales representative with the objective of following up leads, demonstrating products and generating sales orders for Principal, for the Products (as defined in Annex [1] attached to this Contract) ('Products') on a [non-]exclusive basis in the Territory (as defined in the Schedule to this Contract), on the terms and subject to the conditions of this Contract.

Appointment
The Principal appoints the Agent with effect from the Commencement Date (as set out in the Schedule) to be its non-exclusive agent for the marketing of Principal's Products in the Territory on the terms and conditions of this Contract.

Entire Agreement
This Contract (including the Contract Terms and all other agreements and documents signed and/or attached to this Contract by the parties as listed below forming part of the Contract) constitutes the entire understanding between the Parties with respect to the subject matter of this Contract supersedes all prior agreements, negotiations and discussions between the parties relating to it.

Restriction
The Agent shall not without the prior written consent of Principal, during the term of this Contract (and for a period of [ ] months after its termination) in the Territory or any part of the Territory act as agent, representative,

franchisee or distributor for, or otherwise be directly or indirectly concerned or interested in the development, manufacture, sale and supply of, any products that are of a similar description to or compete with the Products. This restriction applies to the Agent, whether on the Agent's own behalf or on behalf of any other person, firm or company whatsoever.

Information
The Principal agrees that during the term of this Contract, the Principal will inform the Agent within a reasonable period of its decision whether or not to enter into a binding contract in respect of any order sourced or obtained for it by the Agent. For the avoidance of doubt, the decision whether or not to enter into any such contract shall be in the absolute discretion of the Principal and the Principal shall have no obligation to give any reason for any refusal to make any such contract.

Remuneration
The commission will be paid in arrears on a monthly basis. The Principal shall provide the Agent with a written statement of the commission due within [five (5)] working days of the end of month. The Agent shall then submit the Agent's invoice for the commission due to the Agent. The Principal shall pay the commission within [ ] days from receipt of the invoice from the Agent.

Entitlement
The Agent shall be entitled to commission on all post-termination sales in so far as the order is received before termination of this Contract. The Agent shall only be entitled to the commission for Products sold by the Principal as regards transactions concluded during the term of this Contract as a result of the Agent's action, or with a third party whom the Agent has previously acquired as a customer for transactions of the same kind.

Data
The Principal maintains a data protection notification under the Data Protection Act 1998 and the Agent must familiarise itself with the Principal's Data Protection and Privacy Policy (a copy of which has been provided and further copies of which are available from the Principal on request) The Agent shall at all times comply with the relevant data protection regulations applicable in the Territory from time to time.

Third Party Information
The Agent acknowledges and recognises that the Agent has received and in the future will receive from third parties their confidential or proprietary information subject to a duty on the Agent's part to maintain the confidentiality of such information and to use it only for certain limited purposes.

Deductions
The Principal reserves the right in its absolute discretion to deduct from the Agent's commission or other sums payable to the Agent or require payment from the Agent of all sums directly or indirectly owed to the Principal.

Freedom
Each party represents and warrants to the other that it is free to enter into this Agreement and is under no restriction or obligation which prevents it from freely entering into this Agreement.

General Commercial Agreements

Appendix 2.4 Representation/Agency Agreement Checklist

In preparing representation/agency agreements, individuals or businesses should consider the following non-exhaustive matters.

Actions/Issues:	Comments:	✎

1   Review the nature of and proposed arrangements for appointment of agent or representative. ☐

2   What type of agent is to be appointed? Ascertain or consider: ☐

    2.1   sales agent or representative; ☐

    2.2   marketing agent; ☐

    2.3   del credere agency; ☐

    2.4   sole representative or agent; ☐

    2.5   exclusive agent; ☐

    2.6   non-exclusive agent or representative; ☐

    2.7   agent for services, goods or both. ☐

3   Set out parties' details including: ☐

    3.1   agent's name and address; ☐

    3.2   principal's name and address; ☐

    3.3   agent's contact details including email, telephone, fax and mobile telephone; ☐

    3.4   commencement date. ☐

4   In relation to the products, specify list of products and right to add new products. ☐

5   Consider and indicate obligation to provide training in relation to product list. ☐

6   Ascertain, consider and specify: ☐

6.1 exact extent of agent's authority and appointment in relation to sales, negotiation, conclusion of contracts and marketing; ☐

6.2 agent's territory; ☐

6.3 the term of the appointment; ☐

6.4 restrictions applicable to the agent in respect of the territory; ☐

6.5 principal's right to sell directly; ☐

6.6 right of appointment of other agents or applicable restriction; ☐

6.7 agent's right to complete unsolicited orders from outside the territory; ☐

6.8 whether agent will have exclusive, non-exclusive or sole rights in specific territories; ☐

6.9 option in respect of future product range; ☐

6.10 representative or agent's defined customer grouping or sector. ☐

7 Ascertain, consider and indicate in relation to term or termination of appointment: ☐

7.1 whether fixed term contract; ☐

7.2 whether for an indefinite period; ☐

7.3 whether terminable by notice; ☐

7.4 applicable principal's notice period to terminate; ☐

7.5 applicable representative or agent's notice period; ☐

7.6 whether appointment is permanent; ☐

7.7 whether term is conditional on occurrence of certain events or performance; ☐

7.8 whether term is conditional on minimum sales targets; ☐

7.9 length and period of agency or representation; ☐

General Commercial Agreements

    7.10   other applicable notice periods; ☐

    7.11   renewal and extension arrangements; ☐

    7.12   any continuance following expiry of fixed term. ☐

8   Commission payment details and remuneration should be set out including: ☐

    8.1   basic commission; ☐

    8.2   percentage rate and payment intervals; ☐

    8.3   basis of calculation; ☐

    8.4   frequency of payments; ☐

    8.5   dates of periodic review of commission and other remuneration; ☐

    8.6   discretionary and/or contractual benefits; ☐

    8.7   any minimum commission payment sums; ☐

    8.8   any advanced commission payments; ☐

    8.9   applicable retainer payments; ☐

    8.10   default interest payments; ☐

    8.11   VAT liability; ☐

    8.12   agreed expenses upfront payment; ☐

    8.13   marketing, promotions and advertising budget; ☐

    8.14   right of audit in relation to remuneration; ☐

    8.15   sliding scale arrangements; ☐

    8.16   provision of statements and audited accounts. ☐

9 Consider and specify obligations and duties of the representative or agent including: ☐

    9.1   to obey the principal's instructions; ☐

    9.2   to act within the expressed authority; ☐

    9.3   to avoid conflicts of interest or make secret profit; ☐

    9.4   not to sub-contract; ☐

    9.5   to act in good faith; ☐

    9.6   not to directly or indirectly compete with the principal; ☐

    9.7   not to incur any unauthorised liability; ☐

    9.8   not to make any representations or give any warranty on behalf of the principal; ☐

    9.9   to provide the principal with periodic reports of promotional activities; ☐

    9.10   to assist the principal as reasonably required; ☐

    9.11   to procure orders from customers within the territory; ☐

    9.12   to diligently and faithfully serve the principal; ☐

    9.13   not to engage in any prejudicial conduct; ☐

    9.14   not to do anything that may prevent the sales of the products; ☐

    9.15   to conduct dealings as agent but without authority to bind the principal; ☐

    9.16   to provide a copy of the principal's standard terms to customers; ☐

    9.17   to use best endeavours to promote sale of the products in the territory; ☐

    9.18   to provide periodic marketing plans; ☐

    9.19   to provide the prencipal with a breakdown of orders and sales; ☐

9.20 to keep information confidential; ☐

9.21 not to use information in any way detrimental to principal. ☐

10 In relation to principal's obligations, consider and indicate as appropriate: ☐

    10.1 to pay commission; ☐

    10.2 to pay approved expenses; ☐

    10.3 to act in good faith; ☐

    10.4 to indemnify agent for certain agreed liability; ☐

    10.5 to support the agent in the sale of the products; ☐

    10.6 to provide timely response to enquiries from the agent; ☐

    10.7 to support the agent in the territory as reasonably required; ☐

    10.8 to supply marketing and technical literature; ☐

    10.9 to inform the agent of contracts entered into with customers; ☐

    10.10 to provide statements of commission due; ☐

    10.11 review the agent's sales activities. ☐

11 Ascertain and set out details of or obligations relating to: ☐

    11.1 intellectual property rights ☐

    11.2 insurance of products; ☐

    11.3 confidentiality obligations; ☐

    11.4 legal compliance; ☐

    11.5 specific data protection policy and compliance; ☐

Commercial Contracts Checklists

    11.6   costs and expense; ☐

    11.7   force majeure; ☐

    11.8   exclusion of liability or limitation provisions; ☐

    11.9   exclusion of third party enforcement rights; ☐

    11.10 restrictions on sub-contracting or assignment; ☐

    11.11 applicable law; ☐

    11.12 jurisdiction submission; ☐

    11.13 dispute resolution procedure; ☐

    11.14 entire agreement; ☐

    11.15 arbitration; ☐

    11.16 rights of set off; ☐

    11.17 compliance with competition law; ☐

    11.18 indemnity in respect of certain matters; ☐

    11.19 reservation of rights; ☐

    11.20 exclusion of compensation at termination (if appropriate); ☐

    11.21 applicable renewal fees; ☐

    11.22 inspection of agent's books; ☐

    11.23 restriction on acceptance of gifts. ☐

12   Termination of engagement and appointment provisions should be specified including termination: ☐

    12.1   by service of written notice; ☐

General Commercial Agreements

12.2 for breach of contract; ☐

12.3 automatically on retirement age; ☐

12.4 specific termination events; ☐

12.5 termination for insolvency, change of ownership of representative, material breach, force majeure, non-performance, conflict of interest or change of control of agent; ☐

12.6 by either party on specified grounds; ☐

12.7 by principal on incapacity of representative; ☐

12.8 for agent's misconduct; ☐

12.9 if representative prohibited from being a director; ☐

12.10 by resignation from appointment; ☐

12.11 following suspension; ☐

12.12 for bringing principal into serious disrepute; ☐

12.13 upon representative being convicted of a criminal offence; ☐

12.14 for agent's acts of dishonesty; ☐

12.15 following representative's bankruptcy; ☐

12.16 on change of control or reorganisation; ☐

12.17 and exclusion of termination payments (if Commercial Agents Regulations do not apply), if appropriate; ☐

12.18 specified termination remedy (compensation or indemnity) under the Commercial Agents Regulations; ☐

12.19 on any other grounds. ☐

13 Ascertain applicable post-termination obligations for required period and specify:

    13.1 restrictions on non-solicitation of staff; ☐

Commercial Contracts Checklists

13.2 restrictions against dealing with suppliers and customers of the business; ☐

13.3 non-competing obligations or involvement in similar business within specified location; ☐

13.4 return of principal's property, documents, materials and equipment. ☐

See Precedent 2.4 on accompanying CD.

General Commercial Agreements

2.5 Marketing Agreement

Overview

Description of Agreement/Document

A marketing agreement is a contract between parties for the marketing and promotion of a business, product or service. The contract sets out the requirement for the marketing of the relevant product, service or business. The detailed arrangements between a company and its client for such marketing services are normally set out in a formal agreement. However, the provision of such services may also be on informal or consultancy terms. The form of agreement sets out the client's marketing requirements, the parties' undertakings together with their respective rights and obligations.

Practical Guidance/Issues List

The parties should consider and provide for the following:
- The client's precise requirements should be set out and agreed by the parties as part of the contract.
- The client may wish to resist general liability limitation or exclusion unless relevant.
- The client may require compliance with its brand guidelines.
- A procedure for amending the marketing requirements and services should be included.
- How performance will be measured, if necessary.
- The arrangements between the parties should be set out clearly in a written contract.
- Reasonable and enforceable restrictions can be negotiated.
- Relevant dispute resolution procedure in the event of disagreement should be set out.
- Ownership rights in relation to intellectual property and other rights should be expressly specified.
- Review and compliance with the appropriate codes should be considered.
- The client may wish to approve marketing material.

Some Key Definitions

'Marketing Materials' means any marketing and press materials as may be developed by and on behalf of the Company relating to the Client and the Client Services including (but not limited to) flyers, posters, videos, billboards, banners, screens, flags, magazines, photographs, internet, CD-ROMs, DVDs and articles.

'Group Company' means a company, a subsidiary or holding company or a subsidiary of that holding company all as defined by section 736 of the Companies Act 1985, as amended by the Companies Act 1989.

'The Client's Links' means any hypertext and/or button links which enable the Users to access to the Client's web site from such other sites as the Company may determine from time to time.

'Brand Guidelines' means the guidelines for the use of the Client's trade marks, names, logos and other intellectual property as set out in the Schedule.

'Intellectual Property Rights' means any and all patents, trade marks, get-up, logos, copyrights (whether registered or not and any applications to register or rights to apply for registration of any of the foregoing), rights in inventions, know-how, and other confidential information, and all other intellectual property rights of a similar or corresponding character which may now or in the future subsist in any part of the world.

Specific Provisions

Joint Efforts
The parties shall jointly from the [commencement date] until the [expiry date] use their respective reasonable endeavours to market and promote [the Products/Business] in the Territory in accordance with the Brand Guidelines as set out in the Schedule.

Service
Throughout the term of this Agreement, the Company shall in good faith provide and carry out the proposed

marketing services and activities relating to the Client and the Client's Services [with the assistance of the Client as provided in this Agreement].

Conduct
The Marketing Company shall not, and shall procure that none of its directors, employees, agents or consultants shall, disclose any confidential information of the Client except as authorised under this Agreement and in particular neither it nor they shall make any derogatory or defamatory statement or participate in conduct which is or may be prejudicial or detrimental to the interests of the Client and its business.

Rights Use
Except as provided in [specify relevant document or guidelines] in relation to specified logos and trade marks, nothing in this Agreement shall entitle [Party Z] to use any of the Intellectual Property of [Party Z] without the prior written consent of [Party Z].

Intellectual Property Rights
Except as expressly provided in this Agreement, nothing in this Agreement shall grant or be deemed to grant to [either party] any right, title or interest in any Intellectual Property Rights owned by or licensed to the [Party A].

Representative
The parties will nominate representatives agreed by the parties from time to time to a [Joint Marketing Project Team] to meet at agreed intervals as determined by the parties but not less than once each [specify period] to manage the marketing efforts set out in [specify relevant Schedule] and strategy development. Notwithstanding the foregoing, [Party A] shall be responsible for all final decisions concerning the marketing strategy of [the Products/Business].

Return of Property
Upon termination of this Agreement both parties shall return to the other all documents and general information including confidential information and/or relating to the Intellectual Property of either party provided by either party to the other at the commencement or during the Term of this Agreement. **Liability**
Neither party shall be liable to the other for any loss or damage whatsoever incurred by the other unless caused by its negligence or that of its employees, representatives, servants or agents.

Confidential Information
The parties agree not at any time during or after the Term to divulge or allow to be divulged to any person any confidential information relating to the business or affairs of the other party to this Agreement or the Intellectual Property [except as expressly provided in this Agreement].

Appendix 2.5 Marketing Agreement Checklist

In preparing a marketing agreement or letter, individuals or businesses should consider the following non-exhaustive matters.

Actions/Issues:	Comments:	✎

1 Recite relevant background information, the nature of the client's business and the client's specific requirements. ☐

2 Set out as appropriate relevant details of the parties to the agreement including names, registration numbers, registered office or business place addresses. ☐

3 Detail the agreement to provide the marketing services on the terms and conditions of the contract. ☐

4 If required, define certain terms for ease of reference: ☐

    4.1   marketing; ☐

    4.2   marketing services; ☐

    4.3   advertiser, client, customer; ☐

    4.4   marketing materials, marketing information; ☐

    4.5   intellectual property; ☐

    4.6   brand guidelines; ☐

    4.7   services; ☐

    4.8   marketing company; marketing agent. ☐

5 As to marketing services, consider and provide: ☐

    5.1   for obligation to provide the marketing services; ☐

    5.2   the terms of reference in relation to such marketing; ☐

    5.3   any professional matters or obligations; ☐

5.4   the consideration payable in respect of the marketing services; ☐

5.5   for the exclusion of all other agreements in relation to the marketing services. ☐

6   Consider warranties, obligations and undertakings from the client. Include as appropriate: ☐

    6.1   to provide required information promptly; ☐

    6.2   to provide such assistance as is reasonably required; ☐

    6.3   to provide certain marketing materials; ☐

    6.4   to promptly provide written approval or disapproval of materials; ☐

    6.5   to be responsible for complying with all applicable rules for regulated marketing; ☐

    6.6   that it has obtained all required consents and has authority to enter into the agreement; ☐

    6.7   to comply with relevant legislation; ☐

    6.8   that information supplied is complete or accurate; ☐

    6.9   that none of the materials supplied will infringe third party rights and an indemnity against third party claims; ☐

    6.10   to make the payment of the marketing fees and expenses on the due dates. ☐

7   The marketing company's service provider warranties, undertakings and obligations should include: ☐

    7.1   to comply with reasonable directions and instructions from the clients; ☐

    7.2   to comply with applicable data protection regulations, laws and policies; ☐

    7.3   to provide the marketing and services in accordance with client's requirements; ☐

    7.4   to use reasonable care and skill; ☐

    7.5   to provide service to a good standard; ☐

    7.6   to keep the client's information confidential; ☐

General Commercial Agreements

	7.7	to comply with legislation and the client's brand guidelines;	☐
	7.8	to prepare, update, develop and implement marketing plan;	☐
	7.9	to liaise regarding new marketing materials;	☐
	7.10	to ensure no prejudicial conduct or detrimental action to the client's logos, trade marks or other intellectual property rights.	☐
8	Review payment terms and set out as appropriate, provisions in respect of:		☐
	8.1	amount of fees;	☐
	8.2	specified and applicable rates;	☐
	8.3	dates of payment;	☐
	8.4	payment structure and payment arrangements;	☐
	8.5	success fees or additional fees;	☐
	8.6	liability for costs and expenses;	☐
	8.7	marketing budget;	☐
	8.8	invoicing arrangements;	☐
	8.9	VAT payment and liability;	☐
	8.10	default interest liability provisions for late payments.	☐
9	Consider:		☐
	9.1	who owns or retains rights in the marketing material;	☐
	9.2	who retains all other intellectual property rights;	☐
	9.3	who owns rights and ideas developed during the provision of marketing services;	☐
	9.4	indemnities for third party infringement claims or other loss.	☐

Commercial Contracts Checklists

10 Indemnity provisions where applicable should be included for specific breaches or issues. ☐

11 Consider infringement of third party rights, claims and non-performance of obligations under the agreement. ☐

12 What is the term of the agreement? Ascertain, review and set out: ☐

    12.1 term of the agreement; ☐

    12.2 who can terminate; ☐

    12.3 when the agreement can be terminated; ☐

    12.4 reasons for terminating the agreement; ☐

    12.5 effect and consequences of termination. ☐

13 As to reasons to terminate, consider termination for: ☐

    13.1 (by marketing company) customer's non-payment on the due date: ☐

    13.2 failure to perform by client; ☐

    13.3 misrepresentations; ☐

    13.4 breach of applicable law; ☐

    13.5 failure to remedy material breach; ☐

    13.6 prejudicial conduct or conflicts of interest; ☐

    13.7 breach of warranties; ☐

    13.8 insolvency or related events by either party. ☐

14 Consider liability provisions including: ☐

    14.1 liability for personal injury or death caused by negligence; ☐

    14.2 fraudulent misrepresentation and non-exclusion of liability; ☐

General Commercial Agreements

14.3 total liability limitation amount; ☐

14.4 consequential loss and exclusion of liability. ☐

15 If applicable, force majeure provisions should be set out including: ☐

15.1 what amounts to force majeure or matter beyond the parties' control; ☐

15.2 undertakings to notify the other party of occurrence; ☐

15.3 obligations during period of delay; ☐

15.4 rights of the client to use an alternative company to market the products, business or service; ☐

15.5 acceptable delay period; ☐

15.6 right to terminate agreement and consequences of such termination. ☐

16 Consider and insert provisions relating to: ☐

16.1 confidentiality undertakings and non-disclosures; ☐

16.2 data protection compliance; ☐

16.3 third party enforcement rights exclusion; ☐

16.4 assignment of the agreement; ☐

16.5 governing law and jurisdiction; ☐

16.6 alternative dispute resolution procedure; ☐

16.7 severance of unlawful or unenforceable provisions; ☐

16.8 non-waiver by delay; ☐

16.9 entire agreement between the parties; ☐

16.10 fact of no partnership or agency between parties; ☐

Commercial Contracts Checklists

16.11 time being of the essence; ☐

16.12 further assurance. ☐

See Precedent 2.5 on accompanying CD.

2.6 Franchising Agreement

Overview

Description of Agreement/Document

A franchise agreement relates to the operation of a business by a party (franchisee) under another entity's (franchisor) trade name, marks, brand and logos. In effect, the agreement governs the commercial and legal relationship between such two parties where one party sets up a similar business. Such new business benefits from the existing goodwill and infrastructure of the franchised business and adopts the other party's manner of business operations subject to the franchisor's guidelines, controls or instructions.

The agreement sets out the type of franchise arrangement, the grant of the licence, the extent of the rights granted and also details the specific agreed terms in relation to the parties duties, rights and obligations. The agreement will normally deal with issues relating to exclusivity, extent of activities and authority of franchisee, renewal rights, use of trade marks, relevant insurance and advertising arrangements. It also details the applicable restrictions, duration of franchise and termination provisions applicable to the appointment.

Practical Guidance Issues List

The appointment terms of a franchise are almost always formal with a neatly presented package including agreement and manuals.

Organisations that operate a franchise network will have a standard form package for franchisees. Even a business starting out on the franchise business expansion road will benefit from having a standard form contract prepared in respect of each type of franchise, including exclusive or non-exclusive franchise arrangements and with regard to relevant territories.

The parties should:
- Provide for adequate training for franchisee and staff to enable proper operation of the franchise.
- Set out expressly what is intended in terms of the arrangement and avoid reliance on any perceived terms of art such as 'sole or exclusive'.
- Detail how problem matters will be dealt with.
- Aim for an agreement that provides adequate protection for both the franchisor and franchisee.
- Secure relevant arrangements in respect of insurance required in connection with the franchisee's business or parties agreement.
- Provide for compliance with applicable laws generally or in the relevant location.
- Detail how product liability and other claims will be handled.
- Carefully recite circumstances surrounding the franchise arrangement as this may assist in the event of litigation or disputes.
- Should provide responsible handover arrangements.

The franchisor:
- Should seek to operate a fair agreement rather than a one sided franchise agreement as this will limit disputes.
- Should have a set of standard and uniformed terms for all franchisees to avoid administrative difficulties as well as difficulties with franchisees as to better or different terms.
- May consider taking a head lease (unless unsuitable financial risk) and granting the franchisee a sub-lease;
- Will need to have appropriate rights to monitor quality of the franchisee's products or services.
- May wish to provide for vacation of the business premises upon termination of the franchise agreement.
- Should impose relevant restrictions during and after the agreement for the protection of its goodwill.
- Should consider the requirement for franchisees to enter into licences in respect of registered trade marks.
- May wish to reserve termination rights where the franchisee fails training in respect of the business.
- Needs to consider the requirement of a guarantor where the franchisee will be a limited liability company.
- May require a right to audit the franchisee or carry out relevant checks on specified notice.
- Will wish to ensure that it is free to appoint the franchisee and is not still bound by any previous exclusive appointment in the relevant territory.
- Should consider the enforceability of any standard restrictions set out in the franchise agreement as they will still need to be considered in the light of reasonableness.

Commercial Contracts Checklists

- Should consider imposing minimum targets (if appropriate) and reserving the right to terminate for failure to meet the target.
- Can obtain a right of first refusal in the event of sale of the franchisee's business.

The franchisee:
- Needs to consider whether there is sufficient demand for the relevant products and services in the proposed territory.
- May wish to resist the requirement for a guarantee.
- May wish to secure exclusivity of a relevant territory.
- Should seek an instalment payment arrangement in relation to the initial fee or any substantial sums due to the franchisor.
- Resist and avoid obligations to use its best endeavours to do anything as this will be onerous.
- May require the franchisor to assist with leasing of equipment on preferable terms available to it.
- Should notify/register under the Data Protection Act 1998 and maintain relevant compliance programme, if applicable.
- May need to secure the position in relation to improvements to the business.
- Can attempt to negotiate the levels of the initial fee and the continuing fees.
- May wish to resist any targets.
- Should resist inappropriate or extensive restrictive covenants.
- Need to consider and investigate whether the franchised business will be sufficiently profitable to justify the initial investment.
- Carefully review the business opportunity.
- Should obtain assistance form accountants or financial advisers in reviewing relevant financial information.
- Should review definitions carefully as they will impact upon the obligations and remedies of the parties.
- Needs to consider the strength of the franchisor's brand and trade marks before signing an agreement.
- Should review the extent of any proposed restrictions on involvement with other businesses during and after termination of the agreement.
- Should secure written guarantees of support required in respect of the franchise arrangement and speak to existing franchisee prior to entry into the agreement.
- May need to consider the efficiency or operability of the franchisor's proposed manual or business systems.
- Needs to ensure the existence of a suitable exit route whether by sale, sub-contract and assignment or disposal to the franchisor.
- Should secure a strong (terminable only for material breach) right of renewal without cost. May require a mechanism to realise the initial investment.

Law/Compliance Requirement

The relationship between the franchisee and the franchisor as set out in the agreement will be governed as a matter of general contract law. Compliance with relevant statutes and regulations may be necessary from time to time.

In addition, other regulations may apply to the relationship and the agreement. There are self regulatory codes such as the European franchising ethics code which may apply to the parties depending on membership or adoption of the relevant organisation.

In relation to advertising, the Control of Misleading Advertisements Regulations 1988 (S1 1988/915) will apply as will the applicable British Code of Advertising Practice.

The franchisee will be subject to the provisions of the Companies Act 1985, if a company. The Trade Marks Act 1994 will apply to arrangements relating to trade marks, registration or infringement.

The Competition Act 1998, the franchising block exemption and the relevant vertical agreements block exemption may need to be reviewed and complied with in relation to certain provisions of the franchise agreement.

Some Key Definitions

'Club' means the Franchisor designed, developed and owned business known as [   ] and trading as the [ ] club managed in accordance with the Manual.

General Commercial Agreements

'Term' means the period from the Commencement to the Expiry Date subject to the termination rights set out in the Agreement.

'Business' means the business of [   ] using the concept and operated from [   ] in accordance with the methods of operating the [ ] using the know-how and systems for contained and detailed in the operations manual.

'Franchise Terms' means this Franchise Contract for the regulation of the appointment of the Franchisee and the arrangements between the parties as further detailed and set out in the attached Schedule.

Customer' means any person firm or company who is contracted or in the process of contracting with the [Business] or any Group Company at any time during [   ] for the supply of any Services of the Business.

'Restricted Area' means the [   ] and any territory in which the Franchisor carries on business, has franchises or is able to demonstrate that it has substantive and developed plans to commence doing business in relation to supply of [the Products and Services].

Specific Provisions

Introductory Recital
The Franchisor wishes to expand its business and reputation. The Franchisee wishes to set up and carry on at the Franchisee's own risk a franchised business in [   ] (Territory). Accordingly, the Franchisee wishes to be granted relevant rights by the Franchisor to carry on the trade of a Franchisor franchised business from [   ]. The Franchisee having taken professional advice wishes to enter into this franchise agreement (Contract) in respect of the franchised business.

Term and Renewal
The Agreement shall remain in force for the term and subject to the provisions of the [Franchisor's Terms and Conditions Of Renewal] set out in the Manual, a copy of which has been provided to the Franchisee,

the Franchisor agrees to grant to the Franchisee a renewal upon the expiry of the current term. Any renewal agreement shall operate from the date of the expiry of this Agreement.

Brand
The Franchisee shall comply with the Franchisor's brand guidelines or instructions (a copy of which has been provided) relating to the form and context in which the Intellectual Property and literature are used. The Franchisee acknowledges that the Franchisee has no rights in or to the Intellectual Property and undertakes not to do or omit to do anything by which the goodwill and reputation associated with the Intellectual Property might be diminished or jeopardised.

Data
The Franchisor maintains a data protection notification under the Data Protection Act 1998 and the Franchisee must familiarise itself with the Franchisor's Data Protection and Privacy Policy (a copy of which has been provided and further copies of which are available from the Franchisor on request) The Franchisee shall at all times comply with the relevant data protection regulations applicable in the Territory from time to time.

Third Party Information
The Franchisee acknowledges and recognise that the Franchisee has received and in the future will receive from third parties their confidential or proprietary information subject to a duty on the Franchisee's part to maintain the confidentiality of such information and to use it only for certain limited purposes.

Deductions
The Franchisor reserves the right in its absolute discretion to deduct from the Franchisee's commission or other sums payable to the Franchisee or require payment from the Franchisee of all sums directly or indirectly owed to the Franchisor.

Freedom
Each party represents and warrants to the other that it is free to enter into this Agreement and is under no restriction or obligation which prevents it from freely entering into this Agreement.

Commercial Contracts Checklists

Appendix 2.6 Franchise Agreement Checklist

In preparing franchise agreements, individuals or businesses should consider the following non-exhaustive matters.

Actions/Issues:	Comments:	✍

1 Review the nature of and proposed franchising arrangements for appointment of the franchisee. ☐

2 Recite in introductory paragraphs relevant information including the franchisor's reputation, goodwill and business, relevant trade marks, ownership of the system and expansion of the franchise network, acknowledgement of business risk and legal advice. ☐

3 What type of franchisee is to be appointed? Ascertain or consider sole franchisee, exclusive franchisee, non-exclusive franchisee or sole and exclusive franchisee. ☐

4 Set out parties details including: ☐

    4.1 franchisee's name and address; ☐

    4.2 franchisor's name and address; ☐

    4.3 guarantor's name and address; ☐

    4.4 franchisee's contact details including email, telephone, fax and mobile telephone; ☐

    4.5 commencement date. ☐

5 In relation to the franchise, indicate the grant of right to carry on business on terms. ☐

6 Consider and indicate obligation to provide initial training in relation to the franchise, business, operations and manual prior to commencement. ☐

7 Define relevant terms as appropriate. Consider the following: system; know-how; equipment; territory; the package; marketing; and promotions contribution; initial charge and the manual. ☐

8 Ascertain, consider and specify the rights granted to the franchisee in relation to: ☐

    8.1 use of system and know-how to operate the business; ☐

    8.2 using the brand and trade marks; ☐

8.3 manual; ☐

8.4 annual sales targets; ☐

8.5 exclusivity of territory and whether subject to target maintenance; ☐

8.6 marketing, promotions or advertising; ☐

8.7 administrative and management support; ☐

8.8 franchisee's territory; ☐

8.9 the term of the appointment; ☐

8.10 other restrictions applicable to the franchisee in respect of the territory; ☐

8.11 franchisor's right to sell directly; ☐

8.12 appointment of additional franchisees or an agent or distributor; ☐

8.13 franchisee's right to complete unsolicited orders from outside the territory; ☐

8.14 option in respect of future renewal of agreement; ☐

8.15 option for franchisee in relation to new or related territories. ☐

9 Ascertain, consider and indicate in relation to the duration of the franchising arrangement:

9.1 whether fixed term contract and if so number of years; ☐

9.2 automatic or conditional renewal right exercisable within specified period; ☐

9.3 whether for an indefinite period; ☐

9.4 whether terminable by notice; ☐

9.5 applicable franchisor's notice period to terminate; ☐

9.6 applicable franchisee's notice period; ☐

9.7 whether appointment is permanent; ☐

9.8 whether term is conditional on occurrence of certain events or performance; ☐

9.9 whether term is conditional on minimum performance targets; ☐

9.10 length and period of franchise; ☐

9.11 other applicable notice periods; ☐

9.12 renewal and extension arrangements; ☐

9.13 any continuance following expiry of fixed term other than express renewal. ☐

10 Financial arrangements, payment details and remuneration structure should be set out including provision for: ☐

10.1 payment of initial fee to the franchisor plus VAT; ☐

10.2 management charge or service fee plus VAT; ☐

10.3 calculation of management charge (with profit element or percentage of receipts); ☐

10.4 advertising, promotions and marketing fee; ☐

10.5 payment without deduction or set off; ☐

10.6 date of payment; ☐

10.7 additional support fees; ☐

10.8 invoicing arrangements or requirements; ☐

10.9 payment of the franchisor's legal costs of preparation, negotiation and implementation of agreement; ☐

10.10 reimbursement or payment of administrative costs and expenses; ☐

10.11 percentage rate and payment intervals; ☐

10.12 basis of calculation; ☐

10.13 frequency of payments; ☐

10.14 dates of periodic review of fees and other remuneration; ☐

10.15 default interest payments; ☐

10.16 general vat liability and payment; ☐

10.17 liability for costs of travel and related expenses of attending training; ☐

10.18 agreed expenses upfront payment; ☐

10.19 marketing, promotions and advertising budget fee review; ☐

10.20 right of audit in relation to remuneration; ☐

10.21 sliding scale arrangements; ☐

10.22 provision of statements and audited accounts. ☐

11 Consider and specify obligations and duties of the franchisee including: ☐

11.1 to use the trade marks and brands for the business; ☐

11.2 to use the brands in accordance with the franchisor's brand guidelines; ☐

11.3 to make the payments promptly; ☐

11.4 not to damage goodwill or franchisor's reputation; ☐

11.5 use the know-how, system and confidential information only for the specified purpose; ☐

11.6 to obtain and maintain insurance as required by the franchisor; ☐

11.7 to operate the system strictly in accordance with the manual; ☐

11.8 maintain records as required by the franchisor; ☐

11.9 compliance with terms of its lease of premises; ☐

Commercial Contracts Checklists

11.10 not to disclose know-how, system and information to any third party; ☐

11.11 providing copies of corporate document including shareholders agreement, partnership agreement, articles and memorandum; ☐

11.12 to obey the the franchisor's reasonable instructions; ☐

11.13 to join in applications to record trade mark licences at registry, if required; ☐

11.14 not to be involved in any other trade or business during the term; ☐

11.15 not to incur any liability, obligation or debt on behalf of the franchisor;

11.16 to disclose all current business interests; ☐

11.17 act within the expressed authority or guidelines; ☐

11.18 to make full disclosure to the franchisor prior to contract; ☐

11.19 not charge excessive prices to customers; ☐

11.20 to immediately notify of any infringements of marks; ☐

11.21 not use any other trading names in connection with business; ☐

11.22 display brand at premises; ☐

11.23 to indemnify the franchisor in relation to the franchised business; ☐

11.24 to ensure retention of sufficient numbers of employees; ☐

11.25 avoid conflicts of interest; ☐

11.26 not sub-contract; ☐

11.27 to act in good faith; ☐

11.28 to comply with the franchisor imposed restrictions; ☐

11.29 provide the franchisor with periodic reports as required; ☐

11.30 assist the franchisor as reasonably required; ☐

11.31 not to engage in any prejudicial conduct; ☐

11.32 not admit liability, settle or make payment in respect of disputes without the franchisor's consent; ☐

11.33 maintain high standards in the franchised business; ☐

11.34 not do anything that may prevent or impair the development of the franchised business; ☐

11.35 comply with confidentiality undertakings; ☐

11.36 use best endeavours to develop and promote the business or supply of services or products in the territory; ☐

11.37 equipping, refurbishing and fitting out premises as specified by the franchisor; ☐

11.38 to only use franchisor supplied stationery; ☐

11.39 not to engage directly or indirectly with competing franchisor's business or the franchised business; ☐

11.40 to comply with information requests and comply with the franchisor's quality control activities or requirements; ☐

11.41 obtain and maintain VAT registration; ☐

11.42 to comply with the guidelines for the premises; ☐

11.43 to allow the franchisor access to premises and employees; ☐

11.44 provide periodic marketing plan, if required; ☐

11.45 notify the franchisor of any customer complaints or disputes; ☐

11.46 provide the franchisor with a breakdown of orders and sales; ☐

11.47 keep information confidential; ☐

11.48 not use information in any way detrimental to the franchisor. ☐

12 In relation to the franchisor's obligations, consider and indicate as appropriate: ☐

Commercial Contracts Checklists

12.1 provision of advice on set up, marketing and launch; ☐

12.2 to provide required advice, support and assistance; ☐

12.3 undertaking to treat the franchisees equally; ☐

12.4 organise annual franchisee's meeting or conference; ☐

12.5 to provide relevant know-how and system relating to the business; ☐

12.6 supply required stationery and agreed products, if applicable; ☐

12.7 provide training for the franchisee and staff; ☐

12.8 to act in good faith; ☐

12.9 to indemnify the franchisee for certain agreed and specified liability; ☐

12.10 support the franchisee in the sale of the products; ☐

12.11 provide timely response to enquiries from the franchisee; ☐

12.12 support the franchisee in the territory and provide continuing assistance as reasonably required; ☐

12.13 supply marketing and technical literature; ☐

12.14 to audit the franchised business periodically; ☐

12.15 to inform the franchisees of any legal changes which affect business; ☐

12.16 review the franchisee's sales activities; ☐

12.17 provide the franchisee with a copy of the manual. ☐

13 Transfer or sale of the franchised business must be subject to the franchisor's consent. Consider grant of pre-emption right to the franchisor in relation to such transfer or sale of the business. Any sale to be subject to conditions including suitability of purchaser, passing training and no debt. ☐

14 Ascertain and set out details or obligations relating to: ☐

14.1   advertising and marketing of the franchised business; ☐

14.2   guarantor's provisions and undertakings; ☐

14.3   approvals, consents, permits or authorisations required or obtained; ☐

14.4   intellectual property rights; ☐

14.5   insurance arrangements; ☐

14.6   confidentiality obligations; ☐

14.7   use of telephones or specified numbers; ☐

14.8   maintenance and use of premises; ☐

14.9   right of first refusal and option for the franchisor to purchase the franchised business; ☐

14.10 trade mark licensing; ☐

14.11 legal compliance; ☐

14.12 specific data protection policy and compliance; ☐

14.13 indemnities; ☐

14.14 improvements and changes to the business; ☐

14.15 data protection compliance provisions and undertakings; ☐

14.16 costs and expenses; ☐

14.17 force majeure; ☐

14.18 exclusion of reliance on representations; ☐

14.19 exclusion of liability or limitation provisions; ☐

14.20 exclusion of third party enforcement rights; ☐

Commercial Contracts Checklists

    14.21 restrictions on sub-contracting or assignment; ☐

    14.22 right to assign agreement; ☐

    14.23 applicable law; ☐

    14.24 jurisdiction submission; ☐

    14.25 dispute resolution procedure; ☐

    14.26 entire agreement; ☐

    14.27 arbitration; ☐

    14.28 rights of set off; ☐

    14.29 death or incapacity of individual; ☐

    14.30 non-competition undertakings and compliance with competition law; ☐

    14.31 indemnity in respect of certain matters; ☐

    14.32 reservation of rights; ☐

    14.33 applicable renewal fees; ☐

    14.34 inspection of the franchisee's books. ☐

15 Renewal rights provisions should be clearly detailed. Consider: ☐

    15.1 automatic renewal; ☐

    15.2 conditional renewal; ☐

    15.3 renewal by service of written notice; ☐

    15.4 setting out conditions precedent to renewal; ☐

    15.5 condition of no material breach; ☐

15.6 requirement to upgrade the premises; ☐

15.7 acceptance of current terms without amendment except for financial arrangements; ☐

15.8 waiver of all claims against the franchisor; ☐

15.9 completion of further training; ☐

15.10 loss of renewal right during the term; ☐

15.11 payment of the franchisor's legal costs. ☐

16 Termination of arrangements should be specified including termination: ☐

    16.1 by service of written notice; ☐

    16.2 for breach of contract; ☐

    16.3 automatically on retirement age; ☐

    16.4 specific termination events; ☐

    16.5 termination for insolvency or analogous events; ☐

    16.6 for change of ownership or control; ☐

    16.7 for material breach of contract; ☐

    16.8 for persistent breaches of obligations; ☐

    16.9 in the event of force majeure; ☐

    16.10 for non-performance; ☐

    16.11 where conflict of interest arises; ☐

    16.12 by either party on specified grounds; ☐

    16.13 by the franchisor on incapacity or death of the franchisee; ☐

16.14 in the event of prejudicial conduct damaging business reputation; ☐

16.15 for the franchisee's misconduct; ☐

16.16 if the franchisee is prohibited from being a director; ☐

16.17 by resignation from appointment; ☐

16.18 following suspension; ☐

16.19 for bringing the franchisor into serious disrepute; ☐

16.20 if the franchisee challenges the franchisor's intellectual property; ☐

16.21 upon the franchisee being convicted of a criminal offence involving dishonesty in respect of the franchise or records (if applicable); ☐

16.22 for the franchisee's acts of dishonesty; ☐

16.23 following the franchisee's bankruptcy or liquidation; ☐

16.24 where the franchisor abandons the business; ☐

16.25 where activities have detrimental effect on goodwill; ☐

16.26 upon provision of false information; ☐

16.27 on unapproved reorganisation which the franchisor considers detrimental to the business; ☐

16.28 breach of provisions of premises lease; ☐

16.29 for failure to maintain standards and following persistent customer complaints relating to quality. ☐

17 Consider post termination effect and consequences. Specify: ☐

17.1 cessation of trading under the franchisor's brand; ☐

17.2 cessation of any dealings whatsoever in relation to the business; ☐

17.3 survival of provisions; ☐

17.4 requirement to pay all sums due and owing; ☐

17.5 restrictions on non- solicitation of staff; ☐

17.6 restrictions against dealing with suppliers and customers of the business; ☐

17.7 non-competing obligations or involvement in similar business within specified location; ☐

17.8 return of the franchisor's property, documents, materials and equipment. ☐

See Precedent 2.6 on accompanying CD.

2.7 Provision of Services Agreement

Overview

Description of Agreement/Document

An agreement for the provision of services regulates the provision of services by a service provider to its client. The services differ but the form of agreement may be the same. Standard conditions of trading are often used and many businesses enter into formal bilateral agreements in relation to the supply of services. The specific terms of such agreements may depend on the nature of the services to be supplied. In general, they will set out the exclusive application of the terms, limit the service provider's liability and set out the arrangements in relation to performance, exclusion of liability, price and payment, warranties and indemnities together with the usual boilerplate provisions.

Practical Guidance/Issues List

Parties to a provision of services agreement should consider the following:
- Where standard terms are used by service providers, such terms should be carefully reviewed as they are usually one sided and may contain onerous provisions.
- Where individuals are party to the contract, any restrictive or unfair provisions will be subject to challenge under consumer protection legislation.
- Provisions seeking to limit liability or exclude certain obligations will be subject to the test of reasonableness or challenge under relevant statutes.
- Exclusion clauses should be properly but reasonably drafted to be effective. Post-termination restrictions will also be challengeable if wide or unreasonable in their terms.
- Protection may also be sought through a guarantor or suitable security arrangements.

Some Key Definitions

'Additional Services' means any other services other than the Services agreed to be provided by the Service Provider to the Client on agreed terms and set out as such in the Services Sheet.

'Service Provider Material' means any Documents or other materials, and any data or other information provided by the Service Provider in connection with or relating to the Services [including any targeted press or mailing list/customer data].

'Documents' includes, in addition to a document in writing, any designed material, map, plan, drawing or photograph, any film, video, tape or other device and any electronic or other material embodying other data.

'Client Material' means any Documents or other materials, and any data or other information provided by the Client relating to the Services.

'Services' means the [specify detail of relevant services], [   ] and [   ] services to be provided by the Service Provider for the Client and specifically set out in the Services Sheet (and the Services shall include the Additional Services where the context permits).

'Term' the period form the [start date] to the [end date] being the minimum period for the provision of the Services as set out in the Contract and continuing thereafter in full force and effect unless terminated in accordance with the provisions of these Conditions.

Specific Provisions

Services
The Services shall in so far as is reasonably practicable be provided in accordance with the specification (if any) set out in the Services Sheet but subject to these Conditions and shall be performed at such times as the Service Provider shall in its sole discretion decide.

General Commercial Agreements

No Warranty
The Service Provider does not warrant, guarantee or undertake on behalf of any third party supplier or service provider that access to any facilities or any products or services will be uninterrupted or of any particular level of availability or quality.

Materials
The Client warrants that any Client Material and its use by the Service Provider for the purpose of providing the Services will not infringe the copyright or other rights of any third party, and the Client shall indemnify the Service Provider against any loss, damages, costs, expenses or other claims arising from any such infringement

Liability
The entire liability of the Service Provider to the Client under or in connection with the Contract shall not in any event exceed the amount of the Charges paid by the Client for the provision of the Services for the minimum period set out in the Contract or for the first year of the Contract, if no minimum period.

Indemnity
The Client agrees to indemnify and keep the Service Provider fully indemnified from and against any loss claim or liability whatsoever incurred or suffered by the Service Provider as a result of negligence or any default by the Client (or its employees, agents or representatives) of its obligations however arising in connection with the Company or the Services, together with expense, claim, loss or damage which the Service Provider (or any of its employees, agents, sub-contractors and other clients) may suffer due to the negligence or breach of the Client (or its employees, agents or subcontractors).

Confidentiality
The Client specifically undertakes at all times to keep confidential any of the Service Provider's confidential information (including this document, the lists or specific customer details and information relating to the Service Provider's business or affairs) confidential and specifically not to disclose (whether or not for profit) such lists or information to any competitor of the Service Provider or any other person, firm or company engaged in similar activity during the Term and at any time following the date of expiry or termination of the Contract.

Appendix 2.7 Provision of Services Agreement Checklist

In preparing a provision of services agreement or letter, individuals or businesses should consider the following non-exhaustive matters.

Actions/Issues: **Comments:**

1   Consider and review the nature of the proposed arrangements. ☐

2   Indicate parties' names and addresses including registered offices and numbers. ☐

3   Recite relevant information in the introduction including, as appropriate: ☐

     3.1   nature of client/customer's business; ☐

     3.2   details of the service provider; ☐

     3.3   nature of the services; ☐

     3.4   agreement to provide the services on the terms but subject to the conditions of the agreement. ☐

4   What needs to be defined? Consider relevant terms having regard to the nature of the service provision: ☐

     4.1   services, additional services; ☐

     4.2   charges, fees; ☐

     4.3   force majeure event; ☐

     4.4   business, business day; ☐

     4.5   client, customer; ☐

     4.6   documents, intellectual property; ☐

     4.7   regulations; ☐

     4.8   service levels, service credits; ☐

     4.9   affiliates, group; ☐

4.10   term, commencement date. ☐

5   Set out: ☐

    5.1   appointment of company to provide services; ☐

    5.2   nature of the services to be provided; ☐

    5.3   client's specification, expectation or requirement; ☐

    5.4   level of service required; ☐

6   In relation to the supply of the services and additional services, specify: ☐

    6.1   right to make changes to the services; ☐

    6.2   manner in which services are to be performed and any specific instructions or requirements; ☐

    6.3   responsibility for obtaining permits, licences, consents or authorisations; ☐

    6.4   provision of the services in consideration of the fees; ☐

    6.5   access to records and any auditing rights; ☐

    6.6   right to suspend provision of services in certain circumstances; ☐

    6.7   provision of services to be with reasonable care and skill; ☐

    6.8   use of suitably qualified or experienced staff to provide services; ☐

    6.9   parties to co-operate and act in good faith; ☐

    6.10   prompt payment of charges and expenses; ☐

    6.11   obligation or option to provide additional services; ☐

    6.12   exclusion of liability for third party provided services; ☐

    6.13   requirement to comply with data protection rules or other specified regulations; ☐

Commercial Contracts Checklists

    6.14   obligation to obtain and maintain insurance; ☐

    6.15   provision of requested information or assistance; ☐

    6.16   record keeping requirement; ☐

    6.17   undertaking to conduct business in reputable manner; ☐

    6.18   arrangements for giving instructions; ☐

    6.19   maintenance of information or materials; ☐

    6.20   exclusion of all other agreements. ☐

7   Payment provisions should be set out. Specify: ☐

    7.1   relevant amount of fees; ☐

    7.2   additional fees and rates; ☐

    7.3   agreed rates or set charges; ☐

    7.4   payment structure; ☐

    7.5   payment periods and dates; ☐

    7.6   costs and expenses liability; ☐

    7.7   invoicing arrangements; ☐

    7.8   liability for tax, duty or VAT payments; ☐

    7.9   default interest liability provisions for late payments; ☐

    7.10   right to suspend services or terminate agreement for late or non-payment. ☐

8   Where relevant, set out intellectual property rights provisions and indemnities for third party infringement claims or other loss. ☐

9   Duration of the arrangements and term of the agreement should be specified. ☐

10 Termination rights should be set out. Consider who can terminate, grounds for termination and timing of termination. ☐

11 As to termination, consider termination for: ☐

    11.1 insolvency of either party; ☐

    11.2 consistent lateness of payments; ☐

    11.3 upon change of control of a party; ☐

    11.4 failure to pay on due date; ☐

    11.5 failure to perform; ☐

    11.6 force majeure following expiry of agreed period of delay; ☐

    11.7 inaccuracy of warranties or representations; ☐

    11.8 without cause but upon service of appropriate notice; ☐

    11.9 breach of applicable law or specific regulations; ☐

    11.10 fraudulent misrepresentations; ☐

    11.11 failure to remedy material breach capable of remedy; ☐

    11.12 breach of related agreement. ☐

12 As to liability, consider: ☐

    12.1 non-exclusion for personal injury or death; ☐

    12.2 liability exclusion for misrepresentation; ☐

    12.3 non-exclusion of liability for fraudulent misrepresentation; ☐

    12.4 total exclusion or limitation of liability, as appropriate; ☐

    12.5 maximum aggregate liability under agreement; ☐

Commercial Contracts Checklists

12.6 consider limiting liability to amount of fees paid; ☐

12.7 indirect loss, loss of profit and consequential loss; ☐

12.8 mutual exclusion of liability for consequential loss; ☐

12.9 exclusion of liability to any third party; ☐

12.10 excluding liability resulting from client's actions or instructions. ☐

13 Consider: ☐

13.1 excluding all other warranties to the fullest extent permitted by law; ☐

13.2 indemnity provisions, where applicable for specific breach or issues; ☐

13.3 liability for infringement of third party rights and claims; ☐

13.4 dispute resolution procedure; ☐

13.5 acknowledgement that no rights of ownership conferred; ☐

13.6 provisions indicating ownership of materials or equipment; ☐

13.7 acknowledgement of reasonableness or fair allocation of risk; ☐

13.8 non-solicitation of employees or business restrictions; ☐

13.9 requirement to comply with conduct of persons rules applicable at premises including security and health and safety issues. ☐

14 Consider force majeure provisions and provide for definition of force majeure, notification obligations and right to terminate in the event of lengthy delays. ☐

15 Consider and insert provisions relating to: ☐

15.1 liability for costs of preparation and implementation of agreement; ☐

15.2 agreement not to make claim against officer or employee of service provider; ☐

15.3 changes to agreement; ☐

126

15.4 service of notices; ☐

15.5 non-reliance on any representations or inducements; ☐

15.6 confidentiality undertakings and non-disclosure; ☐

15.7 data protection compliance; ☐

15.8 third party rights or enforcement rights exclusion; ☐

15.9 assignment of the agreement; ☐

15.10 arbitration; ☐

15.11 mediation or other alternative dispute resolution procedure; ☐

15.12 severance of unlawful or unenforceable provisions; ☐

15.13 non-waiver by delay; ☐

15.14 entire agreement between the parties; ☐

15.15 cancellation rights; ☐

15.16 fact of no partnership or agency between parties; ☐

15.17 further assurance; ☐

15.18 process or agent for service; ☐

15.19 governing law; ☐

15.20 exclusive, non-exclusive or one party submission jurisdiction. ☐

See Precedent 2.7 on accompanying CD.

2.8 Distribution Contract

Overview

Description of Agreement/Document

The distributorship agreement governs the commercial and legal relationship between a supplier/manufacturer and a distributor with regard to the sale of products. The supplier appoints the distributor to resell the supplier's goods in a particular territory and the distributor buys the goods at its own risk selling to its customers as principal.

The agreement regulates the distributorship arrangements and the relationship between the parties, sets out the type of distributorship and the extent of the appointment or rights granted. The agreement will refer to the contract for the sale of goods or the supplier's standard terms, detail the specific agreed provisions in relation to the parties' duties, rights and obligations. As the supplier will not have a direct contractual relationship with the consumer buying from the distributor, the agreement caters for relevant issues. It is normal for the agreement to deal with matters relating to exclusivity, extent of activities and the authority of the distributor, application of relevant regulations and sales targets as well as payment arrangements. It also details the duration and termination provisions applicable to the appointment.

Practical Guidance/Issues List

The distributorship agreement or terms of appointment can easily be set out in a less formal way and is often so set out between the parties in a detailed letter or heads of terms.

The entry into a distribution agreement setting out the respective rights and obligations of the parties is recommended.

If an organisation appoints several distributors in different territories, it is advisable for such an organisation to detail its terms in a standard form contract prepared in respect of each type of distributor and with regard to relevant territories.

The supplier:
- should consider imposing minimum targets and reserving the right to terminate for failure to meet the targets;
- will wish to ensure that there are no restrictions on its ability to appoint the distributor in the relevant territory and is not still bound by any previous exclusive appointment;
- needs to investigate the credit-worthiness of the distributor;
- may wish to consider partitioning the territory to break into a new market taking advantage of the distributor's local knowledge;
- should contrast the benefits of distributorship against agency;
- should undertake rigorous due diligence of any potential distributor;
- should review the distributor's other activities;
- may insist on an automatic right to include updated versions of the goods;
- will wish to consider restrictions on sales of competing product ranges;
- should consider the enforceability of any restrictions as they may still need to be considered in the light of reasonableness;
- will reserve the right to vary the price or list of products.

The distributor:
- may wish to secure exclusivity of a relevant territory;
- should resist and avoid obligations to use its best endeavours as this amounts to an onerous undertaking;
- should secure written guarantees of support required in respect of the distributorship;
- should review definitions carefully (such as 'goods') as they directly impact on its rights and entitlement;
- may require an automatic right to include updated versions of the goods or the right to refuse;
- should reserve the right to accept unsolicited orders from outside the territory;
- may wish to resist any minimum sales targets;
- should resist restrictive covenants that deprive it of its ability to continue earning following termination of the agreement.

The parties should:
- aim for a reasonable agreement that provides adequate protection for both parties;
- set out expressly what type of distributorship is intended in terms of the appointment and avoid reliance on any perceived terms of art such as 'sole', 'selective' and 'non-exclusive or exclusive';
- set out the scope of the agreement clearly to limit disputes;
- define terms fairly and clearly to ensure intention is achieved;
- detail the position with regard to new or improved versions of the products;
- consider the grant to the distributor of an option in respect of new or any improved products;
- clearly detail the extent of the distributor's authority to act on behalf of the principal including marketing, sales, negotiation and conclusion of contracts;
- secure relevant arrangements in respect of insurance required in connection with the products, services or parties' agreement;
- should avoid not entering into a detailed agreement in order to limit the potential disputes;
- decide on who will be responsible for compliance with applicable laws generally or in the relevant location;
- detail how product liability and other claims will be handled;
- should provide responsible handover arrangements;
- detail whether the supplier can make direct sales into the distributor's territory.

Law/Compliance Requirement

The relationship governed under the agreement is a matter of general contract law. Relevant statutes and regulations apply to the sale of goods and the sales relationship. These include the Sale of Goods Act 1979 (as amended), Sale and Supply of Goods and Services Act 1982, Unfair Terms in Consumer Contracts Regulations 1999, Unfair Contract Terms Act 1977, Trade Descriptions Act 1968 and the Consumer Protection Act 1987.

Review of such an agreement for compliance with competition law will be necessary as certain provisions of a distribution agreement may contravene anti-competition provisions set out in the Treaty of Rome and the Competition Act 1998. As distribution agreements are vertical agreements, reference will have to be made to the Vertical Restraints Block Exemption Regulation (EC 2790/99).

Some Key Definitions

'Products' means the products set out in the attached product list together with all applicable accessories manufactured and/or supplied by the Supplier.

'Customer' means any person, firm or company who is listed in the attached customer list or who has contracted, is contracting or may contract with the Distributor at any time during the Term for the supply of any of the Products.

'Year' means each year of this agreement being a period of twelve (12) months commencing on the Effective Date of this Contract and ending on the anniversary of the Effective Date in the following year.

'Restricted Area' means [specify country] and any territory in which the Supplier or Manufacturer carries on business or is able to demonstrate that it has substantive and developed plans to commence doing business in relation to the supply of the Products directly or through its agents and distributors.

'Term' means the period from the Commencement Date and continuing in full force and effect until the Expiry Date unless and until terminated in accordance with the provisions of this Contract.

'Territory' means the territory described in the Schedule;

'Invoice value' means the sums invoiced by the Supplier to the Distributor in relation to the Goods less any VAT and any agreed expenses including transport, loading or insurance costs.

'Person': any reference to a person includes natural persons and partnerships, firms and other such incorporated bodies, corporate bodies and all other legal persons of whatever kind and however constituted.

Specific Provisions

Assistance
The Distributor shall be provided with all required advertising, marketing and promotional materials (including relevant samples, catalogues, brochures and up-to date information concerning the Goods) as the Supplier considers appropriate or as the Distributor reasonably requires in order to assist the Distributor with the sale of the Goods in the Territory.

Delivery Time
Following each Order for the Goods, the Supplier shall [within [state period]/as soon as is reasonably practicable], confirm to the Distributor in writing the proposed delivery date for the Goods provided always that time of delivery shall not be of the essence but the Supplier shall use all reasonable endeavours to meet the proposed delivery date.

Entire Contract
This Contract constitutes the entire understanding between the parties with respect to the subject matter of this Contract and supersedes all prior agreements, negotiations and discussions between the Supplier and the Distributor relating to it.

Restriction
The Distributor, shall not without the prior written consent of the Supplier, during the term of this Contract (and for a period of [specify number] months after its termination) in the Territory or any part of the Territory act as agent, representative, franchisee or distributor for, or otherwise be directly or indirectly concerned with or interested in the development, manufacture, sale and supply of, any products that are of a similar description to or compete with the Products. This restriction applies to the Distributor, whether on the Distributor's own behalf or on behalf of any other person, firm or company whatsoever.

Third Party Information
The Distributor acknowledges and recognises that the Distributor has received and in the future will receive from third parties confidential or proprietary information subject to a duty on the Distributor's part to maintain the confidentiality of such information and to use it only for certain limited purposes.

Estimates
The Supplier requires from the Distributor an indication of its requirements from time to time and accordingly the Distributor shall serve the Supplier with one (1) month's written notice of the Distributor's estimated requirements for the Goods in respect of each month of the Term.

Territory
The parties acknowledge and agree that the Distributor shall not be entitled to seek buyers, establish any branch or maintain any Goods distribution depot in any location outside the Territory but within the European Economic Area, or to solicit Customers for the Goods in any location that is outside the Territory and outside the European Economic Area.

Description
The Distributor must not hold itself out as the Supplier's agent for sales of the Goods or as being entitled to bind the Supplier in any manner whatsoever. The parties agree and acknowledge that Distributor shall be entitled at all times during the Term to describe itself as the 'authorised distributor' of the Supplier in respect of the Goods.

Appendix 2.8 Distributorship Contract Checklist

In preparing a distribution agreement, individuals or businesses should consider the following non-exhaustive matters.

Actions/Issues:	Comments:	✎

1 Review the nature of and proposed distributorship arrangements and requirements for the territory. ☐

2 What type of distributor is to be appointed? Ascertain or consider: ☐

    2.1 selective distributorship; ☐

    2.2 sole distributor; ☐

    2.3 exclusive distributor; ☐

    2.4 non-exclusive distributor or representative; ☐

    2.5 sole and exclusive distributor; ☐

3 Set out parties details including: ☐

    3.1 distributor's name and address; ☐

    3.2 supplier's name and address; ☐

    3.3 distributor's contact details including email, telephone, fax and mobile telephone; ☐

    3.4 commencement date. ☐

4 In relation to the products, specify list of products. ☐

5 Consider and provide for right to add or reject new products (as appropriate). ☐

6 Consider and indicate obligation to provide training in relation to product list. ☐

7 Ascertain, consider and specify: ☐

    7.1 exact extent of distributor's appointment; ☐

7.2 scope of products to be distributed; ☐

7.3 any conditions of exclusivity; ☐

7.4 any required training; ☐

7.5 distributor's lack of authority to bind the manufacturer or supplier; ☐

7.6 distributor's independent status; ☐

7.7 precise extent of distributor's territory; ☐

7.8 the term of the appointment; ☐

7.9 restrictions applicable to the distributor in respect of the territory; ☐

7.10 supplier's right to sell directly into the territory; ☐

7.11 co-ordination of promotional activities with other territories or distributors; ☐

7.12 right of appointment of other distributors, agents, representatives or applicable restrictions; ☐

7.13 distributor's right to respond to or complete unsolicited orders from outside the territory; ☐

7.14 whether distributor will have exclusive, non-exclusive or sole rights in specific territories; ☐

7.15 option in respect of future product range; ☐

7.16 any required consents or permits for distributor. ☐

8 Ascertain, consider and indicate in relation to term or termination of appointment: ☐

8.1 term; ☐

8.2 any renewals or renewal intervals; ☐

8.3 whether fixed term contract; ☐

8.4 whether for an indefinite period; ☐

General Commercial Agreements

    8.5   whether terminable by notice; ☐

    8.6   applicable supplier's notice period to terminate; ☐

    8.7   applicable distributor's notice period; ☐

    8.8   whether appointment is permanent; ☐

    8.9   whether term is conditional on occurrence of certain events or performance; ☐

    8.10   any applicable minimum purchase or sales targets conditionality; ☐

    8.11   other applicable notice periods; ☐

    8.12   renewal and extension notice and new term arrangements; ☐

    8.13   any automatic continuance following expiry of fixed term. ☐

9   Price, payment arrangements and details should be set out including: ☐

    9.1   price; ☐

    9.2   price list; ☐

    9.3   full payment requirement; ☐

    9.4   credit arrangements; ☐

    9.5   price increases; ☐

    9.6   inflation linked price rises; ☐

    9.7   cost of production price increase; ☐

    9.8   retention of title until payment is made in full; ☐

    9.9   payment terms on delivery of invoice or 30 days, etc; ☐

    9.10   payment intervals and frequency of payments; ☐

Commercial Contracts Checklists

    9.11   dates of periodic review of prices; ☐

    9.12   applicable retainer payments; ☐

    9.13   default interest payments; ☐

    9.14   VAT liability; ☐

    9.15   agreed expenses or marketing contribution payments; ☐

    9.16   marketing, promotions and advertising budget; ☐

    9.17   right of audit in relation to sales and remuneration for compliance with agreement. ☐

10   Consider and specify obligations and duties of the distributor including: ☐

    10.1   to purchase the products from the supplier and pay the price on the due date; ☐

    10.2   to obtain all relevant licences and comply with import regulations; ☐

    10.3   to advertise, market and promote the products in the territory; ☐

    10.4   to obey the supplier's instructions; ☐

    10.5   to sell within the territory and act within the expressed authority; ☐

    10.6   to avoid conflicts of interest; ☐

    10.7   not to sub-contract or appoint sub-distributors without supplier's consent; ☐

    10.8   to provide sales forecasts and to act in good faith; ☐

    10.9   not to directly or indirectly compete with the supplier by dealing in competing goods without consent; ☐

    10.10 not to incur any unauthorised liability on behalf of the supplier; ☐

    10.11 not to make any representations or give any warranty on behalf of the supplier; ☐

    10.12 to keep the supplier informed of any change of control in the distributor or any proposed reorganisation; ☐

10.13 to inform the supplier of occurrence of any material adverse event; ☐

10.14 to maintain and insure stock as required by supplier; ☐

10.15 to comply with the supplier's brand guidelines in selling the products under the supplier's marks; ☐

10.16 provide the supplier with periodic reports of promotional activities and assist the supplier as reasonably required; ☐

10.17 to sell or purchase the agreed minimums; ☐

10.18 to service customers within the territory and not actively pursue clients outside the territory; ☐

10.19 not to engage in any prejudicial conduct; ☐

10.20 not to do anything that may prevent the sales of the products; ☐

10.21 to accept the supplier's standard terms and conditions for sale of goods; ☐

10.22 to conduct dealings and sales of the goods as an independent principal reselling the goods; ☐

10.23 to provide a copy of the supplier's standard terms to customers; ☐

10.24 to use best endeavours to develop and promote sale of products in the territory; ☐

10.25 provide periodic marketing plan; ☐

10.26 provide supplier with a breakdown of orders and sales; ☐

10.27 not assign the agreement without consent; ☐

10.28 keep disclosed technical information confidential; ☐

10.29 to respect the supplier's reserved rights. ☐

10.30 not use any disclosed information in any way detrimental to the supplier. ☐

11 In relation to supplier's obligations, consider and indicate as appropriate: ☐

11.1 agreement to supply the goods; ☐

Commercial Contracts Checklists

11.2   to approve promptly the distributors promotional materials; ☐

11.3   to supply spare parts and accessories as required by the distributor ☐

11.4   to act in good faith; ☐

11.5   to indemnify distributor for certain agreed liability; ☐

11.6   support the distributor in the sale of the products; ☐

11.7   provide timely response to enquiries from the distributor; ☐

11.8   support the distributor in the territory as reasonably required; ☐

11.9   supply marketing and technical literature; ☐

11.10   inform the distributor of contracts entered into with customers; ☐

11.11   to fulfil orders promptly; ☐

11.12   supply required training and support; ☐

11.13   to provide advertising and promotional materials in relation to the goods; ☐

11.14   review the distributor's sales activities. ☐

12   Ascertain and set out details of or obligations relating to: ☐

12.1   delivery of goods; ☐

12.2   acknowledgement of no compensation to be payable on termination; ☐

12.3   minimum purchase or sales targets; ☐

12.4   advertising, marketing and promotions requirements; ☐

12.5   requirement to maintain separate bank account; ☐

12.6   grant back of any improvements; ☐

12.7 appointment of sub-distributors; ☐

12.8 intellectual property rights; ☐

12.9 insurance of products; ☐

12.10 confidentiality obligations; ☐

12.11 legal compliance; ☐

12.12 product liability and claims arrangements or indemnities; ☐

12.13 maintenance of data protection policy and compliance; ☐

12.14 costs and expenses; ☐

12.15 force majeure; ☐

12.16 exclusion of liability or limitation provisions; ☐

12.17 exclusion of third party enforcement rights; ☐

12.18 restrictions on sub-contracting, sub-distributor appointment and assignment; ☐

12.19 applicable law; ☐

12.20 jurisdiction submission; ☐

12.21 dispute resolution procedure, arbitration or mediation; ☐

12.22 entire agreement; ☐

12.23 rights of set off; ☐

12.24 compliance with competition law; ☐

12.25 indemnity in respect of certain matters; ☐

12.26 reservation of rights; ☐

12.27 exclusion of compensation at termination (if appropriate); ☐

12.28 applicable renewal fees; ☐

12.29 inspection and auditing of distributor's books. ☐

13 Termination of engagement and appointment provisions should be specified including termination: ☐

13.1 by service of written notice; ☐

13.2 for breach of contract; ☐

13.3 specific termination events; ☐

13.4 termination for insolvency, change of ownership of distributor, material breach, force majeure, non-performance, conflict of interest or change of control; ☐

13.5 by either party on specified grounds; ☐

13.6 by supplier on incapacity of distributor; ☐

13.7 for distributor's prejudicial conduct; ☐

13.8 by resignation from appointment; ☐

13.9 for bringing supplier into serious disrepute; ☐

13.10 upon distributor being convicted of a criminal offence involving dishonesty; ☐

13.11 following distributor's bankruptcy; ☐

13.12 on reorganisation; ☐

13.13 on any other grounds. ☐

14 Consider applicable post-termination obligations for required period and specify: ☐

14.1 sell off stock held; ☐

14.2 restrictions on non-solicitation of staff; ☐

14.3 restrictions against dealing with suppliers and customers of the business; ☐

14.4 non-competing obligations or involvement in similar business within specified location; ☐

14.5 return of supplier's property, documents, materials and equipment. ☐

See Precedent 2.8 on accompanying CD.

Commercial Contracts Checklists

2.9 Consultancy Agreement

Overview

Description of Agreement/Document

The consultancy agreement governs the appointment of a consultant to provide certain services to a company or client. The specific consultancy terms will depend on the nature of the consultancy or type of services to be supplied. In general, it will set out the services to be provided, manner of provision of the services, limit the service provider's liability and set out the arrangements in relation to exclusion of liability, indemnity, quality of service, consultancy fees, charges and expenses, payment provisions, warranties and indemnities together with the usual boilerplate provisions.

Practical Guidance/Issues List

Parties to a consultancy agreement should consider the following:
- Where the consultant is registrable for VAT, the fees may be deemed inclusive of VAT unless otherwise specified in the agreement.
- Validity of any indemnity clause or restrictive provisions may be subject to the Unfair Contract Terms Act 1977.
- Provisions seeking to limit liability or exclude certain obligations will be subject to the test of reasonableness or challenge under relevant statutes.
- Post-termination restrictions will also be challengeable if wide or unreasonable in their terms.
- Protection may also be sought through a guarantor or security arrangements, if necessary.
- Care should be taken in drafting the force majeure provision as the courts construe such provisions as exemption clauses.

Some Key Definitions

'Consultant's Services' means the services to be provided by the Consultant to the Client and specifically set out in the Schedule (and the Services shall include the Ad hoc Services where the context admits);

'Term' means the period from the Commencement Date to the Expiry Date agreed for the provision of the Services until and unless terminated in accordance with the provisions of this Contract.

'Ad hoc Services' means any other services other than the Services agreed to be provided by the Consultant to the Client on an ad hoc basis on agreed terms or as otherwise set out in the Schedule;

'Consultant's Material' means any Documents or other materials and any data or other information provided by the Consultant in connection with or relating to the Services;

Specific Provisions

Discretion
The Services shall in so far as is reasonably practicable be provided in accordance with the requirements (if any) set out in the Schedule but subject to this Contract and shall be performed at such times as the Consultant shall in its sole discretion decide.

Maximum Liability
The entire liability of the Client under or in connection with this Contract shall not in any event exceed the sum of [£   ].

Confidential Information
All information (including, without limitation, the terms of the Contract, business and financial information, customer and vendor lists and pricing and sales information), disclosed by either of the parties (the 'Disclosing

Party') to the other party (the 'Receiving Party') pursuant to the Contract shall be confidential. Except as provided in this Contract, the Receiving Party shall maintain the confidentiality of all such information and shall not, without the prior written consent of the Disclosing Party (i) use the same, directly or indirectly, for its own business purposes or for any other purpose, or (ii) disclose the same to any third party.

Events Beyond Control
Each of the Client and the Consultant shall be released from their respective obligations and shall not be liable to the other or be deemed to be in breach of the Contract by reason of any delay in performing or any failure to perform any of their obligations under the Contract if the delay or failure was due to the occurrence of a force majeure event (being any circumstances or cause beyond the relevant party's reasonable control).

Commercial Contracts Checklists

Appendix 2.9 Consultancy Agreement Checklist

In preparing a consultancy agreement or letter, individuals or businesses should consider the following non-exhaustive matters.

	Actions/Issues:	Comments:	✎
1	Review proposed arrangements and intention of the parties in relation to the consultancy or related services.		☐
2	Consider use of recitals and set out in the introductory paragraph the nature of the consultancy, parties' aims, background and consultancy services relevant information.		☐
3	Review the nature of the client company's business, details of the service provider and nature of the services.		☐
4	Detail operative paragraph to provide that the consultant is to act as consultant and provide the services on the terms but subject to the conditions of the agreement.		☐
5	Set out the parties' names and addresses including registered offices and numbers (if appropriate).		☐
6	For ease of reference, relevant terms should be defined with reference to the nature of the arrangements or services to be provided.		☐
7	Consider relevant terms for definition including:		☐
	7.1 payments, charges, fees, consultancy fee;		☐
	7.2 conditions, currency;		☐
	7.3 services, ad hoc services, specified services, additional services;		☐
	7.4 force majeure;		☐
	7.5 notice, term, instructions;		☐
	7.6 staff, client, customer;		☐
	7.7 confidential information, documents, intellectual property, company materials.		☐
8	Set out in relation to the consultant or consultancy services:		☐
	8.1 appointment of consultant;		☐

General Commercial Agreements

8.2   agreement to provide consultancy services; ☐

8.3   nature of the services to be provided; ☐

8.4   client's service requirements and general consultant duties; ☐

8.5   how the consultant will describe himself or itself in relation to the client; ☐

8.6   how the services will be performed; ☐

8.7   where the services will be provided; ☐

8.8   any specific instructions for consultant to comply with; ☐

8.9   who obtains required consents or permits; ☐

8.10 that the services are provided in consideration of the consultancy fees; ☐

8.11 right to suspend consultant and service provision in certain circumstances; ☐

8.12 level of service and requirement for provision of services to be with reasonable care and skill; ☐

8.13 if appropriate, use of suitably qualified or experienced staff to provide services; ☐

8.14 consultant to act in good faith; ☐

8.15 prompt payment of consultant's fees and expenses; ☐

8.16 obligation to provide additional services on specified basis; ☐

8.17 exclusion of liability for third party actions or services; ☐

8.18 data protection compliance obligations; ☐

8.19 insurance requirements; ☐

8.20 provision of requested information or assistance from time to time; ☐

8.21 obligation to keep certain records; ☐

8.22 maintenance of confidentiality, client information or materials. ☐

9 What are the payment arrangements? Set out applicable fees and charges. Consider: ☐

    9.1 relevant consultancy charge or fees; ☐

    9.2 deposit payable; ☐

    9.3 invoicing arrangements; ☐

    9.4 liability for tax, duty or VAT payment; ☐

    9.5 default interest liability provisions for late payments; ☐

    9.6 applicable additional fees or rates; ☐

    9.7 hourly rates, liability for expenses and set charges; ☐

    9.8 payment dates, periods and discounts; ☐

    9.9 responsibility for costs and expenses (and evidence required prior to payment); ☐

    9.10 right to suspend services or terminate agreement for late or non-payment; ☐

    9.11 set off rights and right of deduction; ☐

    9.12 minimum fees, increases in fees or periodic review of charges; ☐

    9.13 termination or cancellation fee; ☐

    9.14 liquidated damages agreed payments, if appropriate. ☐

10 Detail intellectual property rights provisions and indemnities for third party infringement claims or other loss, where applicable or necessary. ☐

11 Specify how long the appointment will last or set out the term of the agreement. ☐

12 What rights of termination have been agreed. Termination rights should be set out as appropriate, consider: ☐

13 Consider relevant grounds for termination and set out as appropriate: ☐

13.1 insolvency of either party; ☐

13.2 failure to remedy material breach; ☐

13.3 persistent breaches or lateness of payments; ☐

13.4 change of control or ownership; ☐

13.5 failure to make punctual payments; ☐

13.6 failure to perform; ☐

13.7 force majeure; ☐

13.8 levying of distress against party; ☐

13.9 arrangements with creditors; ☐

13.10 insolvency or liquidation; ☐

13.11 prejudicing or putting client's business or intellectual property in jeopardy; ☐

13.12 upon service of appropriate notice; ☐

13.13 in the event of breach of applicable law or specific regulations; ☐

13.14 dishonesty, fraud or fraudulent misrepresentations; ☐

13.15 breach of related agreement. ☐

14 Consider and specify consequences of termination, including: ☐

14.1 payment of all arrears to consultant; ☐

14.2 payment of all other sums due; ☐

14.3 accelerated discount payment in relation to sums that would have fallen due but for determination; ☐

14.4 cessation of services or performance; ☐

14.5 return of client's information and materials; ☐

14.6 non-solicitation of employees or business restrictions and non-compete restrictions; ☐

14.7 certification of compliance with non-disclosure and post-termination obligations. ☐

15 As to liability, consider: ☐

15.1 non-exclusion for personal injury or death; ☐

15.2 liability exclusion for misrepresentation; ☐

15.3 non-exclusion of liability for fraudulent misrepresentation; ☐

15.4 total exclusion or limitation of liability, as appropriate; ☐

15.5 maximum aggregate liability under agreement; ☐

15.6 consider limiting liability to amount of fees paid; ☐

15.7 excluding liability for indirect loss, loss of profit and consequential loss; ☐

15.8 mutual exclusion of liability for consequential loss; ☐

15.9 third party action or liability exclusion; ☐

15.10 no responsibility for liability resulting from client's actions or instructions. ☐

16 Consider: ☐

16.1 excluding all other warranties to the fullest extent permitted by law; ☐

16.2 indemnity provisions, where applicable for specific breach or issues; ☐

16.3 liability for infringement of third party rights and claims; ☐

16.4 mediation, arbitration or other alternative dispute resolution procedure; ☐

16.5 acknowledgement that no rights of ownership are conferred in respect of client's materials or intellectual property; ☐

16.6 acknowledgement of reasonableness or fair allocation of risk; ☐

16.7 requirement to comply with conduct of persons rules applicable at premises including security and health and safety issues. ☐

17 Consider force majeure provisions and provide for definition of force majeure, notification obligation and right to terminate in the event of lengthy delays. ☐

18 Consider and insert provisions relating to: ☐

18.1 liability for costs of preparation and implementation of agreement; ☐

18.2 changes to agreement; ☐

18.3 service of notices; ☐

18.4 non-reliance on any representations or inducements; ☐

18.5 confidentiality undertakings and non-disclosure; ☐

18.6 data protection compliance; ☐

18.7 third party rights or enforcement rights exclusion; ☐

18.8 non-assignment of the agreement; ☐

18.9 legal proceedings or mechanism for referral to alternative dispute resolution; ☐

18.10 severance of unlawful or unenforceable provisions; ☐

18.11 non-waiver by delay; ☐

18.12 entire agreement between the parties; ☐

18.13 cancellation rights; ☐

18.14 fact of no partnership or agency between parties; ☐

18.15 further assurance; ☐

18.16 process or agent for service; ☐

Commercial Contracts Checklists

18.17 governing law; ☐

18.18 exclusive, non-exclusive or one party submission jurisdiction. ☐

See Precedent 2.9 on accompanying CD.

2.10 Management Agreement

Overview

Description of Agreement/Document

A management agreement relating to a club, hotel or other licensed premises is similar but not identical to outsourcing arrangements. It is also similar to a franchise agreement. The owner of a facility or business transfers the management of that business or relevant premises to a third party manager to manage in return for the payment of the management fee. The agreement simply regulates the management of the business, facility or premises (as the case may be) by the manager for retention of all income after payment of the management fees.

The specific terms of such agreements may depend on the nature of the management, the premises or business to be managed. In general, a management agreement will set out the parties' respective obligations. It may concentrate on the owner's obligations in respect of the premises and the manager's obligations in running the business or premises.

The agreement will set out the agreed provisions, indemnity and liability terms, arrangements in relation to performance, exclusion or limitation of liability, fee and basis of calculation, warranties and indemnities together with the usual boilerplate provisions.

Practical Guidance/Issues List

- The owner and manager may have a mutual interest in the management of the premises or business.
- Parties to a management agreement should consider relevant provisions relating to the owner's payment of rent to the landlord, compliance with lease terms and enforcement against the landlord.
- The manager will seek to ensure that the owner gives suitable undertakings in respect of the premises and its maintenance.
- The practical issue of transfer of the liquor licence should be dealt with and any application for a protection order.
- The owner may require the manager's personnel being added to the licence whilst remaining on as a co-licensee.
- The owner should investigate the resources, track record and ability of the manager.
- The parties will wish to deal with the application of the Transfer of Undertakings (Protection of Employment Regulations) 1981 or relevant indemnities in respect of the transfer of employees.
- Responsibility for the management and risk of the business should be clearly stated. The manager will remain liable to pay the management fees regardless of income.
- The owner may consider requiring a guarantor for the payment of the management fees during the duration of the management agreement.
- The manager may not wish to lose out on developed goodwill and negotiate a valued goodwill payment at termination.
- The owner will wish to ensure that no payments are due or payable to the manager for termination.
- The manager should consider securing the owner's consultancy during the term to benefit from the owner's knowledge and experience relating to the business, facility or premises.
- The owner should resist giving the manager trading access to the business, facility or premises prior to agreement.
- The owner should ensure that a confidentiality agreement is signed by the manager prior to disclosure of information in anticipation of agreement.
- The manager may wish to negotiate a trial period of trading with training with an 'out' clause without liability.
- The owner may require the manager to undergo training as with franchising.
- The owner may require a probationary period with a right to terminate.
- The parties may wish to provide for alternative dispute resolution prior to commencement of proceedings.
- All indemnities, force majeure provisions and liquidated damages clauses should be carefully reviewed as they are usually one sided and may contain onerous provisions. They may also be unenforceable as a penalty.
- Provisions seeking to limit liability or exclude certain obligations will be subject to the test of reasonableness or challenge under relevant statutes.

Commercial Contracts Checklists

- Exclusion clauses should be properly but reasonably drafted to be effective. Post-termination restrictions will also be challengeable if wide or unreasonable in its terms.
- The owner may consider alternative protection through use of a guarantor or security arrangements if suitable.

Some Key Definitions

'Owner' means [name of company] (registered number [   ]) whose registered office is at [address] which expression shall include its permitted successors and assigns.

'Name' means [name of company] the name and brand under which the Club and Business is carried on together with all logos and applicable goodwill.

'Equipment' means all the plant and equipment belonging to the Owner and used in the Business as listed in the Schedule.

Specific Provisions

Management Fee
The fees calculated in accordance with the provisions of the Schedule to this Deed being [   ] per cent of the Gross Revenue (as defined in the Schedule) of the Business for the Relevant Period (as defined in the Schedule).

Appointment
The Owner appoints and grants to the Manager and the Manager accepts from the Owner the sole and exclusive right to manage the Business under the Name as provided in this Deed.

Rights
The Owner agrees, in addition to the grant of the right to use the Name, to make available to the Manager the use of all fixtures and fittings, equipment and furnishings presently in and on the Premises.

The Manager shall not use the Name or any derivation of the Name or similar name for any other purpose nor for any other premises other than with the prior written consent of the Owner. The goodwill of the Club and the right to the Name shall not pass to the Manager at any time.

The Fee
The Manager agrees at all times during the Term to pay to the Owner in respect of the rights granted under this Deed the Management Fee on [day] of each [month] from and including the first [day] after [date] by standing order or banker's drafts drawn on a United Kingdom branch of a United Kingdom clearing bank or a combination of such methods of payment.

Income
Subject to payment of the Management Fee, the Manager shall during the Term be entitled to all the income generated from the Business.

Forfeiture of Lease
The Owner undertakes to the Manager that during the Term, the Owner shall, without prejudice to its rights against the Manager, do all acts and things necessary to prevent forfeiture of the Lease. The Owner shall not in any circumstances surrender or agree to surrender the Lease without the Manager's prior written consent.

Permission
This Deed shall create a mere permission to operate and manage the Business at the Premises and not a lease or tenancy of the Premises or an exclusive right of occupation of the Premises and it is agreed by the parties that the Owner has no power or right to confer on the Manager any of the rights, privileges or obligations contained in Part II of the Landlord and Tenant Act 1954.

Payment
The Manager agrees and undertakes with the Owner as follows: to pay all monies due under this Deed punctually and if not paid within seven (7) days of the due date for payment the Manager shall pay interest on at the annual

rate of [ ] per cent above the base rate from time to time of *[name of bank]* Bank plc from the due date until the actual date of payment (whether before or after any judgement).

Guarantee
In consideration of the Owner entering into this deed with the Manager at the request of the Guarantor, the Guarantor irrevocably and unconditionally undertakes and guarantees the performance by the Manager of all its obligations under this Deed and the due and punctual payment of all sums now or subsequently payable by the Manager to the Owner under this Deed when the same shall become due and undertakes that if the Manager shall default in the payment of any sum under this deed the Guarantor will forthwith on demand by the Owner pay such sum to the Owner.

Licences
The Owner warrants to the Manager that the Owner is entitled to the benefit of the Liquor Licence and the Public Entertainment Licence. The Manager will pay all fees and expenses for the transfers and grant of the Licences referred to in this clause and shall be liable for all annual and other renewal fees in respect of such Licences.

Commercial Contracts Checklists

Appendix 2.10 Management Agreement Checklist

In preparing a management agreement or letter for a club, leisure facility or licensed premises, individuals or businesses should consider the following non-exhaustive matters.

Actions/Issues: **Comments:**

1. What kind of premises or business will be managed:

    - hotel;

    - licensed restaurant;

    - licensed bar;

    - leisure premises or facility;

    - club.

2. Set out the manager's and owner's names, addresses and relevant details.

3. Is there a requirement for a guarantor?

4. Detail background and relevant information in the introductory recital paragraph.

5. Consider and define relevant words or phrases:

    5.1 business, business day;

    5.2 liquor licence, public entertainment licence (PEL) protection order;

    5.3 management fees, payment dates;

    5.4 commencement date, expiry period, term;

    5.5 employees, staff;

    5.6 management fees, payment dates;

    5.7 premises, rates, facilities, furnishings;

General Commercial Agreements

5.8 stock in trade, contents, plant, fixtures and fittings; ☐

5.9 rights, name, regulations; ☐

5.10 force majeure event; ☐

5.11 owner, manager, client, customer. ☐

6 Set out: ☐

    6.1 appointment of manager to manage the premises or business; ☐

    6.2 grant of rights to manager on a sole and exclusive basis; ☐

    6.3 manager's right to use the name or any derivation for specified purpose; ☐

    6.4 restriction of the goodwill passing to the manager; ☐

    6.5 manager's right to use all furniture, fixtures, fittings and equipment; ☐

    6.6 payment of the management fee to the owner by the manager; ☐

    6.7 undertaking by the manager to conduct managed business and premises on terms provided; ☐

    6.8 manager's agreement to enter licence agreement in respect of premises; ☐

    6.9 additional services to be provided; ☐

    6.10 owner's management expectation or requirement and level of service required. ☐

7 Will the owner undertake to the manager in respect of the premises or facilities? In relation to the premises or lease, consider and specify (as appropriate) undertakings by the owner:

    7.1 to pay rent under the lease; ☐

    7.2 to pay business and other rates; ☐

    7.3 to provide receipts of paid rental; ☐

    7.4 to enforce landlord's obligations under the lease; ☐

7.5 to seek to prevent forfeiture of lease; ☐

7.6 not to or agree to surrender lease; ☐

7.7 to indemnify the manager for all business rates liability; ☐

7.8 to leave all the equipment, furnishings and fittings at the premises; ☐

7.9 to provide manager with a copy of the lease. ☐

8 In relation to the management of the business or premises, specify the manager's: ☐

    8.1 obligation to make payments punctually; ☐

    8.2 liability for default interest for late payments; ☐

    8.3 obligation to pay all outgoings and running expenses promptly; ☐

    8.4 obligation to refurbish internal customer area as specified or to a high standard; ☐

    8.5 obligation to keep and maintain premises in full state of repair and decorative condition in accordance with lease; ☐

    8.6 obligation not to assign agreement or make changes to the services, business or premises; ☐

    8.7 compliance with the manner in which premises or business is to be run and any specific instructions or guidelines; ☐

    8.8 acceptance of licence or mere permission in respect of occupation of premises; ☐

    8.9 obligation to take reasonable care of owner's equipment; ☐

    8.10 obligation to maintain furnishings subject to wear and tear; ☐

    8.11 obligation to operate business within premises; ☐

    8.12 obligation to use requisite staff in business operation or management of premises; ☐

    8.13 obligation to only operate premises for specified permitted purpose; ☐

    8.14 obligation to pay management fees without deduction or set off in the manner specified; ☐

8.15 responsibility for costs of all utilities; ☐

8.16 entitlement to all income from business or premises subject to payment of management fees; ☐

8.17 obligation to maintain and protect goodwill; ☐

8.18 obligation to keep the business or premises open as specified; ☐

8.19 undertaking not to seek to part with or share possession of any space in the premises; ☐

8.20 obligation not to jeopardise the lease by any action; ☐

8.21 obligation to conduct business or premises in lawful manner; ☐

8.22 obligation to conduct business or premises in a high class manner preserving the character of the premises or business; ☐

8.23 obligation not to permit staff or clients to loiter outside premises; ☐

8.24 obligation to prevent nuisance and disturbance at the premises; ☐

8.25 undertaking to observe rules made by the owner's landlord as to use of the premises; ☐

8.26 undertaking to indemnify the owner against loss from breach; ☐

8.27 undertaking not to impede owner's landlord or owner in respect of possession or access to the premises; ☐

8.28 acknowledgement of no grant of exclusive possession; ☐

8.29 liability for water rates and to indemnify the owner for such liability; ☐

8.30 right to manage the business or premises and to make permitted changes; ☐

8.31 responsibility for obtaining permits, licences, consents or authorisations; ☐

8.32 access to records and any auditing rights; ☐

8.33 management of premises or business with reasonable care and skill; ☐

8.34 use of suitably qualified or experienced staff to manage premises or business; ☐

8.35 undertaking to comply with licensing conditions and regulations; ☐

8.36 undertaking to protect and maintain the liquor licence, public entertainment and games licence applicable to the property; ☐

8.37 undertaking to replace any damaged, broken or destroyed item and indemnify the owner against loss; ☐

8.38 undertaking to comply with fire regulations, health and safety and all other rules applicable to premises; ☐

8.39 undertaking to keep premises open to the public for not less than specified dates and times; ☐

8.40 undertaking to cooperate and act in good faith; ☐

8.41 undertaking to pay promptly management fees, charges and expenses; ☐

8.42 requirement to comply with data protection rules or other specified regulations; ☐

8.43 obligation to obtain and maintain insurance; ☐

8.44 provision of requested information or assistance; ☐

8.45 undertaking to maintain accounts and comply with record keeping requirements; ☐

8.46 undertaking to conduct business in reputable manner; ☐

8.47 undertaking to ensure removal of refuse and proper cleaning of refuse area; ☐

8.48 undertaking to promptly provide copy of any notices from local authority relating to the premises; ☐

8.49 arrangements for giving instructions; ☐

8.50 undertaking to comply with statutory, local government legislation; ☐

8.51 undertaking not to make any licensing applications except for renewals; ☐

8.52 exclusion of all other agreements. ☐

9 Income and payment provisions should be set out. Specify: ☐

9.1 manager's entitlement to all income less management fees and expenses; ☐

General Commercial Agreements

9.2 relevant amount of management fees; ☐

9.3 basis of calculation (percentage of gross revenue or net profit); ☐

9.4 additional or consultancy fees, agreed rates or set charges; ☐

9.5 payment structure; ☐

9.6 payment periods and dates; ☐

9.7 costs and expenses liability; ☐

9.8 invoicing arrangements; ☐

9.9 liability for tax and VAT payment; ☐

9.10 default interest liability provisions for late payments. ☐

10 What are the obligations in respect of the employees employed in the business? Consider application of Transfer of Undertakings (Protection of Employment) Regulations. Employees will normally transfer if going concern. List employees in schedule. ☐

11 Set out matters in connection with the business or premises for which an indemnity is required including (as appropriate):

11.1 owner's indemnity for employees prior to agreement; ☐

11.2 breach of provisions of agreement; ☐

11.3 manager's indemnity for employees after commencement date; ☐

11.4 damage to property, equipment, furnishings and other assets; ☐

11.5 indemnity for liability resulting from negligence or breach. ☐

12 In relation to stock, consider and provide:

12.1 for manager to purchase stock from owner on commencement date; ☐

12.2 for valuation of stock; ☐

Commercial Contracts Checklists

    12.3   for required quality of stock (saleable stock, satisfactory quality); ☐

    12.4   for sale of stock to owner on expiry of management at valuation; ☐

    12.5   for participation of parties' representatives in stock take; ☐

    12.6   valuation of stock at net realisable value or net cost; ☐

    12.7   stock payment arrangements or dates. ☐

13   Will owner agree to provide consultancy and advisory services during the term in relation to the management of the business or premises? Specify arrangements and defined role. ☐

14   Where relevant, set out intellectual property rights provisions and indemnities for third party infringement claims or other loss. ☐

15   Detail warranties (if applicable) of entitlement to liquor or related licences, agreement to consent to protection order, payment of fees for transfers and payment of renewal fees. ☐

16   Duration of the arrangements and term of the agreement should be specified. ☐

17   Termination rights should be set out. ☐

18   Consider who can terminate, grounds for and timing of termination. ☐

19   As to termination grounds, consider termination for:

    19.1   forfeiture of lease; ☐

    19.2   non payment of management fees; ☐

    19.3   closure of the club, facility, business or premises (as the case may be) for a specified period for any reason other than refurbishment; ☐

    19.4   upon damage or destruction of premises; ☐

    19.5   insolvency or bankruptcy (as appropriate) of either party; ☐

    19.6   consistent lateness of fee payments; ☐

    19.7   upon change of control of the manager or owner (as the case may be); ☐

19.8 failure to pay on due date; ☐

19.9 poor performance or failure to perform and provide the management services as required; ☐

19.10 force majeure following expiry of agreed period of delay; ☐

19.11 upon service of appropriate notice; ☐

19.12 breach of applicable law or specific local or licensing regulations; ☐

19.13 dishonesty, fraud or fraudulent misrepresentations; ☐

19.14 failure to remedy material breach capable of remedy; ☐

19.15 breach of related agreement. ☐

20 As to liability, consider:

20.1 non-exclusion for personal injury or death; ☐

20.2 liability exclusion for misrepresentation and non-exclusion of liability for fraudulent misrepresentation; ☐

20.3 total exclusion or limitation of liability, as appropriate; ☐

20.4 maximum aggregate liability under agreement; ☐

20.5 consider limiting liability to amount of fees paid; ☐

20.6 indirect loss, loss of profit and consequential loss; ☐

20.7 mutual exclusion of liability for consequential loss; ☐

20.8 exclusion of liability to any third party; ☐

20.9 exclusion of liability resulting from owner's actions or instructions. ☐

21 Consider:

21.1 excluding all other warranties to the fullest extent permitted by law; ☐

21.2 specific indemnity provisions for breach or identified issues; ☐

21.3 liability for infringement of third party rights and claims; ☐

21.4 dispute resolution procedure; ☐

21.5 acknowledgement that not part of owner, owner's group and that no rights of ownership are conferred; ☐

21.6 confirmation of ownership of materials, furnishings or equipment; ☐

21.7 acknowledgement of reasonableness or fair allocation of risk; ☐

21.8 non-solicitation of employees or business restrictions during and for specified period after end of contract; ☐

21.9 requirement to comply with landlord's rules or other conduct of persons rules applicable at premises including security, health and safety issues; ☐

22 Consider force majeure provisions and provide for definition of force majeure, notification obligations and right to terminate in the event of lengthy delays. ☐

23 Consider and insert provisions relating to: ☐

23.1 severance of unlawful or unenforceable provisions; ☐

23.2 non-waiver by delay; ☐

23.3 entire agreement between the parties; ☐

23.4 liability for costs of preparation and implementation of agreement; ☐

23.5 changes to agreement; ☐

23.6 service of notices; ☐

23.7 non-reliance on any representations or inducements; ☐

23.8 confidentiality undertakings and non-disclosure; ☐

23.9 data protection compliance; ☐

23.10 third party rights or enforcement rights exclusion; ☐

23.11 assignment of the agreement; ☐

23.12 arbitration, mediation or other alternative dispute resolution procedure; ☐

23.13 fact of no partnership or agency between parties; ☐

23.14 further assurance; ☐

23.15 governing law; ☐

23.16 submission to relevant court's jurisdiction. ☐

See Precedent 2.10 on accompanying CD.

3 Computer/Technology Agreements

3.1 Software/Hardware Sale and Purchase Agreement

3.2 Licensing Agreement

3.3 Maintenance and Support Agreement

3.4 Escrow Agreement

3.5 Information Technology Procurement and Turnkey Contract

3.6 Outsourcing/Application Service Provision Agreement

3.1 Software/Hardware Sale and Purchase Agreement

Overview

Description of Agreement/Document

A software/hardware sale and purchase agreement is a contract between a buyer and computer supplier. The contract sets out the arrangements for the purchase of computer hardware products, equipment or software. In certain cases, the agreement extends to the purchase of related services. It is not unusual for the transaction to be effected pursuant to the supplier's standard conditions of sale in relation to the computer equipment. The contract sets out the parties' arrangements in respect of the transaction and in particular details provisions relating to warranties, arrangements for delivery, installations, testing and liability.

Practical Guidance/Issues List

The purchaser of hardware or other computer equipment should take care in entering an agreement on the supplier's standard terms of business.

Where the purchase is by an individual consumer as opposed to a business, consumer protection legislation will apply. The supplier would not be able to rely on any unfair or unreasonable terms.

The buyer should reserve the right to reject the computer hardware/software if it is delivered late, fails testing or does not comply with the specification.

The buyer should be aware that the sale of the hardware may also relate to bundled software which is subject to the licence right of use. Such software is not purchased as part of the computer hardware sales.

Where the sale relates to software, the buyer gets a licence to use such software as provided. Software may also be sold on a package basis, off the shelf or bespoke rather than as a bundle.

The parties should treat the hardware sale as any other normal sale of goods taking into account the usual issues.

For the purchaser, delivery and installation may be significant. The buyer should also ensure that the hardware or software accords with its requirements and any specification.

It may be of assistance to the parties, if the buyer sets out its requirements in a specification.

The buyer should investigate the consequences of any breach of warranty by the supplier. The sufficiency of the remedies on offer (usually repair or replacement) should be considered.

Given the consequences of failure of the purchased hardware or software to a buyer's business, the buyer should resist any unreasonable limitation of liability or exclusion provisions.

If the acquisition is time critical, the buyer should make time of the essence of the agreement.

It may be worthwhile to agree a liquidated damages provision. The buyer should also obtain adequate warranties in relation to the computer hardware and/or software purchased.

An alternative dispute resolution procedure may be more effective for the buyer. The buyer should consider mediation, conciliation or arbitration.

Law/Compliance Requirement

The simple sale and purchase of computer hardware is a matter of sale of goods. The transaction will be subject to the sale and supply of goods legislation including the Sale of Goods Act 1979 and the Sale and Supply of Goods Act 1994.

Where a party to a transaction is an individual, then the contract will be subject to consumer protection legislation. This is in addition to the Sale of Goods Act 1979.

Applicable or relevant legislation includes:
- Sale of Goods Act 1979;
- Unfair Contract Terms Act 1977;
- Unfair Terms in Consumer Contracts Regulations 1999;
- Copyright Design and Patents Act 1988;
- Copyright as Rights in Databases Regulations 1997;
- Supply of Goods and Services Act 1982.

Some Key Definitions

'Products' means any Hardware (computer units, peripherals and other equipment) and/or Software (computer programs, bespoke software, operating software and the other Software products).

'Acceptance Test(s)' means the tests by the Supplier which are suitable to demonstrate that the [Products] comply with and perform in accordance with the Orders.

'Acknowledgement' means the Supplier's acceptance and acknowledgement of the Orders containing the payment schedule, timetable and detailing the implementation and each phase of the relevant Services.

'Contract Price' means the price payable for each of the Services (as the case may be) excluding taxes, specified in the Supplier's payment schedule or price list contained in the Orders.

'Orders' means the instructions and orders of the Customer in respect of its information technology requirements contained in an agreed form (including the specification of the Products describing the intended functions and facilities for the Products and the Customer's particular requirements on each occasion in respect of the Services, maintenance and other matters) from time to time and expressly accepted by the Supplier.

'Timetable' means, as regards any of the Supplier's obligations to deliver any of the Hardware, Software or Documentation (including operating manuals and technical specification) or to perform any of the Services, the relevant date or time agreed or set out in the Orders (if any).

Specific Provisions

Delivery and Installation
The Equipment shall be subject to testing by the Supplier in accordance with its standard works tests prior to delivery to the Customer. The Customer shall be provided with a copy of the test pass certificate together with the specification of the tests.

Off-Loading
On the Delivery Date the Supplier shall deliver the Equipment to the Off-Loading Point but shall not be responsible for off-loading the Equipment or moving it to the Location which shall be undertaken by the Customer at its own expense.

Acceptance
Once the Equipment and every part of the Equipment has successfully passed the Installation Tests the Equipment shall be accepted by the Customer and the Customer shall if required by the Supplier sign a commissioning certificate in the form annexed to this Agreement acknowledging such acceptance.

Costs
The Customer shall, in addition to the Price bear all properly and reasonably incurred costs of the Supplier in connection with the provision of any special equipment, personnel or works necessary to deliver the Equipment to the Location.

Passing Risk and Title
Risk in the Equipment shall pass to the Customer on delivery. The title to the Equipment shall pass to the Customer on payment in full of the Price and any other sums which may then be due under this Agreement.

Information and Access
The Customer undertakes to provide the Supplier with information and access to staff and facilities during normal working hours as may be necessary for the installation of the Equipment.

Post-Delivery Tests
The parties agree that in the event that any part of the Equipment fails to pass the Installation Tests, either party can request that the Installation Tests be repeated on such part of the Equipment within a reasonable time.

Commercial Contracts Checklists

Appendix 3.1 Software/Hardware Sale and Purchase Agreement Checklist

In preparing a software/hardware sale and purchase agreement or letter, individuals or businesses should consider the following non-exhaustive matters.

Actions/Issues:	Comments:	✎

1 Consider: ☐

    1.1   setting out the background to the evaluation; ☐

    1.2   relevant details of the parties; ☐

    1.3   setting out the purpose of the evaluation; ☐

    1.4   effect of a successful outcome or evaluation: ☐

        1.4.1   entry into licence; ☐

2 Review the parties' arrangements, objectives and key terms agreed. ☐

3 Consider specific terms requiring definitions including: ☐

    3.1   product(s), goods, software, hardware, equipment; ☐

    3.2   manufacturer, supplier, customer, purchaser, group company; ☐

    3.3   equipment, price or product price; ☐

    3.4   documentation, manuals, instructions; ☐

    3.5   location, off-loading point, delivery date. ☐

4 What are the products or services to be supplied? Consider any bundled or package software. ☐

5 Consider provisions: ☐

    5.1   for equipment to be sold by seller with full title guarantee and free from lien, charges or encumbrances; ☐

Computer/Technology Agreements

	5.2	for installation of relevant hardware or equipment;	☐
	5.3	in relation to delivery and installation date;	☐
	5.4	relating to the provision of maintenance or any other service following the sale of products;	☐
	5.5	allowing seller to substitute equipment;	☐
	5.6	restricting price increase or loss of quality in the event that seller substitutes product or equipment prior to delivery;	☐
	5.7	specifying what is supplied with the product or equipment purchased (including software, licences, relevant materials or operating supplies).	☐
6	Have all the express terms agreed between the buyer and seller been incorporated into or set out in the contract?		☐
7	Is the buyer relying on the supplier's recommendation as to the suitability of the equipment or product?		☐
8	Are there any specific purposes for which the equipment or product will be used?		☐
9	Has the buyer informed the seller of likely losses from non-compliance with any specification or breach of contract?		☐
10	Consider in relation to cancellation whether:		☐
	10.1	the order is cancellable after specific date or at any time;	☐
	10.2	the consequences of cancellation (prior to delivery or at delivery);	☐
	10.3	who can cancel the order;	☐
	10.4	procedure for cancellation of orders and service of notice;	☐
	10.5	liquidated damages sum payable upon cancellation;	☐
	10.6	forfeiture of deposit;	☐
	10.7	whether the deposit is deductible from cancellation charge;	☐
	10.8	any other obligation or duty in relation to cancellation.	☐
11	Price and payment. Consider or specify:		☐

Commercial Contracts Checklists

11.1 the price payable by the buyer; ☐

11.2 any additional charges; ☐

11.3 any applicable initial fee or licence fee in relation to the software; ☐

11.4 whether the price is inclusive or exclusive of VAT and payment dates or arrangements; ☐

11.5 seller's right to vary price and any consequences of such variation; ☐

11.6 right to charge default interest for late payments at specified rate; ☐

11.7 whether the purchase is by reference to a quoted price, price list or written confirmation; ☐

11.8 if the price includes carriage and delivery; ☐

11.9 whether the price includes packaging and insurance; ☐

11.10 right to unilateral price variations; ☐

11.11 any other costs and expenses including deposit payment or charge for non-return of pallets and reusable packaging; ☐

11.12 method of delivery or service of invoices; ☐

11.13 whether payment is conditional on any matter; ☐

11.14 restriction on additional charges; ☐

11.15 requirements for deposit of pre-payments; ☐

11.16 any discounts or early payment rebates; ☐

11.17 any other remedy for non-payment on due date (suspension of further deliveries or termination); ☐

11.18 any rights of or restriction of set off; ☐

11.19 agreed credit terms limits and obligations; ☐

11.20 required security or parent company guarantee or irrevocable letter of credit; ☐

11.21 whether payment dates and times are of the essence of the supply contract; ☐

12 Specification. In relation to the specification for the equipment or product, consider or specify: ☐

    12.1 who is to prepare the specification; ☐

    12.2 whether the seller can depart from the specification; ☐

    12.3 whether the buyer can terminate or reject the products for failure to meet the specification; ☐

    12.4 any warranties or undertakings in respect of the specification; ☐

    12.5 applicable time limits in respect of the specification and parties' obligations; ☐

    12.6 obligation or procedure to agree or approve the specification. ☐

13 Delivery. Will there be obligations or undertakings: ☐

    13.1 to deliver on or before a specified date; ☐

    13.2 making time or date of delivery of the essence of the contract; ☐

    13.3 to test the equipment or product prior to delivery; ☐

    13.4 relating to attendance or participation in tests or independent verification; ☐

    13.5 to off-load the equipment and deliver to a specific location; ☐

    13.6 for liability as to costs and expenses of delivery including transportation, packaging, off-loading; ☐

    13.7 for the supplier to install the equipment or product on delivery or other specified date; ☐

    13.8 for the buyer to allow access to the location for delivery and installation; ☐

    13.9 for the buyer to obtain necessary third party consents for removal or disconnection of existing equipment; ☐

    13.10 relating to maintenance of insurance; ☐

    13.11 buyer preparing location for installation and providing required assistance; ☐

Commercial Contracts Checklists

    13.12 relating to collection by the buyer, delivery to carrier or other specific arrangements; ☐

    13.13 as to who bears the risk in transit; ☐

    13.14 delayed delivery due to force majeure or other reason; ☐

    13.15 as to delivery of more or less of stated quantities and for delivery by instalments; ☐

    13.16 whether special arrangements are to be made for import/export licences and whether delivery is FOB or CIF. ☐

14   As to risk and title, consider: ☐

    14.1 whether title to the equipment will pass; ☐

    14.2 whether title will pass on payment in full of the price and/or all other sums; ☐

    14.3 when risk in the equipment or product will pass; ☐

    14.4 whether risk should pass on delivery; ☐

    14.5 requirement to insure; ☐

    14.6 obligations in relation to storage; ☐

    14.7 whether the retention of title will cover all equipment not paid for in full; ☐

    14.8 buyer's right to resell prior to payment. ☐

15   Ascertain, review, consider and set out: ☐

    15.1 undertaking for the provision of information or assistance by the buyer; ☐

    15.2 obligation to provide facilities, equipment or access to assist the supplier; ☐

    15.3 requirements for testing the equipment or product upon delivery; ☐

    15.4 procedure for testing the equipment or product together with consequences of failure; ☐

    15.5 who may attend or carry out the tests; ☐

15.6 provisions for acceptance or deemed acceptance of equipment or product following delivery of information; ☐

15.7 requirements and obligation to obtain regulatory or third party approval and consents in relation to equipment, product or installation; ☐

15.8 obligations not to modify the equipment or product and to operate in accordance with instructions; ☐

15.9 liability for costs and expenses of any delay for customer. ☐

16 Term and termination. Ascertain, consider and set out relevant provisions including: ☐

16.1 how long the contract is for; ☐

16.2 commencement date; ☐

16.3 rights of termination if terminable; ☐

16.4 termination upon service of notice stating required period; ☐

16.5 termination by effluxion or expiry of term; ☐

16.6 rights of termination for: ☐

16.6.1 breach; ☐

16.6.2 material breach and failure to remedy; ☐

16.6.3 failure to pay price on due date; ☐

16.6.4 insolvency events; ☐

16.6.5 other agreed basis; ☐

16.6.6 termination immediately upon occurrence of specified default events; ☐

16.6.7 provision for buyer to terminate if the equipment or product is defective, lost, stolen or destroyed; ☐

16.6.8 consequences of termination and accrued rights or provisions surviving termination. ☐

17 Warranties. Consider whether the parties agree express warranties for the supplier and set out: ☐

    17.1   the supplier's warranties; ☐

    17.2   warranty that the equipment will be free from defects (workmanship and installation); ☐

    17.3   relevant warranty period(s); ☐

    17.4   obligation to promptly notify the supplier of defect; ☐

    17.5   supplier's remedy and discretion to repair or replace the equipment or product (or relevant part) at its own cost; ☐

    17.6   conditions (if any) to be satisfied by the buyer (including return of equipment or product); ☐

    17.7   fall back liability cap for failure to comply with repair or replace remedy; ☐

    17.8   exclusions of liability for misuse of equipment, alteration of equipment or product without consent, extraordinary use or accidents; ☐

    17.9   obligation to obtain and maintain insurance; ☐

    17.10   undertaking to pass on manufacturer's warranty (if applicable). ☐

18 Intellectual property rights. Consider provisions for intellectual property rights and indemnity. Ascertain and specify as relevant: ☐

    18.1   warranty of non-infringement of third party rights by the supplier; ☐

    18.2   supplier's indemnity in respect of loss resulting from use or possession of equipment or product which infringes third party rights; ☐

    18.3   relevant conditions to be satisfied by the buyer in the event of a third party claim including: ☐

        18.3.1   notification; ☐

        18.3.2   non-admission of allegation; ☐

        18.3.3   passing claim conduct or negotiations to supplier; ☐

        18.3.4   provide requested reasonable assistance; ☐

Computer/Technology Agreements

18.4 exclusions from indemnity in relation to misuse of equipment; ☐

18.5 obligation to procure the buyer's right to continue using equipment, to replace or modify or refund fee payment in the event of infringement. ☐

19 Supplier's liability provisions. Consider: ☐

19.1 proposed exclusion or limitation of liability; ☐

19.2 liability for death or personal injury; ☐

19.3 liability for damage to property; ☐

19.4 indemnity from supplier for specific loss; ☐

19.5 liability cap for each event or series of events or connected events; ☐

19.6 capping liability for a fixed sum or insurance amount; ☐

19.7 excluding liability for loss of profits, data loss and consequential loss; ☐

19.8 exclude liability for non-fraudulent misrepresentation and mis-description. ☐

20 Consider, review and set out (as appropriate): ☐

20.1 data protection obligations; ☐

20.2 fitness for purpose warranty or exclusion; ☐

20.3 performance criteria warranty or exclusion; ☐

20.4 exclusion of all warranties not expressly set out in contract; ☐

20.5 buyer's warranty and non-reliance on oral representation; ☐

20.6 notice provisions and confidentiality obligation; ☐

20.7 requirement for provision of documentation; ☐

20.8 obligation of supplier to provide training; ☐

Commercial Contracts Checklists

20.9 undertaking to provide support or maintenance for equipment or product; ☐

20.10 boilerplate provisions including (as appropriate or acquired): ☐

    20.10.1 right to assign contract; ☐

    20.10.2 entire agreement provision; ☐

    20.10.3 force majeure provision; ☐

    20.10.4 third party rights; ☐

    20.10.5 notices; ☐

    20.10.6 severance; ☐

    20.10.7 successors; ☐

    20.10.8 waiver of rights; ☐

    20.10.9 time of the essence; ☐

    20.10.10 costs and expenses; ☐

    20.10.11 rights of set off; ☐

    20.10.12 payment currency; ☐

    21.10.13 counterparts; ☐

    21.10.14 governing law and jurisdiction; ☐

    21.10.15 alternative dispute resolution procedure. ☐

See Precedent 3.1 on accompanying CD.

3.2 Licensing Agreement

Overview

Description of Agreement/Document

Licensing agreements in computer and technology contracts simply grant permission to do something that the licensee requires the grant of a right to do. In effect, the owner of software or other licensed products can specifically permit a third party to use such reference for specific purposes.

The licence agreement normally sets out the grant of the right, the extent of the rights granted, any specific restrictions and confidentiality obligations together with the specific obligations of both parties.

Practical Guidance/Issues List

A licence agreement in respect of computer and technology may relate to various subject matters, the type of licensed product and specific requirements of the parties.

The parties should:
- ensure that they have the right to grant the licence and the extent of licence or rights required;
- specify and ensure protection for the licensor's intellectual property rights;
- review any limitation or exclusion of liability provision for reasonableness and consider its unenforceability;
- consider provisions and procedures applicable in respect of acceptance testing, confidentiality, training and support services;
- detail arrangements in respect of deposit of the source code and applicable terms;
- take care in preparing any specification;
- take care in agreeing the terms (and conditions of release) of any escrow agreement in respect of the source code;
- specify the relevant restrictions on use of the licensed product;
- carefully review warranties to be given in the licence agreement;
- consider separate support and maintenance service agreement;
- ensure that the licensor is the correct licensing company with the ability to grant the licence and give the indemnification and ownership warranties;
- ensure that the licensor is capable of giving all of the warranties and guarantees;
- use the recitals and introductory paragraphs to set out the 'story' of the parties entering into the licence together with relevant background.

Law/Compliance Requirement

Apart from the law of contract, various statutes apply to the licensing arrangements. The Copyright, Designs and Patents Act 1988 is applicable to relevant intellectual property together with licensing arrangements. The Unfair Contract Terms Act 1977 and the Unfair Terms in Consumer Contracts Regulations 1999 also apply. Licensing arrangements have generated numerous cases on different matters including reasonableness and enforceability of limitation of liability clauses, misleading instructions in documentation and warranties.

The licensor has a responsibility to provide adequate information as held by the court in Anglo Group plc v *Winther Browne & Co Limited (2000) 72 Con LR 118* and *South West Water Services Limited v International Computers Limited [1998] BLR 420*. The *South West* case dealt with a licensee's entitlement to terminate the agreement for integration of software due to the licensor's inability to comply with the requirements of the specification.

Some Key Definitions

'Additional Charges' means the charges at Licensor's hourly or other specified rates from time to time for work undertaken on a time and materials basis and/or pursuant to provision of the services.

'Authorised Equipment' means the computer equipment with the specification details in the Schedule located at the Premises.

'Business Day' means any day (other than Saturday and Sunday) on which the clearing banks are open for business in the City of London.

'Licensed Products' means the [software programs/services, databases and/or products and/or applications] identified or referred to in greater detail in the Schedule using the software and databases and made available to the Licensee and other users [on the Site] together with the relevant Program Documentation (if any) including any New Release (if appropriate) of the same made or issued pursuant to this Licence constituting the Licensor's [service provider product].

'New Release' means any improved, modified or corrected version of any of the Licensed Products from time to time issued by or on behalf of the Licensor as providing substantial new features sufficient to be separately priced and launched as a separate module.

'Program Documentation' means the instruction manuals, user guides and other information (if any) identified in the Schedule to be made available from time to time during the term of this Licence by or on behalf of the Licensor at its discretion in either printed or machine readable form to the Licensee.

'Use' means the installation, use, storage, access, display, running or otherwise interacting with the Licensed Products, processing or transmission of the Licensed Products [on the Site] or (where in machine readable form) the Program Documentation for the processing of the instructions contained in the Licensed Products or (as the case may be) the Program Documentation [on the Site].

Specific Provisions

Licence Grant
Subject to the terms and conditions of this Licence Agreement the Licensor in consideration of the payment by the Licensee from time to time of the Licence Fee in accordance with this Licence hereby grants to the Licensee a non-exclusive, non-transferable and non-assignable licence to Use the Licensed Products [on the Site] (and where appropriate the Program Documentation) and to possess and refer to the Program Documentation.

Restriction
The Licensed Products are licensed and not sold. Accordingly, all rights not expressly granted in this Licence agreement are expressly reserved by the Licensor and/or its suppliers. Without limiting the generality of the foregoing the Licensee shall ensure that the total number of users of the Licensed Products shall not exceed the number set out in the Schedule and included in the Licence Fee. Additional users for the Use of the Licensed Products may be added upon application to and upon payment of additional user licence fee on the terms of the Licence agreement.

Permitted Use
The Licensee may use the Products only on the [Machine/Equipment] at the Premises and any use by the Licensee or other third party on any other machine, equipment or location shall be with the prior written consent of the Licensor.

No Reverse Engineering
The Licensee undertakes and agrees that it shall not (and shall not permit others to do so) decompile, disassemble or reverse engineer the Products or any part of the Products except as and to the extent permitted by law where this is indispensable to obtain the information necessary to achieve interoperability of an independently provided program with the Products or with another program and such information is not readily available from the Licensor or elsewhere.

Computer/Technology Agreements

Appendix 3.2 Licensing Agreement Checklist

In preparing a licensing agreement or letter, individuals or businesses should consider the following non-exhaustive matters.

Actions/Issues:	Comments:	☐

1 Consider relevant requirements of each party. ☐

2 What type of licence is required? Is the licensor able to grant such a licence? ☐

3 Consider: ☐

    3.1   the extent of the licence. ☐

        3.1.1   will it be a sole licence? ☐

        3.1.2   will it be sole and exclusive licence? ☐

        3.1.3   does the licensor require an exclusive licence? ☐

        3.1.4   will it be non-exclusive? ☐

    3.2   sending out the extent of proposed use or users. ☐

4 Review the relevant territory: ☐

5 Review the relevant territory and consider whether: ☐

- England; ☐
- England and Wales; ☐
- United Kingdom; ☐
- European Union; ☐
- the world; ☐
- M25 or other part of England. ☐

Commercial Contracts Checklists

5.1 specify country or territories. ☐

5.2 the relevant parties details including: ☐

    5.2.1 names and addresses, corporate information and principal place of business; ☐

    5.2.2 details of proposed users including members of the licensee's group of companies; ☐

    5.2.3 details of affiliates; ☐

    5.2.4 information relating to any agent through whom the licensee is acting. ☐

6 Will the agreement require the preparation of a specification? ☐

7 Is the agreement simply to grant a software licence? ☐

8 Are there any other services or matters to be dealt with under the licensing agreement? ☐

9 Consider:

    9.1 provision of maintenance and support services; ☐

    9.2 specific additional licences for group members; ☐

    9.3 software development; ☐

    9.4 installation and testing; ☐

    9.5 software programming; ☐

    9.6 provision of service level agreement; ☐

    9.7 licensing of improvements; ☐

    9.8 data processing; ☐

    9.9 software and related documentation. ☐

10 Specify the grant of the licence (if applicable): ☐

10.1   as being in consideration of the licence fees. ☐

10.2   on an exclusive or non-exclusive basis; ☐

10.3   as a non-transferable and non-assignable licence to use (if appropriate); ☐

10.4   as only right to use and no sale; ☐

10.5   as being subject to reserved rights of the licensor; ☐

10.6   as being subject to specified restrictions; ☐

10.7   relating to a specified licence period. ☐

11   Review, specify or consider: ☐

11.1   whether licence relates to specific existing software; ☐

11.2   whether third party software (by way of sub-licence) licence required; ☐

11.3   commissioned software or data build; ☐

11.4   numbers and copies to be granted; ☐

11.5   restrictions on licensee to use on network, multiple use or single use, machine and specified equipment; ☐

11.6   whether the licensee can further develop the software or carry out any works; ☐

11.7   whether licensee can market and distribute licensed product together with any developments; ☐

11.8   the position in respect of the source code and whether right to have access to the code will be granted; ☐

11.9   terms of any agreed source code access or escrow arrangements; ☐

11.10 any requirement for source code to be deposited with escrow agent or other suitable third party; ☐

11.11 whether the software can be installed directly by the licensee and any obligations in respect of delay; ☐

11.12 whether the relevant software is only operational on certain equipment and set out relevant specification; ☐

Commercial Contracts Checklists

11.13 commencement date of licence and required duration; ☐

11.14 any other feature of the licence or requirements of either party in respect of the subject matter. ☐

12 What will the licensor provide to the licensee? Will it include: ☐

12.1 relevant documentation relating to the software or material? ☐

12.2 access to website for software information or activation of disk? ☐

12.3 provision of the software from a website or by email? ☐

12.4 object code or source code user instructions and manuals? ☐

12.5 training? ☐

12.6 software or material testing? ☐

12.7 confidential information? ☐

13 In relation to the licence fee and payment terms, consider or specify: ☐

13.1 licence fee payable; ☐

13.2 licence fee payment date(s): ☐

13.2.1 monthly; ☐

13.2.2 quarterly on quarter dates; ☐

13.2.3 annually; ☐

13.2.4 30 days after specified period; ☐

13.3 any deposit or initial payments or fees due upon signing licence; ☐

13.4 any time based charges; ☐

13.5 any additional costs/material charges; ☐

13.6 whether any fixed costs are applicable (including staff, material and travel expenses); ☐

13.7 whether fee and sums are inclusive or exclusive of VAT; ☐

13.8 any default interest charges (and at what rates) for late payments; ☐

13.9 whether renewal fees are payable and if so when and at what rate; ☐

13.10 currency of payment and any liability for exchange sale fluctuations (if applicable); ☐

13.11 annual fee increases including: ☐

    13.11.1 contractual; ☐

    13.11.2 materials and costs increases to be reflected; ☐

    13.11.3 retail price index increases; ☐

    13.11.4 standard rates unilateral increases; ☐

    13.11.5 staff and loyalty (increases or decreases); ☐

13.12 any agreed recurring payments (including for new releases and updates); ☐

13.13 any liquidated damages payment provisions (reasonable to avoid being declared a penalty); ☐

13.14 whether payments are to be made in advance or arrears; ☐

13.15 whether payments are to be made by standing order, cheque, cash, telegraphic transfer or other specified/agreed method; ☐

13.16 whether royalty payments are applicable and applicable terms or percentages. ☐

14 Consider and specify in relation to the licensing arrangements: ☐

    14.1 whether agreement comes into force on date of agreement or specified start date; ☐

    14.2 duration of licence and any renewal terms; ☐

    14.3 whether renewal is automatic or optional; ☐

Commercial Contracts Checklists

14.4 whether agreement is terminable by either or both parties and on what grounds; ☐

14.5 whether duration of licence is simply linked to performance or payment of licence fees; ☐

14.6 required approval in respect of specification and any relevant provisions; ☐

14.7 required programming by or for the licensee; ☐

14.8 specific or agreed provisions relating to delivery, installation and access including: ☐

    14.8.1 date of delivery or access; ☐

    14.8.2 what is to be delivered; ☐

    14.8.3 manner of delivery; ☐

    14.8.4 installation arrangements; ☐

    14.8.5 whether time is of the essence; ☐

14.9 what documentation and in what form (disk, paper, web, email) it is to be provided; ☐

14.10 testing and acceptance arrangements (if applicable). ☐

15 Consider other relevant terms of the licence (including restrictions and obligations) and consider or specify. ☐

    15.1 whether copies of the software can be made (how many) and log numbers; ☐

    15.2 the obligations on the licensee to protect the software (what security measures must the licensee take?); ☐

    15.3 whether the licensee is allowed to grant sub-licences; ☐

    15.4 whether any third party can use the software or is it restricted to permitted users only; ☐

    15.5 any restriction as to use for a specified purpose only (internal affairs of the licensee); ☐

    15.6 whether the software can be used in all countries or there is a restriction on export or use in specified countries; ☐

    15.7 whether there is any third party software incorporated into the software or programs; ☐

15.8 any required time scales and whether time (e.g. for delivery or support) is of the essence; ☐

15.9 whether there will be an acceptance testing requirement and include provisions relating to: ☐

    15.9.1 deemed acceptance by licensee; ☐

    15.9.2 period of testing; ☐

    15.9.3 deadlines/preparation for testing; ☐

    15.9.4 testing by both parties, either party or independent third party; ☐

    15.9.5 re-testing requirements; ☐

    15.9.6 testing facilities; ☐

    15.9.7 satisfactory results certificate; ☐

    15.9.8 notification of result and consequence; ☐

15.10 whether any other services including maintenance and support services will be provided – and on what terms (agreement and additional charges). ☐

16 In relation to proprietary rights and restrictions, consider:

    16.1 acknowledgements of confidentiality, title ownership, interest and intellectual property rights of owner or licensor in the licensed product; ☐

    16.2 provisions in respect of back up copying (save as required or permitted by law); ☐

    16.3 restrictions and obligations on the licensee not to: ☐

        16.3.1 modify licensed products; ☐

        16.3.2 incorporate other software; ☐

        16.3.3 assign or transfer, encumber or charge the licensed products; ☐

        16.3.4 remove any copyright or other proprietary notice on the licensed products; ☐

Commercial Contracts Checklists

        16.3.5 circumvent the owner or licensor in connection with the intent of the agreement or agreed services; ☐

        16.3.6 resell, distribute or use except as permitted under the licence agreement. ☐

17 What about confidentiality and related obligations? Consider: ☐

    17.1 definition of confidential information; ☐

    17.2 whether such information will be marked and include codes or oral information; ☐

    17.3 obligations to only use the confidential information; ☐

        17.3.1 for the specified purpose; ☐

        17.3.2 in accordance with provisions of the licence agreement; ☐

        17.3.3 not to disclose to third parties; ☐

    17.4 other obligations:

        17.4.1 not to disclose to employees (except approved employees or on a need to know basis); ☐

        17.4.2 to only disclose to permitted third parties; ☐

        17.4.3 not to disclose pre-agreement information; ☐

        17.4.4 to indemnify the licensor for loss or damage resulting from breach; ☐

        17.4.5 not to directly or indirectly circumvent the licensor or owner; ☐

        17.4.6 to maintain up to date written records of information and documents provided; ☐

        17.4.7 to report knowledge of any unauthorised use of information or licensed product by third party; ☐

        17.4.8 to assist the licensor or owner by taking required steps to protect information; ☐

        17.4.9 to ensure compliance of third parties and employees with confidentiality obligations. ☐

18 What warranties will be given by the licensor? Consider or specify warranties relating to: ☐

18.1 title and right to licensed product; ☐

18.2 software being free and unencumbered; ☐

18.3 performance of any services with reasonable care and skill; ☐

18.4 reliance or non-reliance on any representations or warranties other than the licence; ☐

18.5 performance of software in accordance with (or substantially in accordance with) the specification for the agreed period; ☐

18.6 the licensed product performing the functions and facilities set out as the licensee's requirements; ☐

18.7 freedom from defects for relevant physical media containing licensed product; ☐

18.8 non-infringement of third party intellectual property or other rights of third party. ☐

19 Exclude:

19.1 terms and conditions implied by statute or common law if not expressly stated in the licence; ☐

19.2 grant of any additional rights or licence; ☐

19.3 warranty in relation to readiness for use if licence is for testing and evaluation of software; ☐

19.4 warranty that software will work on every type of system or with every type of software; ☐

19.5 warranty that training will be sufficient for any purpose; ☐

19.6 liability for loss due to failure to meet specifications; ☐

19.7 warranty that software documentation or instruction will enable user to fully use licensed product; ☐

19.8 warranty that software is 'error free' or is rectifiable if defective or will operate without interruption. ☐

20 Consider and/or specify:

20.1 remedy for breach of warranty including: ☐

20.1.1 remedy or defect and time frame within which error is to be remedied; ☐

Commercial Contracts Checklists

    20.1.2 conditions to be satisfied prior to remedy; ☐

    20.1.3 any indemnity for breach of warranty and extent of such indemnity; ☐

    20.1.4 relevant limits of liability and whether based on maximum sum (specified sum or licence fees paid) amount recovered by insurance. ☐

21 Term and termination. Consider and/or specify: ☐

  21.1 initial period of licence and any rolling term; ☐

  21.2 who can terminate the licence (either one or both); ☐

  21.3 how the licence is to be terminated: ☐

    21.3.1 upon expiry of licence period; ☐

    21.3.2 during the licence period by notice (without cause); ☐

    21.3.3 upon service of advance notice in writing; ☐

  21.4 on what grounds can the licence be terminated. Consider: ☐

    21.4.1 failure to pay licence fees or other due sums; ☐

    21.4.2 failure to remedy breach or material breach within specified period; ☐

    21.4.3 breach of agreement; ☐

    21.4.4 either party ceasing to trade; ☐

    21.4.5 non-performance of services such as support and maintenance; ☐

    21.4.6 occurrence of insolvency and related events; ☐

    21.4.7 appointment if received; ☐

    21.4.8 winding up or bankruptcy; ☐

    21.4.9 voluntary arrangement; ☐

21.4.10 administration order; □

21.4.11 inability to pay debts (as provided under section 123 of the Insolvency Act 1986); □

21.4.12 breach of sub-licence. □

22 What will be the consequences of termination? □

    22.1 termination to be without prejudice to accrued or other rights and remedies; □

    22.2 licensee ceases to use licensed products; □

    22.3 licensee to return licensed products and documentation; □

    22.4 certificate of compliance with post-termination obligations; □

    22.5 licensee to return confidential information; □

    22.6 destruction of materials. □

23 In respect of intellectual property rights, consider and/or specify:- □

    23.1 indemnity by licensor owner of the licensee for breach and proven damages awarded to any third party for intellectual property infringement resulting from use; □

    23.2 ownership of licensed products and all related intellectual property rights; □

    23.3 any access to source code by licensee; □

    23.4 ownership of any improvements or modifications by licensor or licensee; □

    23.5 any specific warranties relating to the licensed products and use; □

    23.6 what happens in the event of a claim: □

        23.6.1 who has conduct of claim; □

        23.6.2 any obligations for other party to assist; □

        23.6.3 reimbursement of costs and expenses; □

Commercial Contracts Checklists

  23.7 remedy in event of breach of warranty relating to intellectual property including: ☐

    23.7.1 procure non-infringement use or copies; ☐

    23.7.2 procure right to continue to use; ☐

    23.7.3 make relevant adjustment or alteration pending resolution; ☐

    23.7.4 indemnity from licensee in favour of owner/licensor for breach and against loss or expense resulting from its use or third party claims. ☐

24 Liability provisions should be considered and terms considered in relation to: ☐

  24.1 limiting liability to licence fee; ☐

  24.2 limiting liability to insurance sum; ☐

  24.3 limiting liability to maximum amount; ☐

  24.4 limiting indemnity in favour of licensee to specified amount; ☐

  24.5 non-exclusion of liability for death or personal injury resulting from negligence; ☐

  24.6 damage to tangible property; ☐

    24.6.1 loss of profit, business or revenue; ☐

    24.6.2 consequential loss or incidental loss; ☐

    24.6.3 loss of goodwill; ☐

    24.6.4 loss or corruption of data. ☐

25 Are there any specific matters for which an indemnity is required or suitable? ☐

26 Should each party appoint a representative? ☐

27 What about force majeure provisions? Consider terms of force majeure including: ☐

  27.1 non-liability upon occurrence of event; ☐

27.2 obligation to notify immediately upon occurrence of event; ☐

27.3 obligation to provide full details of nature and length of force majeure; ☐

27.4 what happens during delay? ☐

27.5 any right to terminate as a result of force majeure; ☐

27.6 what will amount to force majeure including specific exclusions? ☐

28 Review and consider (as necessary) provisions relating to:

28.1 waiver; ☐

28.2 notices; ☐

28.3 entire agreement; ☐

28.4 exclusion of pre-licence representations; ☐

28.5 successors and assigns; ☐

28.6 survival of terms; ☐

28.7 conflict between licence and schedule; ☐

28.8 third party rights; ☐

28.9 assignment and sub-licensing; ☐

28.10 status of parties as independent contractors; ☐

28.11 publicity and announcements; ☐

28.12 variation; ☐

28.13 data protection and legal compliance; ☐

28.14 governing law and jurisdiction. ☐

See Precedent 3.2 on accompanying CD.

3.3 Maintenance and Support Agreement

Overview

Description of Agreement/Document

Maintenance and support agreements are normally prepared to accompany the licence agreement of the software licensor. In certain cases, a third party service provider agrees to provide the service. The agreement is simply a provision of services agreement dealing with specific maintenance and support services to be provided. It sets out the parties' respective obligations including any agreed response times or service level agreement.

Practical Guidance/Issues List

A good relationship between the parties is key to a successful maintenance agreement. The parties will seek to clearly state their respective obligations and agree the precise terms of support and maintenance.

Care should be taken in agreeing the terms of the support services agreement as bad service will certainly diminish the use or value of the relevant software.

The parties may wish to:
- enter into a separate maintenance agreement;
- detail arrangements in respect of source code escrow;
- include the support and maintenance provisions in the relevant licence agreement unless services are being provided by a third party;
- carefully consider the effect of the warranties having regard to the maintenance obligations;
- consider and agree the extent of warranties required.

The customer:
- should insist on clear indication of prices and applicable charges;
- will require enforceable service level arrangements; should ensure the provision of all the relevant services it requires;
- should secure the right to use alternative support in certain circumstances;
- should require relevant training, if necessary;
- ensure that the full range of maintenance charges, costs and expenses are set out in the agreement.

Law/Compliance Requirement

The agreement and relevant arrangements are a matter of general contract law. However, any provisions relating to the enforceability of restrictive provisions or limitation and exclusion of liability clauses will be subject to relevant legislation. Such statutes include the Unfair Terms in Consumer Contracts Regulations 1999 and the Unfair Contract Terms Act 1977. Cases such as *St Albans City and District Council v International Computers Limited [1996] 4 All ER 481 (CA)* shed light on the courts' interpretation of the enforceability of such provisions.

Depending on the nature of the business and services, regard may need to be had to compliance with the Data Protection Act 1998.

Some Key Definitions

'Additional Charges' means charges at the Service Provider's rates from time to time for additional services or work undertaken on a time and materials basis or services for charges other than the Fees.

'Licensed Products' means the software programs and products licensed under the Licence Agreement.

'Response Time' means the response times for [Technical Support] in respect of the relevant category as set out in the Agreement.

'Technical Support' means the provision of such categories of technical support in accordance with this Agreement as shall be specified in respect of the Licensed Products in the Schedule and shall mean [specify available levels or categories of support].

'Working Hours' means the business hours 10.00 hours to 16.00 hours local time in the United Kingdom, Monday to Friday, exclusive of United Kingdom Bank Holidays.

Specific Provisions

Provision of Services

The Service Provider, where applicable, in consideration of the payment by the Licensee from time to time of the Fees in accordance with clause [3] below hereby undertakes to the Licensee to provide the Services upon the terms and conditions of this agreement.

Fees

The Service Provider shall be entitled to vary the Fees from time to time upon giving not less than [thirty (30)] days' notice thereof to the Licensee.

Warranty and Liability

Subject to the exceptions set out in clause [9.6] below and the limitations upon its liability in this clause [9] below, the Service Provider warrants that it will perform the Services with reasonable care and skill.

Nothing in this clause shall confer any right or remedy upon the Licensee to which it would not otherwise be legally entitled.

Manager

The Service Provider shall appoint a manager who shall be responsible for the co-ordination of all matters relating to the Services. The parties agree that all documentation, communications and materials shall be sent to such manager. Such manager shall not be replaced without prior written consent of the Licensee.

Appendix 3.3 Maintenance and Support Agreement Checklist

In preparing a maintenance and support agreement or letter, individuals or businesses should consider the following non-exhaustive matters.

Actions/Issues: **Comments:**

1 Review the requirements of the parties in respect of maintenance and support services.

2 Specify what is to be supported or maintained (including any modifications or new releases).

3 What are the services to be provided. Will it be standard support service or are there variations to the standard service.

4 What is the term of the contract?

5 Will the maintenance and support services be provided:

    5.1 for a specific period (licence period);

    5.2 as requested by the Licensee.

6 Will the services be provided:

    6.1 remotely – specified method?

    6.2 by site attendance?

    6.3 by telephone?

    6.4 by internet website access?

    6.5 through email?

    6.6 by disk or CD?

7 Consider any agreed or required response times for provision of the services. Specify whether response shall be:

    7.1 within specified time;

7.2   as soon as reasonably practicable. ☐

8   What is the agreed remedy for failure to meet the responses times? Can the Licensee: ☐

   8.1   terminate the agreement? ☐

   8.2   suspend operation of the agreement? ☐

   8.3   be compensated? ☐

9   What if failure to meet response times is a as a result of the licensee's action. Can the service provider: ☐

   9.1   suspend provision of support service? ☐

   9.2   provide the service at extra cost? ☐

10   Consider and specify: ☐

   10.1   the right for the service provider to modify the software and make corrections or fix bugs and defects; ☐

   10.2   licence from relevant licensor in respect of support services. ☐

   10.3   insurance requirements; ☐

      10.3.1   minimum value; ☐

      10.3.2   employee's liability; ☐

      10.3.3   professional negligence; ☐

      10.3.4   product liability; and ☐

      10.3.5   third party liability; ☐

   10.4   key definitions of 'Additional Charges', 'Response Times', 'Technical Support Services', 'Site' and working hours as relevant; ☐

   10.5   consideration for provision of the services being the service fees. ☐

11   In respect of the fees and payment terms, consider and specify: ☐

Commercial Contracts Checklists

    11.1   amount of fees for standard service; ☐

    11.2   applicable VAT and whether fees are inclusive or exclusive of VAT; ☐

    11.3   date(s) of payment (and whether payable in advance or arrears); ☐

    11.4   additional charges for additional work; ☐

    11.5   entitlement to vary charges upon notice; ☐

    11.6   late payment interest charges. ☐

12   With reference to the technical support service to be provided: ☐

    12.1   specify category of support licensee requires; ☐

    12.2   consider what is comprised in each category of technical support; ☐

    12.3   specify customer's/licensee's preferred method of delivery of service; ☐

    12.4   exclude diagnosis or rectification of fault resulting from customer's/licensee's:

        12.4.1   failure to implement service provider's recommendations or solutions; ☐

        12.4.2   modification of the software; ☐

        12.4.3   merger of software with other programs; ☐

        12.4.4   improper or unauthorised operation of the software; ☐

        12.4.5   use of the software on equipment other than specified equipment; ☐

        12.4.6   permission for use by an unauthorised user; ☐

        12.4.7   breach of the terms of applicable licence agreement in respect of the licensed product or software. ☐

13   What other services are required or will be provided? Consider:

    13.1   consultancy services (outside technical support times) at specified rates; ☐

13.2 training services (as agreed); ☐

13.3 general services on an ad hoc basis upon request. ☐

14 Will the service provider's liability be limited? Set out entire liability sum. Will it be: ☐

    14.1 aggregate of fees paid for specified period; ☐

    14.2 maximum sum; ☐

    14.3 liquidated damages; ☐

    14.4 insurance sum. ☐

15 Consider excluding all other conditions or implied terms to the fullest extent allowed by law. ☐

16 Liability provisions could include: ☐

    16.1 exclusion of liability for consequential loss and loss of profit; ☐

    16.2 non-exclusion of liability for death or personal injury from negligence; ☐

    16.3 exclusion of liability in the event that the customer fails to comply with certain conditions (e.g. notice within time). ☐

17 What is the period of the support services contract and what are the grounds for termination. Consider and specify (as appropriate) termination: ☐

    17.1 upon service of periodic notice (90 days); ☐

    17.2 forthwith upon notice; ☐

    17.3 upon expiry of term by effluxion of time; ☐

    17.4 upon failure to remedy material breach; ☐

    17.5 upon persistent breach; ☐

    17.6 following non-compliance with service levels; ☐

    17.7 on the occurrence of force majeure event or after specified period; ☐

Commercial Contracts Checklists

    17.8   following insolvency of a party on normal insolvency matters including appointment of receiver, arrangement with creditors). ☐

18   Are the parties subject to any confidentiality obligations? Does the obligation survive termination of the agreement. How is confidential information defined and does it include written and oral information? ☐

19   Consider force majeure and relevant provisions including: ☐

    19.1   what amounts to force majeure; ☐

    19.2   effect of occurrence of event; ☐

    19.3   exclude or include payment obligations or failure of domestic or international banking systems; ☐

    19.4   obligation to notify the other party upon occurrence of event; ☐

    19.5   right to terminate for lengthy event. ☐

20   What are the parties obligations. Consider obligations on the licensee to: ☐

    20.1   provide requested information; ☐

    20.2   attend site or premises; ☐

    20.3   provide facilities and related services; ☐

    20.4   operate the software, maintain data and database in accordance with manual; ☐

    20.5   make available staff, office and computer equipment; ☐

    20.6   allow access to premises for customer provider; ☐

    20.7   notify service provider promptly of any fault or requirement for services; ☐

    20.8   allow remote access to licensee's equipment; ☐

    20.9   confirm and inform service providers of latest updates of the software or licensed product; ☐

    20.10   back up and keep copies of software; ☐

    20.11   not to alter, modify or otherwise tamper with software. ☐

20.12 only permit qualified staff to use the software; ☐

20.13 not attempt to fix the fault (without approval). ☐

21 Will the service provider be required to appoint a support manager? Can the support manager be replaced without customer's comment? ☐

22 What are the service levels agreed? Is there need for a service level schedule or agreement? In relation to service levels, consider and specify: ☐

    22.1 agreement of service provider to perform services in accordance with service levels; ☐

    22.2 applicable service credits; ☐

    22.3 required reporting; ☐

    22.4 maintenance record requirement. ☐

23 Consider dispute resolution provision with escalation from manager to independent third party. ☐

24 Consider: ☐

    24.1 non-solicitation obligations; ☐

    24.2 insurance requirements; ☐

    24.3 publicity restrictions. ☐

25 Consider boilerplate provisions and include (if appropriate): ☐

    25.1 entire agreement provisions; ☐

    25.2 waiver or non-waiver; ☐

    25.3 notices; ☐

    25.4 provisions relating to: ☐

        25.4.1 time of the essence; ☐

        25.4.2 severance and invalidity; ☐

Commercial Contracts Checklists

   25.4.3 third party rights; ☐

   25.4.4 entire agreement; ☐

   25.4.5 set off; ☐

   25.4.6 exclusion of representation; ☐

   25.4.7 successors; ☐

 25.5 assignment; ☐

 25.6 governing law. ☐

See Precedent 3.3 on accompanying CD.

3.4 Escrow Agreement

Overview

Description of Agreement/Document

Escrow agreements are agreements for a party to hold on to goods, materials, money, documents or other items on behalf of parties subject to agreed release conditions. The agreement is used mainly in relation to software codes that are deposited for access by the licensee in the event of the licensor's insolvency or failure to maintain. It may also be used in relation to the holding of monies or in respect of security for the payment of a debt or in connection with executed agreements prior to completion. The agreement sets out the owner's undertaking to deliver the relevant item, the escrow agent's duties and protection as well as the agreed grounds for release of the item. The usual boilerplate provisions are also normally set out in the escrow agreement.

Practical Guidance/Issues List

In relation to software, escrow agreements are important because software is normally subject to a licence to use rather than sold outright to the user or licensee. Accordingly a licensee requires protection and access to relevant codes or technical information in the absence or non-performance by the software owner or licensor. Such protection is provided by the requirement for a copy of the source code to be deposited with an escrow agent and to be released upon occurrence of agreed events. The same applies to trusted third party arrangements in relation to holding money, materials or documents by banks or solicitors.

The escrow agent:
- should ensure that the agreement is entered into on its own terms with sufficient protection from liability;
- should require specific and clearly defined release or trigger events;
- should obtain a clear indemnity for any liability it may incur in connection with the arrangements;
- will wish to reserve the right to go to court for declaration or hand the item to a court in certain circumstances.

The supplier (or licensor or owner):
- could wish to protect its intellectual property and the code (if source code escrow);
- should agree or limit the relevant trigger events for release of its code or relevant item;
- may wish to set out dispute resolution procedure.

The licensee or other party:
- will be concerned to broaden the release events;
- should ensure the independence of the agent;
- should ensure clarity with regard to the defined release events;
- should ensure that disputes or requests will be dealt with promptly;
- should require an obligation for updates and improvements to be deposited.

Some Key Definitions

'Authorised Person' means the duly authorised person or signatory in relation to each of the Parties whose details and specimen signatures are set out in the Schedule.

'Relevant Agreement' means the settlement agreement dated the same date as this Agreement and made between the Parties and the Debtor further to the Debt and monies owed to the Lender by the Debtor.

'Materials' shall have the meaning set out in the [Relevant Agreement] together with all materials listed in the Schedule.

Specific Provisions

Resignation
The Escrow Agent may resign at any time upon giving at least [ ] days' written notice to the Parties. Upon resignation of the Escrow Agent or any termination of this Agreement the Escrow Agent shall transfer the

[Materials and Documents] deposited in escrow in accordance with the written reasonable and lawful joint directions of the Parties signed by the Authorised Signatories on behalf of the Parties.

Release
The [Materials/Documents/Share Certificates] shall be released by the Escrow Agent in accordance with clause [ ] of the [   ] Agreement, upon receipt of a joint notice in writing addressed to the Escrow Agent and signed by the Authorised Signatories of each of the Parties instructing the Escrow Agent to release and transfer the [Materials/Documents/Share Certificates] to the Lender or any third party.

Appointment
Each of the Parties [irrevocably] appoints the Escrow Agent, and the Escrow Agent agrees to hold the [Share Certificates/Materials] upon deposit into escrow with it for the Parties on the terms and conditions of this Agreement and in accordance with the provisions of clause [ ] of the Instruction Agreement.

Escrow Agent
The Escrow Agent agrees to hold the [Materials/Documents/Share Certificates] as escrow agent for and on behalf of the Parties and otherwise to release, transfer or otherwise deal with the [Materials] as may be directed in accordance with the terms of this Agreement or otherwise to release, transfer or otherwise deal with the [Materials] as may be directed jointly in writing by the Authorised Signatories of the Parties.

Dispute If there i
s a dispute between the Parties or the Escrow Agent regarding the [Materials] (of which the Escrow Agent has received notice in writing signed by either party (as the case may be), the Escrow Agent shall continue to hold the [Materials] in escrow until the Escrow Agent shall have received a certified copy of an order, decree or judgement of a court of competent jurisdiction regarding the transfer and release of the [Materials], together with an unqualified opinion of counsel confirming the finality of such order or judgement.

Indemnity
The Parties *[jointly and severally]* covenant to indemnify and keep indemnified the Escrow Agent from and against any and all claims, losses, damages, liabilities and expenses and disbursements which may be imposed upon or incurred by the Escrow Agent in connection with the performance of its obligations under this Agreement.

Appendix 3.4 Escrow Agreements Checklist

In preparing an escrow agreement parties should consider the following non-exhaustive matters.

Actions/Issues:	Comments:	✍

1 Review nature of escrow and whether relating to money, technology, software, code, materials or documents. ☐

2 Set out parties' names and addresses including the owner, licensor, supplier, licensee, other contracting parties and/or the escrow agent. ☐

3 Consider: ☐

   3.1 setting out the background to the escrow arrangements; ☐

   3.2 reciting as appropriate, the grant of a software licence or entry into an agreement; ☐

   3.3 detailing the relevant software if technology code escrow; ☐

   3.4 describing technical information (required for maintenance and correction of the software) if source code escrow; ☐

   3.5 owner's acknowledgement of licensee's requirement for access to technical information, material, deposited sum or documents. ☐

4 Set out provisions relating to:

   4.1 appointment of the escrow agent; ☐

   4.2 basis of appointment and whether irrevocable or conditional; ☐

   4.3 basis of instruction to agent; ☐

   4.4 delivery or deposit of the relevant material or transfer of sum; ☐

   4.5 arrangements for escrow including requirements in respect of storage or bank accounts (as the case may be); ☐

   4.6 relevant consideration in respect of agreement or proposed execution as a deed; ☐

   4.7 any restrictions on copying, access or use of the deposited materials, if applicable. ☐

5 In relation to the escrow arrangements and the parties' obligations, specify (as appropriate having regard to whether relating to deposit of code, sums, material or documents) or consider: ☐

Commercial Contracts Checklists

5.1   owner to deposit or deliver; ☐

5.2   owner to update delivered items and further copies or materials; ☐

5.3   compliance with time limits; ☐

5.4   time being of the essence; ☐

5.5   delivery of replacement or update copy by owner or licensor, if code escrow; ☐

5.6   to comply with notices served by the escrow agent; ☐

5.7   deliver or deposit required materials, documents or sum; ☐

5.8   provide requested, relevant or required information; ☐

5.9   supply of additional or requested technical information, if escrow of software code; ☐

5.10   supply relevant or requested contact details of representative; ☐

5.11   notify change of details during the term; ☐

5.12   promptly serve required release event notices; ☐

5.13   appoint agent for service in territory; ☐

5.14   manner in which escrow services are to be performed and any specific instructions or requirements; ☐

5.15   responsibility for obtaining permits, licences, consents or authorisations; ☐

5.16   access to records and any auditing rights; ☐

5.17   parties to co-operate and act in good faith; ☐

5.18   arrangements for giving instructions; ☐

5.19   prompt payment of charges and expenses; ☐

5.20   acceptance of exclusion of all other agreements other than as expressly provided. ☐

6   Consider and review escrow agents duties and obligations including, as appropriate: ☐

    6.1   to accept the appointment as agent on the agreed terms; ☐

    6.2   to acknowledge receipt of the deposited or delivered item; ☐

    6.3   to hold the code, documents, sum or material on the terms of the agreement; ☐

    6.4   to keep relevant items safe and secure; ☐

    6.5   to inform the parties of any loss, damage, destruction or defacing of item, material or documents; ☐

    6.6   provision of services to be with reasonable care and skill; ☐

    6.7   requirement to comply with data protection rules or other specified regulations; ☐

    6.8   maintain confidentiality; ☐

    6.9   obligation to obtain and maintain insurance; ☐

    6.10 record keeping requirement; ☐

    6.11 maintenance of information or materials. ☐

7   Duration of the escrow arrangements and term of the agreement should be specified. ☐

8   Consider detailing required warranties: ☐

    8.1   of authority to enter into agreement; ☐

    8.2   of ownership of the relevant items to be held in escrow; ☐

    8.3   compliance with related agreement; ☐

    8.4   compliance with law or specified requirements; ☐

    8.5   completeness of item supplied. ☐

9   Will there be any obligations to: ☐

9.1   provide details and reports or provide additional items? ☐

9.2   keep information confidential? ☐

9.3   destroy or return the materials at any stage? ☐

10   What are the agreed release events? Specify: ☐

10.1   occurrence of an event specified in relevant instructing document or the governing agreement requiring an escrow; ☐

10.2   entry by specified parties into certain agreement; ☐

10.3   discharge of specified obligation; ☐

10.4   release of certain liability; ☐

10.5   receipt of particular documentation; ☐

10.6   execution of stated document or agreement; ☐

10.7   expiry of an agreed period; ☐

10.8   party or owner enters into liquidation; ☐

10.9   party suffers specified material adverse or other event; ☐

10.10   party ceases to trade; ☐

10.11   party being an individual becomes bankrupt; ☐

10.12   failure to carry out required action by long stop date; ☐

10.13   default of failure to provide maintenance, if software escrow; ☐

10.14   receipt of certified copies or originals of certain executed contracts; ☐

10.15   receipt of joint instruction from relevant parties to release. ☐

11   Consider reservation of agent's right to require sworn declaration of compliance or occurrence of release event. ☐

12 Specify means of service of notice on agent in relation to release event. ☐

13 Reserve agent's rights to release material, sum, item or documents without liability in absence of fraud or gross negligence. ☐

14 Consider and provide as necessary in respect of intellectual property rights and confidentiality. ☐

15 Reserve agent's protection to seek court direction at parties' cost in the event of dispute or uncertainty about its duties. ☐

16 Payment provisions should be set out. Specify: ☐

    16.1 relevant fees; ☐

    16.2 payment of agreed fees; ☐

    16.3 payment of standard published fees; ☐

    16.4 additional fees and changes in published rates; ☐

    16.5 agreed rates or set charges; ☐

    16.6 payment structure or schedule; ☐

    16.7 payment periods and dates; ☐

    16.8 costs and expenses liability; ☐

    16.9 invoicing arrangements; ☐

    16.10 liability for tax, duty or VAT payment; ☐

    16.11 default interest liability provisions for late payments; ☐

    16.12 right to suspend services or terminate agreement for late or non-payment. ☐

17 What are the provisions for verification, if relevant, and related costs. ☐

18 Provide for a joint and several indemnity by the parties in favour of the escrow agent against all liability or costs. ☐

19 Arrangements for successor escrow agent should be provided and relevant transfer of materials. ☐

Commercial Contracts Checklists

20 Will the: ☐

    20.1 agreement terminate for late or non-payment of fees? ☐

    20.2 agreement terminate on the expiry of a specified period? ☐

    20.3 agreement terminate forthwith upon service of notice in writing by the parties to the agent? ☐

    20.4 agreement require termination upon service of written notice giving a specified period? ☐

    20.5 agreement be terminable by the escrow agent upon material breach or insolvency of any of parties? ☐

    20.6 agreement terminate upon termination of governing or other agreement? ☐

    20.7 agreement contain relevant post-termination obligations? ☐

    20.8 escrow agent be required to re-deliver the items to the owner or an appointed independent party on termination? ☐

    20.9 the agent or any party be entitled to terminate for:

        20.9.1 insolvency of either party? ☐

        20.9.2 upon change of control of a party? ☐

21 Consider intellectual property provisions including: ☐

    21.1 setting out ownership of intellectual property notwithstanding deposit of materials or escrow; ☐

    21.2 making provision for modifications and improvements; ☐

    21.3 relevant indemnity for breach of third party intellectual property rights; ☐

    21.4 requirement of acknowledgement of ownership and undertaking not to assert claim on the intellectual property. ☐

22 Consider force majeure provisions, if relevant, in favour of the escrow agent. Provide as appropriate for definition of force majeure, notification obligation and right to terminate in the event of specified lengthy delays. ☐

23 As to liability, consider: ☐

    23.1 non-exclusion for personal injury or death; ☐

23.2 liability exclusion for non-fraudulent misrepresentation; ☐

23.3 total exclusion or limitation of liability, as appropriate; ☐

23.4 maximum aggregate liability under agreement for escrow agent; ☐

23.5 consider limiting liability to amount of fees paid or required level of insurance held by escrow agent; ☐

23.6 indirect loss, loss of profit and consequential loss; ☐

23.7 mutual exclusion of liability for consequential loss; ☐

23.8 exclusion of liability to any third party. ☐

24 Consider general provisions including: ☐

24.1 relevant warranties (if any); ☐

24.2 further assurance provisions or obligations to assist in specific ways; ☐

24.3 disclaimers of liabilities and limitation of liability provisions; ☐

24.4 an exclusion of liability for indirect and consequential loss; ☐

24.5 force majeure acknowledgements including termination for long delays; ☐

24.6 notices/service of notice; ☐

24.7 relevant boilerplate provisions and detail as necessary; ☐

25 Are any approvals or consents required? ☐

26 Consider relevant schedules setting out details of the items, materials or software delivered or deposited. ☐

27 Consider and insert provisions relating to: ☐

27.1 liability for costs of preparation and implementation of agreement; ☐

27.2 agreement not to make claim against officer or employee of escrow agent; ☐

Commercial Contracts Checklists

27.3 changes to agreement; ☐

27.4 service of notices; ☐

27.5 non-reliance on any representations or inducements; ☐

27.6 confidentiality undertakings and non-disclosure; ☐

27.7 data protection compliance; ☐

27.8 third party rights or enforcement rights exclusion; ☐

27.9 assignment of the agreement; ☐

27.10 arbitration; mediation or other alternative dispute resolution procedure; ☐

27.11 severance of unlawful or unenforceable provisions; ☐

27.12 non-waiver by delay; ☐

27.13 entire agreement between the parties; ☐

27.14 fact of no partnership or agency between parties; ☐

27.15 further assurance provision; ☐

27.16 process or agent for service; ☐

27.17 governing law; ☐

27.18 exclusive, non-exclusive or one party submission jurisdiction. ☐

See Precedent 3.4 on accompanying CD.

3.5 Information Technology Procurement and Turnkey Contract

Overview

Description of Agreement/Document

The agreement for IT procurement and/or turnkey solutions relates to the supply of a fully operational system to a customer. The contract with the supplier relates to procuring the customer's various requirements to enable the customer to simply turn a key. The supplier under the contract will be responsible for procuring all relevant components to achieve the turnkey or procurement contract according to the customer's requirements.

Practical Guidance/Issues List

The parties should consider the obligations of each party and consider:
- clearly stating the user's requirements as comprehensively as possible;
- agreeing the exact tests and acceptance criteria required;
- specifying liquidated damages provision and an effective remedy in relation to specific breaches;
- ensuring the grant of relevant third party licences to the customer;
- ensuring that any relevant manufacturer's warranties are assigned (if assignable);
- obtaining any third party approval as may be required for delivery of the procurement or turnkey solution;
- clarity in respect of the price payable, terms of payment and whether any additional costs will be incurred;
- avoiding any unilateral variations of prices, services or contract terms;
- relevant arrangements for delivery of any codes (particularly in relation to bespoke software);
- entering into escrow arrangements;
- negotiating and agreeing all ancillary contracts (training, project management, support, etc.) at the same time;
- avoiding unenforceable provisions such as 'agreement to agree';
- setting out the user's specification in plain English with comprehensive requirements relating to functionality, technical requirements or details, what the system is to achieve;
- setting out specific team for the project;
- agreeing clear timetables;
- obtaining third party assistance as required.

Some Key Definitions

'Acceptance Test(s)' means the tests by the [Contractor] which is suitable to demonstrate that the System complies with and performs in accordance with the Orders.

'Acknowledgement' means the Contractor's acceptance and acknowledgement of the Orders containing the payment schedule, timetable and detailing the implementation and each phase of the relevant Services.

'Customer Equipment' means the equipment, communications links, computer programs, apparatus, materials and or other items (other than the System) to be provided (including the installation of them) by the Customer at the Location for use in association with the System.

'Location' means the Customer's offices or such other location(s) set out in the Customer's Requirements where the System or parts of it will be installed.

'Operating Software' means the computer programs and associated documentation (if any) supplied by a manufacturer in connection with the operation of a Hardware item.

'Orders' means the instructions and orders of the Customer in respect of its information technology requirements contained in an agreed form (including the specification of the System describing the intended functions and facilities for the System and the Customer's particular requirements on each occasion in respect of the Services, maintenance and other matters) from time to time and expressly accepted by the Contractor.

'Timetable' means as regards any of the Contractor's obligations to deliver any of the Hardware, Software or Documentation or to perform any of the Services, the relevant date or time agreed or set out in the Orders (if any).

Specific Provisions

Sub-Contractors
The Contractor may employ Sub-Contractors for carrying out any part of the Services provided that the Contractor will not be relieved of any of its obligations under this Agreement by entering into any sub-contract for the performance of any part of the Services, and will at all times remain primarily responsible and liable to the Customer for the conduct of the Sub-Contractors.

Required Skill
The Contractor shall use its reasonable endeavours to provide and carry out the Services with reasonable care and skill using appropriately qualified and experienced persons.

Change(s)
Except as expressly provided, no changes to this Agreement or any Orders shall be binding unless agreed in writing between the authorised representatives of the Contractor and Customer provided always that any changes to this Agreement shall be authorised by a partner of the Contractor.

The Contractor may make a reasonable charge for investigating a proposed change and preparing an impact assessment or a quotation or estimate for that change (whether or not subsequently implemented) subject to agreeing the basis of charging for doing so with the Customer in writing before proceeding with the investigatory work.

Responsibilities
The Customer will provide the Contractor with such information as it may reasonably need concerning the Customer's operations and answers to queries, decisions and approvals which may be reasonably necessary for the Contractor and its Sub-Contractors to undertake the Services. The Customer is responsible for ensuring that such information and answers are accurate and complete.

Checklist 3.5 IT Procurement and Turnkey Agreement Checklist

In preparing information technology procurement and turnkey contracts, individuals or businesses should consider the following non-exhaustive matters.

Actions/Issues: **Comments:**

1 Consider the scope of the agreement and the parties' requirements or objectives. ☐

2 Set out background, history and summary in recital. ☐

3 Ascertain and consider relevant service to be provided in connection with: ☐

    3.1 information technology procurement; ☐

    3.2 turnkey contract; ☐

    3.3 software development and supply; ☐

    3.4 installation ☐

    3.5 testing; ☐

    3.6 maintenance and support; ☐

    3.7 integration services; ☐

    3.8 training; ☐

    3.9 escrow arrangements; ☐

    3.10 consultancy. ☐

4 Is there an agreed specification and/or list of customer's requirements? ☐

5 As to the parties to the agreement, consider: ☐

    5.1 parties' names, addresses, registered offices and numbers; ☐

5.2 parties' details for service of notices including email and fax; ☐

5.3 requirement for guarantor (parent company or other); ☐

5.4 any other contracting party or related third party. ☐

6 Consider key terms and relevant definitions including: ☐

    6.1 bespoke software, operating software, hardware; ☐

    6.2 contract price; ☐

    6.3 order, delivery, acceptance tests; ☐

    6.4 customer equipment, system, documentation; ☐

    6.5 sub-contractor, timetable. ☐

7 Review requirements for IT procurement and/or turnkey solution agreement. Consider and specify the scope of the solution or services to be provided including: ☐

    7.1 appointment as contractor to supply solution or service; ☐

    7.2 basis of appointment (exclusive, sole or non-exclusive); ☐

    7.3 procedure for orders and specification; ☐

    7.4 variation or acceptance in writing; ☐

    7.5 obligation to deliver and install hardware and software at location; ☐

    7.6 obligation to carry out installation tests on the system; ☐

    7.7 supply of orders; ☐

    7.8 provision of consumable supplies by contractor; ☐

    7.9 procure licence and third party licence for use of relevant software; ☐

    7.10 supply of documentation; ☐

7.11 assisting the contractor with acceptance tests; ☐

7.12 agreement to procure or provide training, support and maintenance and consultancy services; ☐

7.13 use of sub-contractors for performance of services; ☐

7.14 use of reasonably skilled and experienced persons; ☐

7.15 entering into further agreements. ☐

8 Change request procedure in connection with agreement including:

8.1 request in writing; ☐

8.2 specify required change; ☐

8.3 analysis of impact; ☐

8.4 estimates or liability for expense and cost of review, investigation or implementation; ☐

8.5 formal acceptance or adoption of change. ☐

9 Ascertain, review and specify obligations or responsibilities of the customer including:

9.1 provision of required information; ☐

9.2 provision of facilities; ☐

9.3 allowing access to premises; ☐

9.4 permission and use of customer's equipment; ☐

9.5 liaising with contractor's representative; ☐

9.6 satisfying specified conditions and providing required environmental conditions for solution; ☐

9.7 ensuring adequate security for system; ☐

9.8 ensuring proper and satisfactory installation; ☐

Commercial Contracts Checklists

    9.9   preparation of specification. ☐

10   Will the contract be for a defined period or will it continue until delivery of solution or termination. Consider and specify: ☐

    10.1   how long contract is for; ☐

    10.2   provisions for extension or roll over; ☐

    10.3   length of subsequent terms; ☐

    10.4   applicable extension or option to extend procedure. ☐

11   Consider administration of project and requirements for: ☐

    11.1   each party to appoint a representative or account manager; ☐

    11.2   periodic written reports; ☐

    11.3   regular progress meetings; ☐

    11.4   replacement of representative. ☐

12   How will payment be made and what are the agreed pricing arrangements? Consider or specify as follows: ☐

    12.1   amount of contract price; ☐

    12.2   method of calculation of contract price; ☐

    12.3   whether price is all inclusive; ☐

    12.4   whether exclusive of VAT; ☐

    12.5   payment timing and dates; ☐

    12.6   procedure for varying price; ☐

    12.7   whether additional charges applicable; ☐

    12.8   basis upon which payment can be withheld; ☐

12.9 default interest penalty provisions; ☐

12.10 liability for additional duties, surcharges or tax; ☐

12.11 remedy for late payment in addition to default interest; ☐

12.12 price increases due to law and regulatory changes; ☐

12.13 price adjustments, discounts or rebates. ☐

13 In relation to software procurement or solution, consider:

    13.1 responsibility for installation; ☐

    13.2 arrangements for code and escrow; ☐

    13.3 delivery of bespoke software; ☐

    13.4 any relevant licensing arrangement or third party approvals. ☐

14 Consider the following in relation to hardware:

    14.1 ensuring compliance with environment conditions; ☐

    14.2 delivery and off-loading arrangements; ☐

    14.3 installation obligations; ☐

    14.4 responsibility for costs; ☐

    14.5 when risk passes to the customer; ☐

    14.6 when title passes to the customer (payment in full of relevant price for item or all outstanding sums). ☐

15 What are the terms of the required solution? Is the specification together with required functionality agreed? ☐

16 Timetable obligations should be considered including:

    16.1 setting out relevant phases and compliance periods or dates; ☐

Commercial Contracts Checklists

    16.2   whether dates are target dates only; ☐

    16.3   whether time is of the essence of the contract; ☐

    16.4   procedure for extension of time if delayed due to force majeure event or customer's action. ☐

17   Consider and specify: ☐

    17.1   relevant installation tests; ☐

    17.2   what is to be submitted for testing; ☐

    17.3   applicable testing or re-testing procedure; ☐

    17.4   preparation for acceptance tests; ☐

    17.5   responsibility for carrying out the acceptance test; ☐

    17.6   any maintenance or support requirement or obligation to enter into agreement. ☐

18   What warranties have the parties agreed? Consider warranties relating to: ☐

    18.1   quality of service; ☐

    18.2   quality of solution or turnkey product; ☐

    18.3   prompt installation; ☐

    18.4   non-reliance (by customer) on representations; ☐

    18.5   defects warranty (repair and/or replace) and warranty period; ☐

    18.6   conditions of warranty; ☐

    18.7   ownership of systems and non-infringement of third party rights. ☐

19   Review liability requirements and consider provisions relating to: ☐

    19.1   agreement being exhaustive in respect of parties' obligations and liabilities; ☐

19.2 exclusion of all implied, statutory or other warranty; ☐

19.3 responsibility of customer for use of system; ☐

19.4 exclusion of liability for indirect, consequential loss or damage, loss of profits or data; ☐

19.5 capping liability at contract price or insurance sum; ☐

19.6 indemnity for breach (and whether within liability cap) or third party claims; ☐

19.7 acknowledgement of risk – fair/reasonable risk allocation. ☐

20 Are there any indemnity provisions in respect of intellectual property rights infringement? Is the indemnity conditional? Consider and specify applicable conditions. Are there any contractor exclusions in respect of infringement of third party rights? ☐

21 Will the customer be required to give any warranties? Consider warranty that: ☐

    21.1 specification, design or instruction will not infringe third party rights; ☐

    21.2 customer will indemnify contractor for third party claims. ☐

22 Specify obligations of confidentiality. Consider definition of 'confidential information' as any specific obligations or undertakings. Will the undertaking survive termination of contract? Are there any exclusions from non-disclosure restrictions? ☐

23 Ascertain, consider or specify: ☐

    23.1 undertaking in relation to continuity of personnel by contractor; ☐

    23.2 consent requirement prior to key personnel replacement; ☐

    23.3 customer right to require replacement of project personnel; ☐

    23.4 requirement to comply with health and safety, site regulations and other relevant policies; ☐

    23.5 non-solicitation undertakings in relation to employees for specified period; ☐

    23.6 statement of requirements; ☐

23.7 provisions for serving notices; ☐

23.8 dispute resolution provisions; ☐

23.9 relevant schedules to agreement and requirement to prepare documents or agreements; ☐

23.10 force majeure provisions, obligation to notify, discretion to terminate, responsibility for costs and what amounts to a matter beyond a party's control; ☐

23.11 conflict resolution between agreement and schedules; ☐

23.12 project management obligations; ☐

23.13 required performance parameters; ☐

23.14 implementation plan and acceptance procedures; ☐

23.15 liquidated damages for failure to attain specific milestones or customer's loss due to lateness; ☐

23.16 insurance requirements; ☐

23.17 ancillary services; ☐

23.18 data protection obligations, requirements and undertakings; ☐

23.19 regulatory approvals; ☐

23.20 compliance with relevant laws; ☐

23.21 further assurance provisions; ☐

23.22 relevant guarantee provisions. ☐

24 Ascertain and set out acceptance testing provisions including: ☐

24.1 acceptance testing criteria and scope of testing; ☐

24.2 conduct of tests and attendance; ☐

24.3 user's requirements; ☐

24.4 assistance with testing; ☐

24.5 delays in testing; ☐

24.6 user as final arbiter or independent verification/assessment; ☐

24.7 preliminary testing by contractor; ☐

24.8 final testing by customer or user; ☐

24.9 revealed defects or system failure; ☐

24.10 warranty period for remedies for minor defects; ☐

24.11 retesting failed system; ☐

24.12 payment of liquidated damages pending re-submission for testing; ☐

24.13 option to accept defective system with price reduction. ☐

25 Termination provisions to be set out including considering provisions relating to:

25.1 circumstances permitting customer to terminate; ☐

25.2 termination by either party with or without cause; ☐

25.3 termination notice periods; ☐

25.4 limits on timing of termination; ☐

25.5 post-termination consequences; ☐

25.6 post-termination obligations; ☐

25.7 termination immediately for specified events of default; ☐

25.8 termination for insolvency; ☐

25.9 applicable charges for cancellation or termination; ☐

25.10 accrued rights of the parties prior to termination. ☐

26 Review and consider relevant provisions relating to: ☐

    26.1 waiver of rights by either party; ☐

    26.2 agreement being complete; ☐

    26.3 exclusion of all other terms; ☐

    26.4 third party rights exclusion; ☐

    26.5 severance of unenforceable or illegal provisions; ☐

    26.6 right to assign agreement or sub-contract; ☐

    26.7 effect of contract on affiliated or group companies; ☐

    26.8 remedies to be cumulative; ☐

    26.9 parties not being partners or agents; ☐

    26.10 who is responsible for legal costs; ☐

    26.11 any rights of set off; ☐

    26.12 restriction on publicity or press announcement without approval; ☐

    26.13 waiver of right to terminate for non-fraudulent misrepresentation; ☐

    26.14 signing contract in counterparts; ☐

    26.15 varying or altering the contract. ☐

See Precedent 3.5 on accompanying CD.

3.6 Outsourcing/Application Service Provision Agreement

Overview

Description of Agreement/Document

An outsourcing agreement or application service provider (ASP) contract relates to the provision of services by one party to another. However, with an outsourcing contract, the entity that previously provided the relevant services in-house transfers some of its employees and assets to an external service provider to enable them to provide the entity with the services. The agreement details the arrangements between the parties including where relevant, the transfer of employees and assets, agreement to purchase the services and re-transfer provisions.

In relation to ASP services, the service provider details and manages applications and technology services from a remote location to users via the internet or a private network. The agreement details the service arrangements, partner obligations, service levels and liability provisions. The customer buys the use of the application without having to transfer any internal resources to the ASP service provider.

Practical Guidance/Issues List

The parties should take great care with the contract as it governs a long term relationship between the parties.

Parties should consider:
- the necessity to transfer employees;
- relevant assets required for provision of the services;
- each party's requirements and objectives;
- what the outsourcing arrangement is intended to achieve;
- suitable restrictions in the contract to provide the relevant 'contracting back in' protection for the company outsourcing the services at the end;
- setting out arrangements for replacing the service provider;
- the appropriate duration of the outsourcing arrangements;
- ensuring that the agreement is subject to review during the term.

In relation to ASP services, the parties should also consider the following:
- The confidentiality and data protection provisions are important. The parties will need to ensure that they are carefully drafted to protect the parties in relation to relevant proprietary information and compliance with data protection. The provision of services online also increases security risks and it will be important for the provider to demonstrate that it has adequate data protection mechanisms in place.
- The provider will require time to fix problems. The service level agreement (SLA) should clearly set out the relevant period allowed for a provider to fix any problems it may have with its service before penalties are imposed. Where the problem is likely to last for an unreasonable period of time there should be a provision requiring the provider to make alternative arrangements for provision of the services to the customer, for example by way of a back up system or through another provider. Security is always a very important issue for the customer. The customer should satisfy itself and make provision in the contract for the SLA to include detailed security requirements used in providing the services. There should also be adequate provision requiring the provider to take certain specific steps, including notification to the customer, in the event of a breach of security.
- Security provisions will relate both to offline and online issues. In relation to offline issues, the SLA may detail the protections in relation to the data centre: 24 hour security, CCTV and other physical protections in place could be outlined. These security measures may be implemented by third parties.
- In relation to online protections, the SLA will need to address the various mechanisms in place guaranteeing security of the service to the customer, such as use of domain structures to centralise login and account information in secure locations, rotation of passwords for routers, account login and server and local administration. The installation and updating of virus protection software by the provider would also be crucial from the customer's perspective.
- The provider will need to deal with issues relating to scheduled and unscheduled maintenance and provide for this appropriately in the contract.

Commercial Contracts Checklists

- The customer should ensure that the data centre or location from which services are provided is equipped with and will maintain an uninterruptible power supply and power regulators capable of ensuring that the operation of the necessary equipment located in the data centre is unhindered by any fluctuations or interruptions in the power supply.
- The responsibility for upgrading and maintaining the application software should be clearly dealt with as this is important for the customer.
- Customers should require information on upgrade obligations, timing and any additional costs involved.
- The provider will need to ensure that the SLA not only covers the service requirements for the customer but that it is commercially achievable for the provider.

Law/Compliance Requirement

Apart from general contract law, the arrangements may require reference to the Transfer of Undertakings (Protection of Employment) Regulations 1981 (as amended), which are relevant to the transfer of employees to the service provider.

The Data Protection Act 1998 is of importance in an ASP relationship. ASPs may require access to sensitive data needed to put in place relevant compliance procedures. The Act was introduced due to increasing concerns about how data on individuals is handled and protected by organisations. The parties will need to comply with the provisions of the Act.

Some Key Definitions

'Intellectual Property Rights' means all copyrights, patents, utility models, trade marks, service marks, registered designs, moral rights, design rights (whether registered or unregistered), technical information, know-how, database rights, semiconductor topography rights, business names and logos, computer data, generic rights, proprietary information rights and all other similar proprietary rights (and all applications and rights to apply for registration or protection of any of the foregoing) as may exist anywhere in the world.

'Operating Rules' means any Provider rules or protocols, in whatever form recorded, that affect the Customer's access to or use of the Services, and made available by the Provider from time to time to the Customer.

'Services' means the software applications services of the Provider, as specified in Schedule 1, made available to the Customer (together with any Operating Rules) and including any computer software programs and, if appropriate, Updates thereto.

'Updates' means any new or updated applications services or tools (including any computer software programs) made available by the Provider as part of the Services.

'Required Service Level' in respect of any Service in any period means the standard of performance referred to in clause [ ] in the provision of that Service in the period in question.

'Service Charges' means the charges levied by the Provider for the Services in accordance with the tariffs, scales, charges, invoicing methods and terms of payment as set out in Annex [ ]

'Service Credits' means the credits which become payable to the Client by way of a reduction in the Service Charges where the Required Service Levels are not as achieved as set out in Annex [ ]

Specific Provisions

Implementation
The Provider agrees to provide the Services in accordance with the Implementation Plan. Notwithstanding the foregoing, the parties agree that the Implementation Plan shall be amended to the extent reasonably necessary in order to reflect any breach of the Customer's obligations, negligence by it or any force majeure event preventing the Provider from providing the Services.

Records
The Provider shall keep records of the service levels achieved for the Services it is providing to the Customer for

each [ ] month period throughout this Agreement and provide copies of such records to the Customer upon request.

Service Level
In the event that the service levels achieved by the Provider fall short of the Required Service Level in any [specified] period or the goals set out in the Implementation Plan are not achieved, the Provider shall provide the Service Credits as specified in Annex [ ]. If the Provider fails to provide the Services in accordance with the Required Service Levels measured over any [ ] month period, the Customer shall incur Service Credits as set out in Annex [ ]. Such Service Credits shall be calculated [monthly] and applied as a deduction to any Service Charges payable under this Agreement.

Price Increase
The Provider reserves the right, by giving notice to the Customer at any time before performance of the relevant Services to increase the price of such Services to reflect any increase in the cost to the Provider which is due to an act or omission of the Customer including but not limited to any change in the date for the performance of Services or any delay caused by any instructions of the Customer or failure by the Customer to give the Provider adequate information or instructions.

ASP Warranty The Provider warrants that by performing the Services it will not knowingly infringe the rights of any third party (including but not limited to Intellectual Property Rights) in any jurisdiction or be in breach of any obligations it may have to a third party. The Provider further warrants that it is not prohibited from providing the Services by any statutory or other rules or regulations in any relevant jurisdiction.

ASP Licence
Subject to the Customer's payment of the Fees, the Customer is granted a non-exclusive and non-transferable licence to use the Services (including any associated software, Intellectual Property Rights and Confidential Information) during the Term. Such licence shall permit the Customer to make such copies of software or other information as are required for the Customer to receive the Services.

IPR of ASP
Nothing in this Agreement shall be construed to mean, by inference or otherwise, that the Customer has any right to obtain source code for the software comprised within the Services. All Intellectual Property Rights and title to the Services (save to the extent they incorporate any Customer or third party owned item) shall remain with the Provider and/or its licensors and no interest or ownership therein is conveyed to the Customer under this Agreement. No right to modify, adapt or translate the Services or create derivative works is granted to the Customer.

Checklist 3.6 Outsourcing Agreement/Application Service Provision Checklist

In preparing an outsourcing agreement or letter, individuals or businesses should consider the following non-exhaustive matters.

Actions/Issues:	Comments:	✎

1 General. What are the parties' requirements and objectives? What is being outsourced? Consider relevant services to be provided and how. ☐

2 Introduction. Indicate background – parties' status, history or objectives including parties' group structure in the recitals and introductory paragraph. ☐

3 Parties. Consider and specify the parties to the agreement including: ☐

   3.1 the client company/customer's name, address, registration number and other contract details; ☐

   3.2 the service provider's address details and contract information; ☐

   3.3 whether a guarantee is required by either party; ☐

   3.4 any third party contractor involved in the outsourcing process. ☐

4 Definitions. Consider definition of key terms, words or phrases including: ☐

   4.1 change request, change control procedure; ☐

   4.2 continuous performance assessment; ☐

   4.3 dispute resolution procedure; ☐

   4.4 cut-over date; ☐

   4.5 exit management plan; ☐

   4.6 force majeure; ☐

   4.7 key personnel, third party provider, replacement service provider; ☐

   4.8 persistent failure; ☐

4.9 quality management plan, requirements plan, transition plan, disaster recovery plan; ☐

4.10 request for service; ☐

4.11 service level agreement; ☐

4.12 support, service charges. ☐

4.13 object code, source code. ☐

5 Service Provider. Specify provision of services by service provider: ☐

    5.1 to the customer/client or users with effect from specified date; ☐

    5.2 on the terms of agreement; ☐

    5.3 with reasonable care and skill; ☐

    5.4 in accordance with stated principles and agreed service levels; ☐

    5.5 through agreed or specified methods; ☐

    5.6 for a specified period; ☐

    5.7 in accordance with implementation plan; ☐

    5.8 obligation to keep records of services provided and service levels; ☐

    5.9 subject to customer complying with its obligations; ☐

    5.10 having regard to the customer's specific standards or policies (including security, premises, health and safety, IT and data protection policy). ☐

6 Services. What are the services to be provided by the service provider? Consider: ☐

    6.1 information technology services; ☐

    6.2 business process services; ☐

    6.3 required resources; ☐

6.4 whether the service provider will agree to service levels for all services or only specified services; ☐

6.5 whether the parties are willing to accept service credits as remedy for breach of service level agreement; ☐

6.6 whether the customer will be entitled to change the services required from time to time; ☐

6.7 whether the service provider will be providing all services or if a third party provider will be involved. ☐

7 Service levels. What are the provisions relating to service levels? ☐

    7.1 Consider and indicate: ☐

        7.1.1 service level commencement date; ☐

        7.1.2 any initial grace period(s); ☐

        7.1.3 which services the service levels apply to; ☐

        7.1.4 relevant remedies for failure to meet service levels; ☐

        7.1.5 how the service levels are set or agreed; ☐

        7.1.6 how performance will be verified against service levels; ☐

        7.1.7 whether the applicable remedies relate to all services; ☐

        7.1.8 measurement periods, methods and tools in relation to performance; ☐

        7.1.9 periodic reporting obligations; ☐

    7.2 in relation to the remedies for breach of service level agreement by failure to attain service levels, consider: ☐

        7.2.1 damages; ☐

        7.2.2 set off; ☐

        7.2.3 service credits; ☐

        7.2.4 termination; ☐

7.2.5 suspension; ☐

7.2.6 liquidated damages; ☐

7.3 consider calculation of service credits liability for failure to meet service levels; ☐

7.4 specify effect of force majeure on liability for failure to meet service levels; ☐

7.5 exclude liability for failure to attain levels resulting from outsourcer customer's breach or force majeure event; ☐

7.6 insert dispute resolution obligation reference in the event of dispute over reason for failure to reach required level of service. ☐

8 Transition. Ascertain and specify the required transitional arrangements. Consider: ☐

8.1 undertaking to co-operate in process; ☐

8.2 obligation to obtain third party consents; ☐

8.3 effect of transitional arrangements on performance following commencement; ☐

8.4 effect of incomplete arrangements prior to start of service; ☐

8.5 variation of third party contracts position in the event that third party consents are not obtained; ☐

8.6 due diligence, staff transition, contract assignment; and ☐

8.7 specify the transitional obligations of each party. ☐

9 Standards. Are there any applicable standards in respect of: ☐

9.1 data protection? ☐

9.2 information technology? ☐

9.3 security policy? ☐

9.4 access to premises policy? ☐

9.5 health and safety? ☐

Commercial Contracts Checklists

10 Personnel. What about the personnel engaged to provide the services? Consider: ☐

    10.1 obligation to keep key personnel for the term (if practicable); ☐

    10.2 specifying key personnel; ☐

    10.3 specific requirements in relation to key personnel or other personnel engaged to provide the services; ☐

    10.4 prohibition of changes to personnel without consent; ☐

    10.5 restrictions on the use of key personnel on similar projects with or for competitors. ☐

11 Access. The obligations in respect of access and use should be considered including: ☐

    11.1 access to customer's premises to be provided as reasonably required on agreed terms; ☐

    11.2 undertakings and obligations of service provider in relation to access or attendance at customer's premises; ☐

    11.3 liability exclusions or obligations in respect of premises or access and use; ☐

    11.4 use of relevant equipment and facilities; ☐

    11.5 required authorisation process for use and access; ☐

    11.6 licence grant for service provider in respect of customer's intellectual property (if applicable); ☐

    11.7 applicable indemnities in respect of use of and access to premises, equipment and intellectual property; ☐

    11.8 obligations relating to performance of third party contracts together with applicable indemnity. ☐

12 Outsourcer's obligations. Consider the respective duties and obligations of each party. In relation to the customer: ☐

    12.1 ensure use and supply of suitable and experienced staff; ☐

    12.2 comply with provisions of agreement and applicable policies; ☐

    12.3 maintain specified third party agreements including support and maintenance services contracts; ☐

    12.4 permit access to its premises, equipment, facilities and intellectual property; ☐

12.5 grant the service provider and its agents required licences; ☐

12.6 provide such assistance as reasonably required; ☐

12.7 provide information and documents promptly; ☐

12.8 indemnify service provider in respect of specified breach of warranty or contract; ☐

12.9 prepare required plans. ☐

13 Service provider's obligations. Consider: ☐

13.1 provision of services for the term; ☐

13.2 compliance with service levels; ☐

13.3 assistance or preparation of specified plans; ☐

13.4 provide the services with reasonable skill and care; ☐

13.5 its experienced and suitable personnel; ☐

13.6 maintain key personnel; ☐

13.7 comply with all relevant policies of the customer. ☐

14 Fees. Consider applicable provisions in respect of service charges, fees and expenses including: ☐

14.1 obligation to pay the fees; ☐

14.2 the amount and rate of charges; ☐

14.3 charges schedule detailing applicable sums and terms; ☐

14.4 invoicing arrangements; ☐

14.5 dates of payment; ☐

14.6 whether VAT is inclusive or exclusive; ☐

Commercial Contracts Checklists

14.7 any agreed advance or estimates payments; ☐

14.8 reconciliation provisions for relevant periods; ☐

14.9 liquidated damages provision; ☐

14.10 rights of set off, withholding or deduction and disputed payments; ☐

14.11 late payment or default interest payment provision; ☐

14.12 indemnity for third party costs; ☐

14.13 accounting obligations and auditing rights; ☐

14.14 obligation to pass on price reductions and other benefits; ☐

14.15 additional charges and expenses; ☐

14.16 rights to vary charges; ☐

14.17 remedy in the event of non-payment on due date including: ☐

    14.7.1 default interest payment; ☐

    14.7.2 suspension of services pending payment; ☐

    14.7.3 termination of agreement or particular service; ☐

    14.7.4 additional costs and expense for delay; ☐

    14.7.5 enforcement costs liability. ☐

15 Changes. As changes may be required in long term contracts, parties should consider and agree the relevant procedure. Consider: ☐

    15.1 how changes will be originated; ☐

    15.2 information required and impact assessment; ☐

    15.3 discretion to agree to change request or order; ☐

15.4 cost of implementing a change request or order; ☐

15.5 changes related to work undertaken prior to order (effect or impact analysis); ☐

15.6 reservation of right to change services without notification for compliance with safety and statutory requirement; ☐

15.7 limitation of variation for safety without consent where quality or performance will be affected; ☐

15.8 service representations to handle change of control requests and procedures; ☐

15.9 regular periodic review meeting. ☐

16 Consider and specify any liquidated damages provision applicable to the agreement or any particular provision or service. ☐

17 Will there be an obligation on the parties to co-operate? What about a further assurance provision? Can the parties' representatives be indicated? ☐

18 Termination. What is the term of the contract? Consider:

18.1 whether the contract is for a specified period; ☐

18.2 option to renew upon expiry; ☐

18.3 roll over of term to periodic term upon expiry; ☐

18.4 continuous term until terminated by notice; ☐

18.5 grounds for termination and specify if the agreement will be terminable:

18.5.1 upon service of notice; ☐

18.5.2 with or without cause; ☐

18.5.3 during the term; ☐

18.5.4 subject to any dispute resolution procedure; ☐

18.5.5 with immediate effect in certain circumstances; ☐

18.5.6 for material breach of service level agreement; ☐

Commercial Contracts Checklists

            18.5.7   upon insolvency or related event in respect of either party. ☐

      18.6   Consider the consequences of termination including: ☐

            18.6.1   implementation of exit management plan; ☐

            18.6.2   return of materials; ☐

            18.6.3   migration of service to new provider; ☐

            18.6.4   certification of compliance. ☐

19   Disputes. Is there a dispute resolution procedure? Consider ☐

      19.1   meeting of service managers; ☐

      19.2   meeting of senior officers or directors; ☐

      19.3   request to enter procedure with mediator; ☐

      19.4   relevant periods for seeking to resolve dispute; ☐

      19.5   whether binding; ☐

      19.6   confidentiality of negotiations; ☐

      19.7   right to interlocutory relief; ☐

      19.8   restriction on commencement of legal proceedings; ☐

      19.9   agreed or mediated settlement; ☐

      19.10 costs and expenses of procedure; ☐

      19.11 payments during procedure. ☐

20   IPR. In relation to intellectual property rights, consider or specify: ☐

      20.1   who owns the intellectual property; ☐

20.2 any required rights of use; ☐

20.3 any licence granted; ☐

20.4 warranties of ownership and non-infringement; ☐

20.5 vesting and ownership of created intellectual property; ☐

20.6 indemnity for breach; ☐

20.7 procedure for claims or defence of third party claims. ☐

21 Confidentiality. Obligations relating to non-disclosure and confidentiality should be considered: ☐

21.1 mutual non-disclosure; ☐

21.2 required acknowledgements; ☐

21.3 disclosure exceptions; ☐

21.4 record keeping obligations; ☐

21.5 relevant undertakings. ☐

22 General. Consider provisions relating to: ☐

22.1 further assurance and assistance; ☐

22.2 force majeure; ☐

22.3 compliance with general law; ☐

22.4 co-operation between parties; ☐

22.5 insurance (public liability); ☐

22.6 compliance with data protection regulations; ☐

22.7 non-solicitation; ☐

22.8 remove access control; ☐

22.9 customer's data; ☐

22.10 preparation of plans; ☐

22.11 regulatory approvals; ☐

22.12 sale, restructuring or joint ventures; ☐

22.13 escrow and third party software; ☐

22.14 bench marking; ☐

22.15 staff; ☐

22.16 disaster recovery. ☐

23 Warranties. Specify relevant warranties in relation to: ☐

23.1 equipment and facilities; ☐

23.2 premises; ☐

23.3 intellectual property; ☐

23.4 existing agreement; ☐

23.5 employees and personnel; ☐

23.6 performance of services and standards; ☐

23.7 time and periods; ☐

23.8 experience; ☐

23.9 authority and approval to enter into contract, parties' status and capacity; ☐

23.10 non-infringement of third party rights; ☐

23.11 compliance with applicable laws and regulations; ☐

23.12 transitional arrangements. ☐

24 Liability. What are the provisions relating to liability? Consider: ☐

    24.1 exclusion of liability for force majeure; ☐

    24.2 client non-performance; ☐

    24.3 third party acts; ☐

    24.4 non-payment by customer; ☐

    24.5 exclusion of liability for consequential loss or loss or profit; ☐

    24.6 obligation to insure and indicate required sums and liability; ☐

    24.7 acceptance of liability for death or personal injury caused by negligence; ☐

    24.8 applicable indemnities; ☐

    24.9 limitation of liability to specific amount, the charges or insurance, acknowledgement and declaration that provisions are reasonable. ☐

25 What about transfers of: ☐

    25.1 assets? ☐

    25.2 premises? ☐

    25.3 employees? ☐

    25.4 contracts? ☐

See Precedent 3.6 on accompanying CD.

4 Lending and Security Documents

4.1 Loan Agreement

4.2 Security Document (Legal Charge/Debenture)

4.3 Guarantee

Lending and Security Documents

4.1 Loan Agreement

Overview

Description of Agreement/Document

The loan facility agreement is a contract between a lender and borrower. The borrower agrees to pay the loan sum and abide by the terms of the agreement in exchange for the loan. The loan agreement sets out the terms of the loan arrangement including amount of loan, any conditions to be satisfied prior to drawing the loan, interest payment provisions, undertakings of the borrower and warranties and deprecations. The agreement also sets out applicable security with provisions relating to the term and termination of the agreement upon occurrence of default events.

Practical Guidance/Issues List

The borrower is normally in a weaker position than the lender in negotiating a loan agreement depending on the circumstances. In entering such arrangements, the borrower and lender should consider matters generally including (as appropriate):

- the solvency of the borrower;
- existing debts and contractual obligations;
- whether there is an existing charge over the assets of the borrower;
- the available assets and applicable value;
- the borrower's ability to satisfy the conditions precedent;
- whether there is a need to take advice from local lawyers if any relevant entity (including a subsidiary, if relevant) or the borrower is non-UK resident;
- legal status of the borrower and capacity;
- required security;
- cancellation and prepayment obligations or penalty;
- whether the borrower can comply and continue to comply with the representation and undertakings;
- effect on representations of group if applicable.

The borrower may wish to resist:

- certain events on default;
- inclusion of a material adverse change provision;
- personal guarantees;
- extensive or irrelevant representations;
- indemnities or extensive restrictions;
- the lender's decision being final in relation to disputed matters set out in the agreement;
- restrictions on assignment to group members.

The process should be recorded by the company or borrower following board approval. Relevant resolutions and minutes should be filed.

Law/Compliance Requirement

The loan arrangements between the parties are a matter of contract. However, the corporate borrower would need to ensure that it is within its borrowing limits or has power to borrow and enter into the agreement under its constitution. Any security involving a charge over the assets of the borrower will need to be registered at Companies House within 21 days of its creation or grant . Relevant minutes and resolutions should be filed. The borrower will need to comply with the relevant provisions of the Companies Act 1985.

Some Key Definitions

'Business Day' means a day (other than Saturday and Sunday) on which banks are open for normal banking business in London.

Commercial Contracts Checklists

'Loan' means the aggregate principal amount for the time being advanced and outstanding under this Letter.

'Indebtedness' means the Loan together with all interest (if any) thereon and all other sums owing from time to time under this Agreement from the Borrower to the Lender.

'Security Document' means the debenture and charge document dated [date] and any other documents now or after the date of this Agreement entered into in connection with the security arrangements between the parties or evidencing or creating any security in respect of any obligations of the Borrower to the Lender together with such variations of and supplements to any of the foregoing as may from time to time be in force.

'Encumbrances' means any mortgage, charge, pledge, lien, assignment, hypothecation, title retention, right of set off or any security interest whatsoever, howsoever created or arising and whether related to existing or future assets.

Specific Provisions

The Lender will (in consideration of the Borrower agreeing to repay the Loan on the terms of this Agreement) advance up to the amount of [sum] pounds in full to the Borrower in respect of [purpose].

The Borrower shall repay the Loan together with all Indebtedness without deduction or set off on the first to occur of the following:

- an Event of Default; or
- the Repayment Date being the [thirtieth (30th)] day following a written demand by the Lender to the Borrower requesting repayment of the Loan.

Should the Lender waive the right to repayment on the Repayment Date under [clause] above the Loan together with all Indebtedness shall be payable upon demand by the Lender.

The repayment of the Loan and Indebtedness will be secured by way of a fixed and floating charge over the assets of the Borrower as specified in the Security Document.

The Borrower shall at its cost and expense ensure that all documents, registrations, consents, licences and other matters and things reasonably required by the Lender in connection with the security afforded to the Lender are promptly produced, executed, obtained, filed or made as required by law or by the Lender.

Checklist 4.1 Loan Agreement Checklist

In preparing a loan agreement or letter, individuals or businesses should consider the following non-exhaustive matters.

	Actions/Issues:	Comments:	✎

1. Ascertain and consider the terms of the loan and set out background arrangements in the recitals. ☐

2. Consider details of the Borrower together with the relevant legal status and capacity. Is there a guarantor? ☐

3. Review terms and consider relevant terms to be defined including:- ☐

    3.1 company, borrower, or lender, guarantor; ☐

    3.2 business day; ☐

    3.3 event of default; ☐

    3.4 indebtedness, loan, purpose, security document; ☐

    3.5 repayment date. ☐

4. Review provisions and specify loan amount or advance. ☐

5. What is the consideration for the loan or will the agreement be entered into as a deed? ☐

6. What notice of draw down is required: ☐

    6.1 is it written notice? ☐

    6.2 is it acceptance of advance? ☐

7. Are there any conditions to be satisfied prior to draw down? Consider submission of: ☐

    7.1 certified complete copy of Memorandum of Articles of Association of the Borrower (if applicable); ☐

    7.2 certified copy of Borrower contribution or constitutional documents; ☐

    7.3 an executed security document; ☐

7.4   copy of approving board resolution certified by secretary; ☐

7.5   confirmation as proof of proposed signatory's authority to sign; ☐

7.6   certificate of Company Secretary confirming that no event of default has occurred. ☐

8   What is the loan advance to be used for? Are there any restrictions? Consider: ☐

    8.1   general working capital; ☐

    8.2   repayment of existing loan; ☐

    8.3   other specified or agreed purpose. ☐

9   What are the terms of the loan agreement? Consider: ☐

    9.1   fixed terms; ☐

    9.2   terminable on demand; ☐

    9.3   terminable on occurrence of event of default. ☐

10   In relation to repayment, specify: ☐

    10.1   obligation and undertaking to repay the loan amount together with any applicable interest or cost; ☐

    10.2   repayment without deduction or set off; ☐

    10.3   repayment on specified date or from specified bank account; ☐

    10.4   repayment upon occurrence of event of default; ☐

    10.5   repayment on the first to occur of a specified date or event of default; ☐

    10.6   lender's ability to waive repayment on repayment date; ☐

    10.7   lender's right to require repayment on demand at any time following waiver of repayment date; ☐

    10.8   currency of repayment or any currency exchange rate fluctuation provisions; ☐

Lending and Security Documents

    10.9   repayment to be on a Business Day; ☐

    10.10 borrower's ability to repay the loan (and whether or not any repaid sum can be re-borrowed); ☐

    10.11 the periodic payment obligations; ☐

    10.12 any right to extend the final repayment date; ☐

    10.13 early repayment right or restriction. ☐

11   What is the applicable interest date for sum payable? Consider or specify:

    11.1   how the date is fixed or variable; ☐

    11.2   interest payment dates; ☐

    11.3   application of loan repayment proceeds first to principal sum and interest. ☐

12   What is the security for the loan? Consider:

    12.1   guarantors; ☐

    12.2   charge on property; ☐

    12.3   debenture (fixed and floating charge); ☐

    12.4   charge on shares; ☐

    12.5   charge on account. ☐

13   Who is responsible for:

    13.1   costs and expenses relating to the security documents? ☐

    13.2   registration and filing of the security documents? ☐

    13.3   obtaining required consents of licences? ☐

    13.4   filing company forms? ☐

Commercial Contracts Checklists

    13.5   loan fees or costs? ☐

14   Are there any other charges applicable to the loan: ☐

    14.1   commitment fees? ☐

    14.2   placement fees? ☐

    14.3   application fee? ☐

    14.4   administration fee? ☐

15   What warranties and representations are required from the borrower? Consider : ☐

    15.1   the borrower is duly incorporated; ☐

    15.2   the loan agreement will be binding; ☐

    15.3   the borrower has authority to enter into agreement; ☐

    15.4   performance of the agreement is within the borrower's corporate powers; ☐

    15.5   the borrower is not in breach of any law or regulation; ☐

    15.6   there are no security interest in existence ☐

    15.7   the borrower is not involved in any disputes or litigation; ☐

    15.8   the borrower owns its assets and intellectual property rights; ☐

    15.9   the loan will rank as indicated; ☐

    15.10   the loan is within the borrower's borrowing limits; ☐

    15.11   the information supplied is accurate and true; ☐

    15.12   no termination event or event of default has occurred; ☐

    15.13   all stampable documentation has been stamped; ☐

15.14 the borrower (and its subsidiaries) is in compliance with its licences, permits and contracts; ☐

15.15 the financial information provided is accurate; ☐

15.16 the borrower has paid all relevant taxes; ☐

15.17 there is no adverse charge in the borrower's business; ☐

15.18 the borrower is solvent and has made full disclosure of all relevant matters; ☐

15.19 all required or necessary insurance is in place; ☐

15.20 the assets of the borrower are free from encumbrances other than as expressly disclosed. ☐

16 What undertaking and convents are required by the lender? Review and specify whether the borrower is requested to undertake that is shall:

16.1 not carry out specified activities without the lender's prior written consent; ☐

16.2 not dispose of whole or substantial part of its business or assets; ☐

16.3 keep the lender fully informed of matters as required by the lender; ☐

16.4 give to the lender notice of occurrence of default events; ☐

16.5 not create any mortgage security interest or liens over its assets; ☐

16.6 not enter into unusual material contracts without notice to the lender; ☐

16.7 carry on business in a proper and efficient manner; ☐

16.8 keep proper books of account and permit access or audit by the lender; ☐

16.9 settle all debts in the ordinary course of business; ☐

16.10 provide periodic financial statements; ☐

16.11 maintain insurance as required or necessary for the business; ☐

16.12 comply with the terms of the facility loan agreement; ☐

Commercial Contracts Checklists

  16.13 indemnify the lender for all loss related to its action or breach; ☐

  16.14 not prepay the advance or loan amount; ☐

  16.15 not take on further loans without prior consent of lender; ☐

  16.16 not acquire further subsidiaries or merge with another company. ☐

17 Ascertain as necessary and specify obligations to insure and keep assets insured. Consider the necessary invoices against specific or general assets, insurance against loss or damage, third party insurance replacement value or reinstatement value. ☐

18 Specify applicable events of default entitling termination of loan agreement or making loan immediately due and payable. Consider the following as appropriate: ☐

  18.1 failure to pay on specified date; ☐

  18.2 judgments against the borrower; ☐

  18.3 insolvency or bankruptcy of borrower or any guarantor; ☐

  18.4 breach of covenants and undertakings given by borrower; ☐

  18.5 breach of warranties or representations of the borrower; ☐

  18.6 breach of terms of the security document; ☐

  18.7 material adverse charge to borrower's financial condition; ☐

  18.8 provision of unsatisfactory information or discovery of inaccuracy or incorrectness of representations made; ☐

  18.9 presentation of winding up petition or passing of resolution; ☐

  18.10 insolvency related to occurrence including appointment of administrators, receiver, encumbrances or other matters such as inability to pay debts or voluntary arrangement; ☐

  18.11 breach of other contract of indebtedness; ☐

  18.12 change of contract of borrower; ☐

18.13 if borrower changes constitutional documents, issues or redeems shares or alters rights without notice; ☐

18.14 occurrence of any event which would be an event by default following service of notice. ☐

19 Will the borrower be requested to pay the lender's fees: ☐

19.1 on demand and on a full indemnity basis? ☐

19.2 inclusive or exclusive of VAT? ☐

19.3 relating to preparation, negotiation and implementation of documents? ☐

19.4 connected with lender's enforcement or preservation of its rights? ☐

20 Will all payments be requested to be made in a specific currency? Specify currency and payment to be made without counterclaim or withholding. ☐

21 Review and specify as appropriate: ☐

21.1 notice provisions (post, personal, fax and email); ☐

21.2 restriction on assignment for borrower; ☐

21.3 lender's express right to assign; ☐

21.4 exclusion of waiver of rights by delay; ☐

21.5 provision for joint and several liability; ☐

21.6 that remedies are cumulative and not exclusive of other legal rights; ☐

21.7 whether lender's decision is final and binding in relation to agreement or any calculation (in absence of manifest error); ☐

21.8 any dispute resolution procedure; ☐

21.9 that the document represents the entire agreement between the parties; ☐

21.10 severance of unenforceable provisions; ☐

21.11 agreement as binding on successors and assigns; ☐

Commercial Contracts Checklists

    21.12 lender's right to disclose information to assignees; ☐

    21.13 modification or amendment by parties or effects of changes in law; ☐

    21.14 obligation to maintain records; ☐

    21.15 rights of set off and counterparts; ☐

    21.16 waiver of right to object to forums or court; ☐

    21.17 time being of the essence; ☐

    21.18 announcements and confidentiality; ☐

    21.19 exclusion of third party rights; ☐

    21.20 further assurance obligations. ☐

22   Relevant provisions relating to governing law and jurisdiction. ☐

See Precedent 4.1

4.2 Security Documentation (Legal Charge/Debenture)

Overview

Description of Agreement/Document

The nature of the debenture is that it is security for debt. It contains fixed and floating charges used to secure debt. Many lenders use a standard form debenture document. The debenture normally sets out the covenant to repay and assumes the terms of the loan are regulated by a separate document. The terms of the debenture will include specific borrower obligations, protection of the lender's rights, covenants of the borrower restricting its dealing with certain assets, together with provisions relating to enforcement.

Practical Guidance/Issues List

Debentures are mostly in standard form and leave little room for negotiation. It is still necessary, however, to carefully review the terms of any debenture to ensure it accords with expectations or understanding.

It should be noted that the debenture will need to be registered at Companies House within twenty one (21) days of creation of the charge or grant of the debenture. This is registered on the relevant company form 395.

Care should be taken in the definition of 'secured liabilities'.

A default interest provision is subject to attack on a penalty if shown to be excessive.

Charges on property or buildings will normally require registration at the Land Registry.

The parties should review and note the difference between fixed and floating charges.

The creation of a debenture may give rise to claims of transaction at an undervalue or as a preference. The parties should ensure that the debenture is executed as a deed.

The borrower should resist:

- an all assets debenture if not intended, required or necessary;
- an excessive provision in relation to costs and should seek to limit the amount recoverable under this provision;
- any requirement for deemed receipt or service of notice;
- blanket ban on assets disposal and seek to reserve the right to dispose following substitution of assets;
- irrelevant or inapplicable events of default;
- restrictions on transfer of debenture to a group company;
- extensive representations and warranties.

The lender should:

- review the borrower's memorandum and articles of association to ensure relevant powers or limits;
- obtain a certified copy of the borrower's resolution authorising agreement;
- investigate covenants, consents or authorities required;
- take great care with the drafting of a fixed or floating charge over certain assets (accounts and book debts) having regard to the varying interpretation of such charges by the courts;
- carry out a search on the borrower (Companies House/bankruptcy search) and pursue due diligence correspondence with the borrower;
- set out required restrictions.

Law/Compliance Requirement

A debenture in its operation and application relates to various areas of law. Applicable legislation includes:

Commercial Contracts Checklists

- Law of Property Act 1925;
- Companies Act 1985;
- Insolvency Act 1986.

There is a requirement to register the debenture (on a Form 395) pursuant to the Companies Act 1985 at Companies House. Charges on land or buildings will need to be registered at the Land Registry.

Various cases deal with several aspects of interpretation of provisions of a debenture.

Depending on the circumstances, the grant of a debenture on security for indebtedness may be challenged as a preference or a transaction at an undervalue.

Some Key Definitions

'Assets' means all the undertaking, property and assets of the Company whatsoever and wheresoever present or future including as listed in the Schedule.

'Debts' means all book and other debts now or in the future owing to the Company (whether alone or jointly with any other person), whenever payable and whether liquidated or unliquidated (including any rent or income arising from, due or attributable to land), certain or contingent, balances on bank accounts but 'Debts' does not include any asset or right effectively charged by way of fixed charge under any other provision of this Deed.

'Encumbrance' means any mortgage, charge, pledge, lien, hypothecation or other security interest of any kind, and any right of set off, assignment, trust, flawed asset or other agreement or arrangement whatsoever for the purpose of providing security or having a similar effect to the provision of security, other than liens arising by operation of law in the ordinary course of the Company's business.

'Intellectual Property' means all the right, title and interest of the Company (now or in the future) in or to any of the following:

- the customer list of the Company from time to time including the database containing names, addresses, purchasing and enquiry history;
- any registered intellectual property right in any territory, including without limitation patents, trade marks, service marks, registered designs, and any similar right in any territory and any applications or right to apply for any of the above;
- any invention, copyright, design right or performance right;
- any trade secrets, know-how and confidential information;
- any the benefit of any agreement or licence for the use (by the Company and any other person) of any such right;
- the domain names of the Company.

'Land' means any right or interest in or over land or property wherever situated, including without limitation any buildings and fixtures on land, and the benefit of any covenants or rights owed to any person or enforceable by such person by virtue of the ownership, possession or occupation of land.

'Secured Liabilities' means all money, liabilities and obligations now or in the future owed or incurred by the Company to the Lender of any kind, however arising and in any currency, whether or not immediately payable, whether certain or contingent, whether sole or joint, whether as principal or as surety, whether or not the Lender was the original creditor in respect of liability, and including (without limitation) interest, commission, costs, charges and expenses charged by the Lender at rates agreed between it and the Company or, in the absence of express agreement, in accordance with the Lender's normal practice for the time being.

'Securities' means all the right, title and interest of the Company, now or in the future, in any stocks, shares, instruments creating or acknowledging any debt, or other securities issued by any person.

Specific Provisions

Company's Obligations
The Company covenants to pay or discharge the Secured Liabilities to the Lender on demand and without

prejudice to the generality of the foregoing to pay all monies advanced under the Loan Agreement upon demand.

Default Interest
The Company shall be liable to pay interest to the Lender upon any sum so demanded until payment (both before and after any judgment) at [   ] per cent ([   ]%) per year above the base rate as varied from time to time of [name] Bank plc accruing daily.

Conversion
The Lender may from time to time by notice in writing to the Company convert any floating charge created by this Debenture into a fixed charge in respect of any Assets which are specified in any such notice.

Continuing Security
This Debenture shall be a continuing security to the Lender and shall remain in force until expressly discharged in writing by the Lender notwithstanding any intermediate settlement of account or other matter or thing whatsoever, and shall be without prejudice and in addition to any other right, remedy or security of any kind which the Lender may have now or at any time in the future for or in respect of any of the Secured Liabilities.

Covenants
While this Debenture continues in force the Company shall provide to the Lender all information and copies of all documents which the Lender may require relating to the financial affairs of the Company and any Group Company and in particular, without limitation, shall provide not later than [twenty one (21)] days after the end of each month (or such other period as the Lender may at any time specify in writing) copies of management accounts and financial information in such form as the Lender may require in respect of the Company and each Group Company;

Receivers
At any time after this Debenture has become enforceable, or if the Company so requests at any time, the Lender may appoint any person or persons ('the Receiver') to be a receiver or receivers of all or any part of the Assets hereby charged. An appointment over part only of the Assets shall not preclude the Lender from making any subsequent appointment over any other part of the Assets.

The appointment of a Receiver shall be in writing, and may be signed by any director or employee on behalf of the Lender. Where more than one person is acting at any time as Receiver, they shall have power to act severally as well as jointly.

Company Agent
The Receiver shall be the agent of the Company (which shall be solely liable for his acts, defaults and remuneration) unless and until the Company goes into liquidation, whereafter he shall act as principal and shall not become the agent of the Lender, and the Receiver shall have and be entitled to exercise in relation to the Company all the powers set out in the Insolvency Act 1986.

Protection of Third Parties
In favour of any purchaser, the statutory powers of sale and of appointing a receiver which are conferred upon the Lender, as varied and extended by this Debenture, and all other powers of the Lender, shall be deemed to arise and be exercisable immediately after the execution of this Debenture.

Checklist 4.2 Security Document (Legal Charge/Debenture) Agreement Checklist

In preparing a lending security agreement or letter, individuals or businesses should consider the following non-exhaustive matters.

Actions/Issues:	Comments:	✎

1 Set out the parties to the security document and refer to related transactions or agreement. ☐

2 Consider relevant definitions of key terms including: ☐

   2.1 assets, fixed plant and equipment, loose plant and equipment; ☐

   2.2 debts; ☐

   2.3 encumbrances; ☐

   2.4 group company; ☐

   2.5 loan agreement, facility, advance; ☐

   2.6 intellectual property; ☐

   2.7 secured liabilities. ☐

3 Specify the borrower's covenant to pay and discharge the secured liabilities (including interest) on demand. ☐

4 In relation to the charging provisions, set out in the charge as security for payment of outstanding sums. ☐

5 What does the company/borrower charge to the lender? Consider (as appropriate): ☐

   5.1 all land by way of [first] legal mortgage; ☐

   5.2 future acquired land by way of [first] fixed equitable charge; ☐

   5.3 all other assets below by way of [first] fixed charge: ☐

      5.3.1 intellectual property; ☐

      5.3.2 stocks; ☐

	5.3.3	loose plant and equipment;	☐
	5.3.4	fixed plant and equipment;	☐
	5.3.5	debts and other claims;	☐
	5.3.6	insurances;	☐
	5.3.7	securities and shares;	☐
	5.3.8	stocks in trade;	☐
	5.3.9	all other assets not effectively charged as fixed charge by way of [first] floating charge	☐
6	In relation to protection of the lender's rights. Consider:		
	6.1	covenants by the borrower not to create any encumbrance over the assets;	☐
	6.2	covenant not to dispose of any assets subject to fixed charge;	☐
	6.3	covenant not to dispose of any assets subject to floating charge except in ordinary course of business;	☐
	6.4	ability to do any of the foregoing with the prior written consent of the lender.	☐
7	Consider and specify the lender's right to convert any floating charge into a fixed charge by notice.		☐
8	Can the floating charge automatically convert into a fixed charge? In what circumstances? Consider:		
	8.1	immediately prior to creation of encumbrances over assets;	☐
	8.2	if company ceases to carry on business;	☐
	8.3	if voluntary arrangement or compromise with creditor is entered into by the borrower.	☐
9	Consider and indicate whether:		
	9.1	debenture is to be continuing security and remain in force until discharged;	☐
	9.2	debenture is in addition to other rights and remedies or security;	☐

Commercial Contracts Checklists

9.3 the security document will prejudice or determine or otherwise affect any other security; ☐

9.4 any prior security held will merge with the newly created security. ☐

10 Specify what covenants the borrower gives during the term of the debenture. Review and indicate appropriate undertakings to: ☐

10.1 provide information and documents; ☐

10.2 take action to maintain intellectual property registrations and applications; ☐

10.3 procure that the lender's representative is a signatory to the borrower's bank account; ☐

10.4 apply proceeds of any litigation to discharge the sums incurred; ☐

10.5 provide the lender with financial information on a periodic basis and as required; ☐

10.6 comply with statutes and notices; ☐

10.7 deposit with the lender deeds and documents; ☐

10.8 pay monies into designated or separate account; ☐

10.9 pay rents and taxes promptly; ☐

10.10 observe covenants related to the property; ☐

10.11 apply insurance proceeds to make good or repay loan; ☐

10.12 keep buildings, fixtures and equipment in good repair; ☐

10.13 pay all premiums and maintain all insurances; ☐

10.14 put and keep buildings in good and substantial repair; ☐

10.15 provide copies of audited accounts within specified period; ☐

10.16 provide management accounts and financial documents in required form and within specified period; ☐

10.17 not grant or accept surrender of any lease; ☐

10.18 conduct business properly and efficiently. ☐

11 What if the borrower is in default of covenants? Can the lender (at its discretion): ☐

    11.1 remedy the default? ☐

    11.2 make good its effects? ☐

    11.3 pay any amount due by the company borrower? ☐

    11.4 authorise persons to enter buildings? ☐

    11.5 put in place or review insurance? ☐

12 Who is entitled to the proceeds of insurance? Specify instruction to insurer to pay and take further instructions from lender. Will all proceeds of insurance to be used to make good the damage or used towards discharge of loan? Does the lender have a discretion as to the application of insurance proceeds? ☐

13 What provisions apply in respect of demand and enforceability? When will the debenture be enforceable? Consider enforceability upon: ☐

    13.1 demand by lender; ☐

    13.2 occurrence of a loan agreement event of default; ☐

    13.3 passing of resolution or presentation of petition for winding up; ☐

    13.4 conversion of a floating charge into a fixed charge; ☐

    13.5 appointment of a receiver; ☐

    13.6 occurrence of any other event which in the lender's opinion puts security in jeopardy; ☐

    13.7 occurrence of a event with material adverse effect on borrower. ☐

14 Consider and indicate procedure for service of demand for payment notice. ☐

15 Following debenture becoming enforceable, can the lender exercise a power of sale under the Law of Property Act 1925? Consider whether there are applicable restrictions to such power. Can the power be delegated to a third party or receiver? ☐

16   In relation to receivers, consider and indicate: ☐

   16.1   appointment of receiver of or over assets; ☐

   16.2   manner of appointment; ☐

   16.3   appointment of joint receiver and powers; ☐

   16.4   right to determine remuneration of receiver; ☐

   16.5   right to remove receiver from office; ☐

   16.6   receiver an agent of the company until liquidation; ☐

   16.7   where company remains solely liable for defaults and acts of receiver; ☐

   16.8   other applicable provisions and specify general powers or duties of the receiver; ☐

17   Confirm appointment of lender and receiver as attorney of the borrower. Indicate the grant of power of attorney and extent of the power. Will the borrower be obliged to satisfy and confirm attorney's acts? ☐

18   How will monies received by the receiver be applied? What is the applicable priority? Consider funds to be used in satisfaction of: ☐

   18.1   costs and expenses of receivership together with remuneration of receiver; ☐

   18.2   secured liabilities; ☐

   18.3   payment to any person so entitled to any surplus. ☐

19   Consider the lender's right to place monies secured or released on a suspense or separate account, without obligation to apply it to discharging the secured liabilities. ☐

20   Consider and specify provisions relating to: ☐

   20.1   consolidation of rights of lender; ☐

   20.2   lender's right to set off liabilities and obligations; ☐

   20.3   availability and application of rights whether or not demand made; ☐

Lending and Security Documents

    20.4   protection of third parties and the statutory powers of sale being deemed to arise upon execution of debenture; ☐

    20.5   third parties not enquiring as to rights or powers of sale arising, whether the secured liabilities are outstanding or in relation to the occurrence of an event; ☐

    20.6   receipt of lender or receiver an absolute and conclusive discharge to the borrower ☐

    20.7   protection of the lender and receiver by exclusion of liability in relation to exercise of powers; ☐

    20.8   lender's possession of assets and any attendant obligations; ☐

    20.9   indemnity by the borrower of the lender and receiver; ☐

    20.10   provisions surviving termination and discharge of debenture or receiver. ☐

21   Consider and specify provisions relating to: ☐

    21.1   lender's right being cumulative; ☐

    21.2   lender's right to be waived in writing; ☐

    21.3   delay to not amount to waiver; ☐

    21.4   severance of invalid provisions; ☐

    21.5   responsibility for costs and expenses of the lender related to the debenture or enforcement; ☐

    21.6   authority to seek information from third parties about the borrower; ☐

    21.7   appointment of investigating accountants; ☐

    21.8   rights to assign or restriction on assignment; ☐

    21.9   further assurances and obligation to sign deeds and do things (at whose costs). ☐

22   In relation to the schedule, consider setting out: ☐

    22.1   company/borrower details; ☐

    22.2   details of property, land and buildings charge; ☐

22.3　vehicles list; ☐

22.4　computers and other equipment list; ☐

22.5　intellectual property details (including trade marks, patent rights, copyright, database right, service marks, designs); ☐

22.6　general assets list as charged. ☐

See Precedent 4.2 on accompanying CD.

4.3 Guarantee

Overview

Description of Agreement/Document

The guarantee is a contract where one party agrees to pay money or perform an obligation owed to the other party by a third party. In effect, it is a promise to be responsible for another person's default. The guarantee provides for the guarantor's liability to pay or perform if the relevant third party fails to pay or perform. The guarantor's liability only becomes effective upon default by the principal debtor or party. The guarantee normally sets out the principal obligation together with provisions relating to protection of the creditor, an indemnity, avoidance or discharge of the guarantee provisions together with express rights of the guarantor.

Practical Guidance/Issues List

The parties should note the distinction between a guarantee and an indemnity: the legal implications are different as the guarantee is conditional.

The guarantor:

- may wish to consider resisting an express indemnity provision being included in the guarantee;
- can insist that information is provided on an ongoing basis by both parties in order to keep an eye on potential defaults;
- should consider ensuring that rights are first exhausted against the principal debtor or party before the guarantor is pursued;
- restrict internally the rights of officers or directors to give guarantees without board approval;
- may wish to resist a continuing guarantee;
- can insist on a limited guarantee setting out a limitation on the total amount for which it will be liable;
- may wish to reserve rights against any co-guarantor or enter into a contribution agreement in relation to any guaranteed liability;
- should obtain an indemnity from the principal debtor;
- should seek to obtain a written release at the end of the term to ensure proper discharge of the liability;
- may reserve its rights against the principal debtor or party;
- should insist on discharge of the guarantee in the event that the underlying contract or obligations are varied without the guarantor's consent.

The party accepting the guarantee:

- needs to review the guarantor's capacity and authority to enter into the contract of guarantee;
- should avoid accepting oral guarantees to limit enforcement difficulties;
- should review the relevant constitutional documents of the corporate guarantor for specific power to give guarantees.

Law/Compliance Requirement

The formal and essential elements of a guarantee are the same as with any other contract. A valid guarantee must be a binding legal contract involving an offer and acceptance, relevant consideration and an intention to create legal relations.

The Statutes of Frauds 1677 as amended may in certain circumstances apply to particular forms of guarantee, but essentially, legal compliance in relation to a guarantee is a matter of general contract law.

Specific Provisions

Payment
If the [Provider O] shall default in the payment of any sum under this Guarantee the Guarantor(s) will

immediately on demand by [Company X] pay such sum to [Company X]. Such guarantee and undertaking is a continuing guarantee and undertaking and shall remain in force until all the obligations of the [Provider O] under this Guarantee have been fully performed and all sums payable to [Company X] have been fully paid

Continuing Security
This guarantee and indemnity is to be a continuing security to [Company X] for all obligations, commitments, warranties, undertakings, indemnities and covenants on the part of the [Provider O] under or pursuant to the Guarantee notwithstanding any settlement of account or other matter or thing whatsoever.

Obligation
In consideration of [Company X] entering into this Guarantee, the Guarantor(s) unconditionally and irrevocably [jointly and severally] undertake and guarantee to [Company X] the due and punctual performance and observance by the [Provider O] of all its obligations, commitments, undertakings, warranties, indemnities and covenants under or pursuant to the Guarantee and the due and punctual payment of all sums now or subsequently payable by the [Provider O] to [Company X] under this Guarantee when the same shall become due.

Indemnity
The Guarantor further agrees to indemnify [Company X] against all losses, damages, costs and expenses (including legal costs and expenses) which [Company X] may incur or suffer through or arising from any breach by the [Provider O] of such obligations, commitments, warranties, undertakings, indemnities or covenants.

Checklist 4.3 Guarantee Checklist

In preparing a guarantee or letter, individuals or businesses should consider the following non-exhaustive matters.

Actions/Issues:	Comments:	✎

1 Ascertain and consider guarantor details. ☐

2 What are the terms of the guarantee? Will the guarantee include an indemnity? ☐

3 What is the consideration for the guarantee? ☐

4 Will the liability of guarantors be joint and several? ☐

5 Consider type of guarantee in terms of the obligation or liability guaranteed. Consider and specify whether guarantee is: ☐

    5.1 for a specified sum; ☐

    5.2 for a specified obligation or undertaking unlimited in amount or subject to a cap; ☐

    5.3 continuing; ☐

    5.4 in respect of whole or part of debt; ☐

    5.5 subject to effect for a specified period; ☐

    5.6 subject to liability proof by lender or relevant party; ☐

    5.7 applicable to contingent liabilities; ☐

    5.8 unconditional and irrevocable. ☐

6 Consider definitions of relevant terms including: ☐

    6.1 debenture; ☐

    6.2 indebtedness; ☐

    6.3 loan agreement; ☐

	6.4	guarantor;	☐
	6.5	principal debtor.	☐
7	In respect of the guarantee clause, specify:		☐
	7.1	consideration for guarantee;	☐
	7.2	whether joint and several;	☐
	7.3	the guaranteed obligation or undertaking;	☐
	7.4	undertaking to pay and discharge indebtedness;	☐
	7.5	the guarantor as primary obligator;	☐
	7.6	that guarantor acts not only as guarantor but as a surety;	☐
	7.7	obligation to indemnify on demand against loss;	☐
	7.8	maximum sum recoverable under guarantee.	☐
8	Consider and indicate that guarantee:		☐
	8.1	shall be continuing security;	☐
	8.2	is in addition to other security;	☐
	8.3	shall not merge with or otherwise prejudice any other right or remedy;	☐
	8.4	is not to be affected by defect or informality of any document or security;	☐
	8.5	amount shall be conclusively set as indicated by the creditor/lender.	☐
9	Consider and specify provisions relating to avoidance, discharge and enforcement. Insert provisions to protect against discharge of guarantor. Consider non-discharge of guarantor as a result of:		☐
	9.1	assignment of the loan agreement;	☐
	9.2	assignment or novation of the main relevant agreement containing the principal obligation or obligations guaranteed by the guarantor ;	☐

9.3 release of the principal by law; ☐

9.4 release of any applicable security; ☐

9.5 impairment of any security; ☐

9.6 release or discharge of principal or joint guarantors; ☐

9.7 giving time or indulgence to principal debtor; ☐

9.8 variation of the applicable principal contract; ☐

9.9 liquidation or insolvency of principal; ☐

9.10 setting aside of any payment or security on a preference by transaction at undervalue. ☐

10 Are there any express rights of the guarantor? Consider: ☐

10.1 right to require that principal be pursued and rights exhausted prior to claim from guarantor; ☐

10.2 limit on liability amount; ☐

10.3 specific rights where joint guarantors; ☐

10.4 right for guarantor to pursue principal following claim; ☐

10.5 requirement for information and documents from time to time; ☐

10.6 any conditions precedent to liability. ☐

11 Consider and specify provisions relating to: ☐

11.1 payments of guarantor to be without set off, counterclaim, lien or other right; ☐

11.2 specific obligations, undertakings, limits or rights applicable to each joint guarantor; ☐

11.3 defences applicable to principal debtor; ☐

11.4 appropriation of payments; ☐

11.5 payment currency and account of payment; ☐

11.6 indemnity provisions and extent of loss indemnified; ☐

11.7 insolvency or bankruptcy of any party and consequences; ☐

11.8 service of demand under the guarantee; ☐

11.9 specific form of guarantee and if it relates to guarantee: ☐

    11.9.1 for goods and services supply; ☐

    11.9.2 for payment of fixed amount; ☐

    11.9.3 of one off obligation, undertaking or transaction; ☐

    11.9.4 of continuing obligations; ☐

    11.9.5 of money lent and existing indebtedness; ☐

    11.9.6 for cross-guarantee obligations or inter-company liability; ☐

    11.9.7 in addition to an indemnity in relation to continuing obligations; ☐

    11.9.8 of specific obligations or transactions relating to factoring; ☐

11.10 restriction on the guarantor taking action against the principal; ☐

11.11 the creditor not having to pursue the principal prior to claim under guarantee; ☐

11.12 rights of set off; ☐

11.13 warranties by the guarantor that: ☐

    11.13.1 it will not to take security over principal; ☐

    11.13.2 it is entitled to give the guarantee; ☐

    11.13.3 entry into this guarantee is not in breach of any contract or law. ☐

Lending and Security Documents

12 Specify: ☐

    12.1 governing law; ☐

    12.2 jurisdiction; ☐

    12.3 exclusion of third party rights to enforce guarantee; ☐

    12.4 notice provisions; ☐

    12.5 guarantee is binding on successors and assigns; ☐

    12.6 restrictions on or rights of assignment; ☐

    12.7 waiver or non-waiver provisions; ☐

    12.8 rights on cumulative; ☐

    12.9 notice to determine guarantee. ☐

See Precedent 4.3 on accompanying CD.

5 Intellectual Property and Media-Related Agreements

5.1 Sponsorship Agreement

5.2 Technical Services/Know-How Agreement

5.3 Data Processor Agreement

5.4 Presenter's Agreement

5.5 Contributor's Agreement

5.6 Research and Development Agreement

Intellectual Property and Media-Related Agreements

5.1 Sponsorship Agreement

Overview

Description of Agreement/Document

The agreement sets out the relationship between a sponsor and a right holder. In return for payment of sponsorship monies, the right holder grants the sponsor certain sponsorship rights. The sponsorship agreement seeks to record the obligations of the parties in relation to the sponsored event or entity. The rights granted to the sponsor vary depending on the nature of the sponsorship.

Practical Guidance/Issues List

The success of the sponsorship arrangement will depend on the parties' efforts and the practical precautions taken as expressly provided in the agreement. Certain relevant matters are set out below:
- Consider the parties objectives and type of sponsorships.
- What are the sponsor's requirements?
- Review the legal status of the parties to the contract and confirm legal capacity.
- Ascertain sponsor's financial status and confirm ability to make relevant payments.
- Consider proposed promotional campaigns and suitability.
- What about the reputation of the sponsor? Consider available resources.
- Ascertain need for third party consents or approvals.
- Ascertain, review and ensure:
  - that the right owner is the appropriate contracting party;
  - that the rights are available and owned by the specified entity;
  - that information is provided about intellectual property protection;
  - that there are no existing adverse agreements or rights;
  - the type, nature and extent of rights to be granted.
- Consider and ensure insurance arrangements are put in place.
- Review proposed position in respect of cancellation of sponsored event, dissolution or insolvency of entity.
- Who is liable for any costs, cancellation claims, third party claims or force majeure event?
- Review and ensure that the proposed sponsorship agreement contains all the main agreed terms.
- Ensure clarity of drafting to avoid enforcement difficulties resulting from uncertainty.
- The agreement may be best executed as a deed or consideration should be specified.
- Will there be an increase in payments required in the event of renewal or occurrence of specified event.
- Define exactly what rights are being granted for exploitation. Consider the following depending on nature of agreement and sponsorship:
  - exclusivity;
  - use of logo, rights, broadcast coverage or video;
  - photographs;
  - advertising;
  - title branding;
  - advertising boards and signage;
  - programmes;
  - personal appearances/association;
  - entertainment and hospitality;
  - seating and free entry.
- The sponsor should ensure that it has an adequate period built into the arrangements to enable full exploitation of the rights.
- Reserve the right to extend the sponsorship rights or renew the contract on (no less favourable) agreed terms.
- It is advisable to register all applicable trade marks to give greater chance of policing any infringement.

Some Key Definitions

'Advance' means the advance sum of £[ ] solely recoupable from income received from the Event Agreements and payable by [Party A] in accordance with clause [ ] comprising initial funding towards the overall costs of staging the Event.

'Broadcast Rights' means the right to broadcast the Event in the [United Kingdom and abroad] by any means of broadcast including (but not limited to) terrestrial, satellite, cable, pay or free television or otherwise.

'Designated Account' means a separate bank account set up by and under the sole control of [specify party] which shall be operated as set out in clause [ ] of this Agreement.

'Event Exploitation Revenue' means all gross revenues received from the Event Agreements and exploitation of the rights generally in relation to the Event and granted to [Party X] in accordance with the Underlying Rights, but excluding [specify relevant exclusion] Introduction Revenue.

'Event Marks' means the event logo to be created by [indicate creator] in conjunction with [specify applicable partner or party] and subject to the approval of [   ], which may include the use of the [specify relevant] Marks.

'Expenses' means all costs and expenses incurred by [   ] as set out in the Event Budget or otherwise agreed by the parties in writing.

'Merchandising Rights' means the right to manufacture and sell products and goods containing the Event Marks or [specify relevant marks] Marks.

'Sponsorship Rights' means the sponsorship and hospitality rights to be exercised by [   ] as detailed in the Schedule.

Specific Provisions

Condition Precedent
Save as provided in clause [ ], this Agreement is subject to and conditional upon [specify relevant party] being granted the Underlying Rights from the [Event].

Notices
Any notice given under this Agreement shall be in writing and shall be sent to the party to be served at the address at the top of the Agreement or such other address of which notice has been previously given to the other party in accordance with this clause. All notices shall be delivered by hand or sent by fax (with a copy posted) or by registered or recorded delivery or by registered airmail letter. All notices shall be deemed to have been received if delivered by hand on the date of delivery, if posted on the expiration of *[48]* hours or (in the case of airmail) *[seven]* days after posting and if sent by fax at the time of transmission.

Renewal
Three months before the completion of the Event in the [specify relevant event period or season] Season, the parties shall enter into good faith negotiations to renew the Agreement for a further period of [   ] months on terms no less favourable than under this Agreement.

In the event that [Party Z] does not renew the Agreement under clause [ ], [Party X] shall be entitled to continue to provide services in relation to the Event and [Party Z] agrees that it will not directly or indirectly enter into any arrangements with any company in the same or 'similar field' of interest as [Party A] to become a title sponsor of the Event for the following Season only and acknowledges that it shall not be entitled to use the [specify marks] Marks or Event Marks in any way nor imply that the Event has any continuing connection with [specify party or organisation].

Obligations
Subject always to having the requisite Underlying Rights and [Party A's] prior written approval (such approval not to be unreasonably delayed or withheld), [Party B] shall use reasonable endeavours to source parties willing to enter into agreements with [Party A] relating to Merchandising Rights and other business opportunities relating to the Event. [Party B] shall submit the proposed commercial terms relating to the grant of Merchandising Rights to [Party A] for [Party A] to approve.

[Party B] shall keep [Party A] fully informed of all progress or anticipated setbacks in respect of the Event.

Sponsorship Monies

In consideration of the Sponsorship Rights the Company shall pay by way of sponsorship of the Events the following sums exclusive of VAT that is to say:
- in the Year ending [2005] the sum of £[   ];
- in each subsequent Year a sum equal to the Sponsorship Monies payable in the immediately preceding Year increased by RPI or [10%] whichever is the lower.

Obligations of the Company

The Company undertakes with the [specify relevant party] and [specify relevant party] that it shall not use any of the rights and licences granted herein in a manner which in the reasonable opinion of [specify relevant party] is prejudicial to the image of [   ] and/or [the sport].

Commercial Contracts Checklists

Checklist 5.1 Sponsorship Agreement Checklist

In preparing a sponsorship agreement or letter, individuals or businesses should consider the following non-exhaustive matters.

Actions/Issues:	Comments:	✍
1 Ascertain and review proposed terms of sponsorship.		☐
2 Consider the legal status of sponsored entity and ensure it has relevant legal capacity.		☐
3 Consider the type of sponsorship proposed and form of agreement:		☐
3.1 letter and acceptance;		☐
3.2 formally drafted legal agreement;		☐
3.3 memorandum of understanding;		☐
3.4 legally binding heads of terms.		☐
4 Who will be the parties to the agreement?		☐
5 Recite the parties' intention, proposed sponsorship, background and general requirements.		☐
6 Will there be third party involvement or requirement for a guarantor?		☐
7 Consider definitions for relevant terms (as appropriate):		☐
7.1 advance;		☐
7.2 broadcast rights;		☐
7.3 sponsorship monies;		☐
7.4 event or tournament;		☐
7.5 sponsorship rights;		☐
7.6 merchandising rights;		☐

7.7 secondary sponsors and secondary rights; ☐

7.8 venue; ☐

7.9 organisers; ☐

7.10 term. ☐

8 Consider and specify any conditions precedent. Will the agreement be terminable in the event of non-fulfilment by a specified long stop date? Can the conditions be waived? Can the long stop date be extended? ☐

9 What is the proposed duration of the contract? Consider: ☐

    9.1 fixed term; ☐

    9.2 indefinite term and terminable on notice; ☐

    9.3 renewal and extension obligation; ☐

    9.4 rolling term; ☐

    9.5 commencement date; ☐

    9.6 specific event, seasons or tournament. ☐

10 Ascertain, review and specify the provisions relating to sponsorship monies. Consider: ☐

    10.1 sponsorship monies due for relevant period; ☐

    10.2 payment dates and arrangements; ☐

    10.3 requirement for advance or deposit payments; ☐

    10.4 retail price index increases; ☐

    10.5 whether inclusive of exclusive of VAT; ☐

    10.6 variation to payment terms; ☐

    10.7 default interest payment at specified date; ☐

Commercial Contracts Checklists

    10.8   reduction of amount in the event of default or other situations (e.g. relegation). ☐

11   Set out the consideration: ☐

    11.1   grant of sponsorship rights; ☐

    11.2   payment of sponsorship monies. ☐

12   Specify what rights are granted in definition of sponsorship rights or in the schedule. Consider: ☐

    12.1   rights of exclusivity; ☐

    12.2   use of logo, trademarks and names; ☐

    12.3   photographs, television and/or video coverage; ☐

    12.4   right to display screens, signage and boards at the event; ☐

    12.5   use of specific title such as 'official sponsor' or 'official [product] for [Event]'; ☐

    12.6   personal appearances and association; ☐

    12.7   complimentary tickets and specific seating; ☐

    12.8   Credit in official programme or on screen; ☐

    12.9   title branding; ☐

    12.10   entertainment and hospitality. ☐

13   Consider and specify obligations of the event organiser or right holder including obligations to: ☐

    13.1   provide specified services; ☐

    13.2   organise and manage event; ☐

    13.3   provide required assistance; ☐

    13.4   assist with obtaining underlying or required rights; ☐

13.5 ensure adequate level of staff; ☐

13.6 ensure non-infringement of third party rights; ☐

13.7 perform services to a specified standard or at least with reasonable diligence, skill and care; ☐

13.8 keep sponsor informed of progress or problems; ☐

13.9 restrict competitive advertising to sponsor's product; ☐

13.10 assist with exploiting underlying rights and broadcast rights; ☐

13.11 not carry out any prejudicial conduct; ☐

13.12 maintain good name, image and reputation; ☐

13.13 not engage in acts which may damage or bring event and sponsor into disrepute; ☐

13.14 obtain and maintain required insurance; ☐

13.15 comply with relevant specific regulations (e.g. data protection) or general compliance with legislation; ☐

13.16 submit or approve publicity and marketing information; ☐

13.17 ensure sponsor's rights are upheld and maintained; ☐

13.18 ensure sponsor's signage is not obscured; ☐

13.19 stage the event in accordance with previous events or specified format of events; ☐

13.20 grant access to premises and facilities. ☐

14 What are the sponsor's obligations? Consider obligations to: ☐

14.1 make payments promptly; ☐

14.2 pay sponsorship sum and increases; ☐

14.3 provide required assistance, information and documents; ☐

14.4 provide relevant branding, signage, artwork, logos and other material; ☐

14.5 comply with the branding, promotions and advertising regulations of the entity or event; ☐

14.6 introduce the entity or event organisers to relevant secondary sponsors; ☐

14.7 only use the sponsorship rights as specified; ☐

14.8 not use any rights in a manner likely to bring entity or event into disrepute; ☐

14.9 not conduct its business or association with the organiser/event in a manner prejudicial to image of the organiser and/or event; ☐

14.10 comply with applicable rules and regulations. ☐

15 Review, consider or specify: ☐

15.1 exclusion of responsibility for event organisation or operation; ☐

15.2 options to acquire equipment or further rights; ☐

15.3 option to renew or extend sponsorship; ☐

15.4 exclusivity of sponsor's appointment; ☐

15.5 any provisions relating to payments into or administration of any designated accounts; ☐

15.6 fee arrangements for any services; ☐

15.7 responsibility for costs and expenses; ☐

15.8 obligations to render statements or provide requested information; ☐

15.9 auditing rights in relation to any revenue or accounting arrangements; ☐

15.10 commission arrangements or obligations; ☐

15.11 terms relating to accounting; ☐

15.12 periodic audits in relation to costs verification, books of account, contracts and other records; ☐

15.13 insurance requirements and obligations; ☐

15.14 rights of set-off and retention; ☐

15.15 arrangements for service of notices. ☐

16 Specify applicable termination rights: ☐

    16.1 by either party; ☐

    16.2 upon non-remedy of material breach; ☐

    16.3 upon written periodic notice; ☐

    16.4 in the event of insolvency or related specified matter; ☐

    16.5 in the event of prejudicial conduct; ☐

    16.6 for bringing event or organiser into disrepute; ☐

    16.7 on occurrence of scandal or controversy; ☐

    16.8 for force majeure event; ☐

    16.9 for non-fulfilment of condition (e.g. sale of broadcast rights, failure to attain specified level of coverage); ☐

    16.10 for cancellation or postponement; ☐

    16.11 if sponsor is prevented from exploiting sponsorship rights for whatever reason; ☐

    16.12 for specified default events; ☐

    16.13 change in legislation with adverse event; ☐

    16.14 for sponsor's failure to exploit rights granted; ☐

    16.15 in the event of charge of control; ☐

    16.16 for non-payment of sums on payment date. ☐

Commercial Contracts Checklists

17   Consider and specify consequences of termination. ☐

18   What are the post-termination obligations and/or undertakings? ☐

19   Will any provisions survive termination? Consider a general provision in respect of terms capable of surviving termination. ☐

20   Specify the force majeure provisions. Ascertain and define relevant events. Will there be any termination rights? What about obligations during the event or following occurrence of the event? ☐

21   Specify confidentiality undertakings and consider definition of Confidential Information. Are there any permitted disclosures? ☐

22   In relation to intellectual property, consider or specify: ☐

     22.1   who owns what; ☐

     22.2   non-transfer of rights unless express; ☐

     22.3   what happens to jointly created rights or materials; ☐

     22.4   grant of right to use any rights; ☐

     22.5   requirement for approval for representation of design logos or marks; ☐

23   With reference to an indemnity: ☐

     23.1   will either party be required to provide an indemnity? ☐

     23.2   what are the terms of any such indemnity? ☐

     23.3   who is indemnified? ☐

     23.4   what is the extent of the indemnity and does it cover costs? ☐

     23.5   is consequential loss excluded? ☐

     23.6   is there a cap? ☐

     23.7   are there any exclusions? ☐

     23.8   will the indemnity be mutual? ☐

24　Consider relevant limitation or exclusion of liability provision? ☐
　　Consider:

　　24.1　excluding liability for specified matters; ☐

　　24.2　exclusion of consequential loss or damage; ☐

　　24.3　liability for death or personal injury; ☐

　　24.4　specify liability and limiting to specific sum or insurance; ☐

　　24.5　liquidated damages provision for specific breach. ☐

25　Specify relevant boilerplate provisions including: ☐

　　25.1　governing law and jurisdiction; ☐

　　25.2　severance of illegal or unenforceable provisions ☐

　　25.3　procedure for variation or amendment of agreement; ☐

　　25.4　whether the agreement is assignable; ☐

　　25.5　no relationship of agency or partnership; ☐

　　25.6　the agreement being all inclusive of agreed terms; ☐

　　25.7　third party to have right to enforce agreement. ☐

　　25.8　headings not to affect interpretation ☐

See Precedent 5.1 on accompanying CD.

5.2 Technical Services/Know-How Agreement

Overview

Description of Agreement/Document

A technical services and know-how agreement details the transfer of know-how on a licence and the provision of services by the grantor, owner or possessor of such know-how. The specific terms of such agreements may depend on the nature of the know-how to be licensed or the services to be supplied.

In general, such an agreement will set out the exclusive application of the terms and the arrangements in relation to products, training, support and provision of technical services. In addition, the agreement will contain relevant provisions for the protection of the know-how and the owner's interest, certain restrictions on the licensee, licensing of improvements, licensing fee payment, applicable warranties and indemnities. The standard boilerplate provisions are also set out.

Practical Guidance/Issues List

Parties to a know-how licence and technical assistance agreement should consider the following:
- The owner or grantor should ensure sufficient protection will be in place for the licensed know-how.
- The licensee should seek relevant warranties in respect of service provision and the know-how provided.
- Where applicable, suitable indemnity should be included for required comfort.
- The owner should resist any warranties relating to the adequacy of training provided.
- The owner may wish to reserve a right of first refusal in the event that the licensee proposes to sell the production facility.
- Strict compliance with confidentiality undertakings will be necessary.
- A liquidate damages provision may be useful to regulate or deter breach under the licence agreement.
- The licensee should require that trainers or providers of support are highly experienced.
- The owner may require a nominal percentage of the sales revenue from the products.
- Where standard terms are used by the owner or grantor for the provision of services, this should be properly incorporated. The licensee should ensure that any such terms are carefully reviewed as they are usually one sided and may contain onerous provisions.
- Parties should note that provisions seeking to limit liability or exclude certain obligations will be subject to the test of reasonableness or challenge under relevant statutes.
- Exclusion clauses should be properly but reasonably drafted to be effective.
- Post-termination restrictions should be set out clearly to limit disputes.
- The owner may require further protection of a guarantor or other security arrangements in respect of the licensee's commitments under the agreement.

Some Key Definitions

'Products' means the products listed in the Schedule which have been developed by the [Grantor/Owner/Licensor] and manufactured in accordance with the secret formula and Know-How.

'Know-How' means the know-how of the [Grantor/Owner/Licensor] relating to [specify relevant matter or process] and the [Products] including specified computer software, oral and written instructions, drawing, photograph, any film, video, tape or other device, any electronic or other material embodying other data, plans, graphs, diagrams and related materials or information required for the manufacture of the [Products].

'Expiry Date' means the date on which the Contract terminates in accordance with its terms as a result of passing of required specified period or early proper termination under the Contract.

'Technical Services' means the assistance and technical services to be provided by the [Owner/Grantor/Licensor] to the Licensee, further details of which are set out in the Schedule together with such other technical services or assistance required on an ad hoc basis and requested in writing by the Licensee.

Specific Provisions

Services
The Services shall in so far as is reasonably practicable be provided in accordance with the specification (if any) set out in the Services Sheet but subject to these Conditions and shall be performed at such times as the Grantor shall in its sole discretion decide.

No Warranty
The Grantor does not warrant, guarantee or undertake on behalf of any third party supplier or service provider that access to any facilities or any products or services will be uninterrupted or of any particular level of availability or quality.

Sale
In the event of a proposed sale by the Licensee of the Production Facility used in the manufacture of the Products, the Grantor shall be entitled to a right of first refusal. The Licensee shall notify the Grantor of the proposed sale and offer to sell the Production Facility to the Grantor. If the Grantor accepts such offer, the Grantor shall purchase the Production Facility at the price and on the terms agreed with the Licensee.

Indemnity
The Licensee agrees to indemnify and keep the Owner fully indemnified from and against any loss, claim or liability whatsoever incurred or suffered by the Owner as a result of negligence or any default by the Licensee (or its employees, agents or representatives) of its obligations however arising in connection with this Agreement.

Confidentiality
The Licensee agrees and specifically undertakes at all times to keep confidential the Know-How disclosed to the Licensee under or pursuant to this Agreement and the Licensee shall use the Know-How in connection with the specified purpose.

Commercial Contracts Checklists

Checklist 5.2 Technical Services/Know-How Agreement Checklist

In preparing a know-how agreement or letter, individuals or businesses should consider the following non-exhaustive matters.

Actions/Issues:	Comments:	☐

1 Review proposed licence and services arrangements. ☐

2 Recite background information, as appropriate and set out: ☐

    2.1   nature of grantor's business; ☐

    2.2   details of development of technology and know-how acquisition by grantor; ☐

    2.3   fact that know-how is exclusive and valuable; ☐

    2.4   licensee's need for the know-how to produce the products; ☐

    2.5   nature of the services to be provided; ☐

    2.6   licence and services agreement on the terms and conditions. ☐

3 Detail parties' names and addresses including registered offices and numbers. ☐

4 Define relevant terms for ease of reference and certainty including, as applicable: ☐

    4.1   research, development; ☐

    4.2   product, know-how; ☐

    4.3   relevant technology; ☐

    4.4   term, commencement date. ☐

    4.5   services; ☐

    4.6   charges, fees; ☐

    4.7   event of force majeure; ☐

	4.8	business, business day;	☐
	4.9	grantor, owner, licensor, licensee, user;	☐
	4.10	intellectual property rights.	☐
5	Set out grant of know-how licence in connection with the products.	☐
6	Detail consideration for grant.	☐
7	Set out obligation not to disclose know-how to other manufacturers.	☐
8	Set out:	
	8.1	appointment of grantor to provide services;	☐
	8.2	nature of the services to be provided;	☐
	8.3	required training and support services;	☐
	8.4	hours of training and support services;	☐
	8.5	grantor's obligation to provide experienced trainers and support service providers;	☐
	8.6	licensee's obligation to provide facilities for grantor's staff;	☐
	8.7	parties' respective confidentiality undertakings;	☐
	8.8	licensee's undertaking not to disclose technology and know-how;	☐
	8.9	permission to disclose know-how to approved persons;	☐
	8.10	disclosure to persons bound by a non-disclosure agreement;	☐
	8.11	use of know-how for specified purpose only;	☐
	8.12	liability to liquidated damages if know-how used for unauthorised purpose;	☐
	8.13	licensee's undertaking not to use or abuse grantor's name or marks;	☐

Commercial Contracts Checklists

    8.14   licensee's agreement not to apply for registration of associated mark; ☐

    8.15   right of first refusal on any development or improvement. ☐

9   Consider and provide for indemnity in favour of grantor for third party liability resulting from unauthorised use of know-how. ☐

10   Set out mutual obligation to notify and share improvements by grant of non-exclusive licence. ☐

11   Set out procedure for agreed or joint patent applications. ☐

12   In relation to the supply of the technical services, specify: ☐

    12.1   right to make changes to the technical services; ☐

    12.2   manner in which technical services are to be performed; ☐

    12.3   responsibility for obtaining permits or consents; ☐

    12.4   provision of the technical assistance or services in consideration of the fees; ☐

    12.5   right to suspend provision of services; ☐

    12.6   provision of services to be with reasonable care and skill; ☐

    12.7   use of suitably qualified or experienced staff to provide services; ☐

    12.8   parties to co-operate and act in good faith; ☐

    12.9   prompt payment of charges and expenses; ☐

    12.10   exclusion of liability for third party provided services; ☐

    12.11   requirement to comply with data protection rules or other specified regulations; ☐

    12.12   obligation to obtain and maintain insurance; ☐

    12.13   required prompt compliance with requests for information or assistance; ☐

    12.14   record keeping requirement; ☐

12.15 maintenance of information or materials. ☐

13 Payment of fees in consideration of supply of know-how, assistance and services. Specify: ☐

    13.1 relevant amount of fees or basis of calculation; ☐

    13.2 method of payment; ☐

    13.3 additional fees and rates; ☐

    13.4 agreed expenses or charges; ☐

    13.5 payment in instalments; ☐

    13.6 payment periods and dates; ☐

    13.7 costs and expenses liability; ☐

    13.8 invoicing arrangements; ☐

    13.9 liability for tax and VAT payment; ☐

    13.10 default interest liability provisions for late payments; ☐

    13.11 grantor's right to suspend services or terminate agreement for late or non-payment. ☐

14 Set out any agreed percentage fee in relation to sales of products, licensee's obligation to keep books for continuing fees and grantor's right of audit or review. ☐

15 If appropriate, provide a right of first refusal for grantor in the event of licensee's sale of manufacturing facility. Set out applicable procedure. ☐

16 Where relevant, set out intellectual property rights provisions and indemnities for third party infringement claims or other loss. ☐

17 Specify the duration of the arrangements and whether the term can be extended. ☐

18 Consider and provide for grounds, terms, fee and procedure for extension of term. ☐

19 Consider termination rights, grounds and timing of termination. ☐

20 Detail or consider termination: ☐

Commercial Contracts Checklists

    20.1   upon expiry of fixed period; ☐

    20.2   for non-performance or failure to meet targets; ☐

    20.3   on engagement in prejudicial conduct; ☐

    20.4   upon insolvency of either party; ☐

    20.5   in the event of consistent lateness of fee payments; ☐

    20.6   on change of control or ownership of a party; ☐

    20.7   as a result of failure to pay on the due date; ☐

    20.8   for excessive delay from force majeure occurrence; ☐

    20.9   for failure to remedy material or fundamental breach; ☐

    20.10 upon service of appropriate notice; ☐

    20.11 for breach of applicable law or specific regulations; ☐

    20.12 for fraudulent misrepresentations; ☐

    20.13 for breach of related agreement. ☐

21   Provide for termination consequences and obligations. Obligations to include: disposal of stock of products; return or destruction of confidential information; return of grantor's materials, know-how, documents and software; payment of outstanding fees to grantor; certification of compliance with obligations. ☐

22   Will licensee be entitled to compensation for grantor's wrongful or early termination? Set out agreed liquidated damages. ☐

23   Reservation of accrued rights notwithstanding termination. ☐

24   Detail liability provisions: ☐

    24.1   non-exclusion for personal injury or death; ☐

    24.2   total exclusion or limitation of liability, as appropriate; ☐

24.3 specify maximum aggregate liability under agreement; ☐

24.4 consider limiting liability to amount of fees paid; ☐

24.5 mutual exclusion of liability for consequential loss, indirect loss, loss of profit and consequential loss. ☐

25 Consider: ☐

25.1 excluding all other warranties to the fullest extent permitted by law; ☐

25.2 indemnity provisions, where applicable for specific breach or issues; ☐

25.3 liability for infringement of third party rights and claims; ☐

25.4 alternative dispute resolution procedure; ☐

25.5 provisions indicating ownership of materials or equipment; ☐

25.6 non-solicitation of employees or business restrictions; ☐

25.7 requirement to comply with conduct of persons rules applicable at premises including security and health and safety issues; ☐

26 Consider force majeure provisions and provide for definition of force majeure, notification obligation and right to terminate in the event of lengthy delays. ☐

27 Consider and insert provisions relating to: ☐

27.1 required currency payment; ☐

27.2 set off and deduction rights; ☐

27.3 warranty of authority to contract; ☐

27.4 grantor's right of inspection of production units or facility; ☐

27.5 requirement for change of control approval by grantor; ☐

27.6 non-exclusivity of grant to licensee in territory; ☐

27.7 definition of territory. ☐

Commercial Contracts Checklists

27.8 data protection compliance. ☐

27.9 liability for costs of preparation and implementation of agreement; ☐

27.10 agreement not to make claim against officer or employee of grantor or licensee; ☐

27.11 changes to agreement; ☐

27.12 service of notices; ☐

27.13 non-reliance on any statements or inducements; ☐

27.14 confidentiality undertakings and non-disclosure; ☐

27.15 data protection compliance; ☐

27.16 third party rights or enforcement rights exclusion; ☐

27.17 assignment of the agreement; ☐

27.18 successors and continued payments to grantor's personal representative on death; ☐

27.19 arbitration; ☐

27.20 retention of title; ☐

27.21 severance of unlawful or unenforceable provisions; ☐

27.22 non-waiver by delay; ☐

27.23 entire agreement between the parties; ☐

27.24 fact of no partnership or agency between parties; ☐

27.25 further assurance; ☐

27.26 survival of terms; ☐

27.27 process or agent for service; ☐

27.28 governing law; ☐

27.29 exclusive, non-exclusive or one party submission jurisdiction. ☐

See Precedent 5.2 on accompanying CD.

Commercial Contracts Checklists

5.3 Data Processor Agreement

Overview

Description of Agreement/Document

The data processor agreement is a product of the Data Protection Act 1998. It sets out the requirements of one of the data protection principles. The agreement details the provision of data processing services to a data controller by a data processor. Apart from the main processing obligations, the agreement also sets out the commercial terms. A data processor agreement will normally provide for the respective obligations of the parties, ownership of intellectual property rights, specific acknowledgements, security guarantees and restrictions. The standard boilerplate provisions will also apply.

Practical Guidance/Issues List

The agreement can be entered into as supplemental to other agreements between the parties, such as a database build or management contract or a bureau service agreement.

Compliance with the obligations set out in the Data Protection Act 1998 is recommended. The data controller should:

- ensure appropriate notification of its processing to the Information Commissioner;
- maintain appropriate procedures;
- process the personal data in accordance with the principles of the Data Protection Act including requirement for a data processor written agreement;
- include all other applicable commercial terms in the data processor agreement;
- consider imposing a liquidated damages provision for specific breaches;
- consider using service levels or providing written instructions;
- ensure that it owns all rights created in connection with the personal data and obtain an assignment;
- impose restrictions on overseas transfers of data by the processor without the data controller's written request or approval;
- ensure it is made clear who owns the results of services (i.e. spending habits profile) provided;
- consider post-termination obligations and consequences of termination;
- consider restricting the appointment of sub-processors except as agents of the data controller or enter into direct agreements with each sub-processor;
- provide that the agreement is enforceable by the data subject.

The data processor should consider:

- using specific personnel for the services to comply with the requirements of the Data Protection Act 1998;
- restricting its liability for certain matters;
- requesting processing instruction to be in writing only;
- training employees in data protection issues and providing adequate practice updates to avoid careless breaches;
- requirements to comply with other or related regulations;
- whether it will be able to comply with specified obligations;
- insisting that the data controller carries and pays costs of complying with subject access requests;
- reviewing applicable data protection notice and ensure processing is within or as specified;
- specifically setting out permitted disclosures in writing;
- excluding liability for disclosures requested by law or a court;
- keeping detailed records;
- maintaining required practical, commercial, technological or organisational security measures;
- insisting on an indemnity against third party (data subject or regulatory authorities) claims;
- reserving any specific rights in relation to its processing tools.

Law/Compliance Requirement

The data processor agreement is a product of the Data Protection Act 1998. The data controller is obliged to comply with the obligations under that Act including the principles set out in the Act.

The seventh data protection principle requires a contact in writing between a data controller and data processor in connection with any processing. Such contract is to contain terms specified under the Act including guarantees in respect of applicable technical and organisational measures for security of personal data.

The data processor is required to only use the personal data in accordance with the express instructions of the data controller.

The seventh principle contains specific requirements for data controllers who use data processors. A breach of any of the principles of the Data Protection act could lead to enforcement action by the Information Commissioner.

Some Key Definitions

'Data Subject' means an individual who is the subject of Personal Data.

'Personal Data' has the meaning set out in the Data Protection Act 1998 and relates only to personal data of the Data Controller's customer, and prospective customers, together with all other personal data from time to time for which the Data Controller is the data controller (as such term is defined in the Data Protection Act 1998) and in relation to which the Data Processor is providing Services.

'Processing' and 'process' have the meanings set out in the Data Protection Act 1998.

'Confidential Information' means any information relating to the Data Controller's customers and prospective customers, current or projected financial or trading situations, business plans, business strategies, developments and all other information relating to the Data Controller's business affairs including any trade secrets, know-how and any information of a confidential nature imparted by the Data Controller to the Data Processor during the term of this Agreement or coming into existence as a result of the Data Processor's obligations, whether existing in hard copy form, in electronic form or otherwise, and whether disclosed orally or in writing. This definition shall include all Personal Data.

Specific Provisions

Data
All processing of Personal Data pursuant to this Agreement shall be strictly according to its terms and the written instructions of the Data Controller from time to time.

Laws
The Data Processor shall comply with applicable laws and ensure that the Personal Data is processed in accordance with the data protection legislation applicable in the United Kingdom. The data processing facilities and procedures of the Data Processor shall be subject to inspection and audit on notice by the Data Controller (or its agents) during the Term of this Agreement.

Sub-Processor
The grant of any approval by the Data Controller under this clause in respect of the appointment of any sub-processor shall not relieve the Data Processor from any liability under this Agreement and the Data Processor shall remain responsible for obligations, services and functions performed by any of its sub-processors to the same extent as if those obligations, services and functions were performed by the Data Processor.

IPR
If the Data Processor creates any intellectual property rights, including copyright and database rights, in the Personal Data in the course of providing the Services, the Data Processor hereby assigns such intellectual property rights to the Data Controller with full title guarantee, free from third party rights and for the full term during which those rights and any renewals or extensions subsist.

Service Levels
The service levels specified in the Schedule shall apply to the Services and the Data Processor shall during the Term comply with the service levels and provide the services in accordance with any timetable specified in the Schedule. Where a timetable is not specified, the Data Processor shall provide the Services within a reasonable time.

Checklist 5.3 Data Processor Agreement Checklist

In preparing a data processor agreement or letter, individuals or businesses should consider the following non-exhaustive matters.

Actions/Issues: **Comments:**

1 Review nature of data controller's business and use of data. ☐

2 Consider the data processor's details and set out the parties' registration numbers, registered office address and place of incorporation. ☐

3 Ascertain background and recite position in introductory paragraphs. Consider reciting: ☐

    3.1   data processor's experience; ☐

    3.2   data controller's wishes and requirement; ☐

    3.3   proposed appointment of data processor; ☐

    3.4   requirement for disclosure of personal data to data processor; ☐

    3.5   intent to process data in accordance with instructions and requirements; ☐

    3.6   entry into agreement to regulate the disclosure, use and processing of the personal data. ☐

4 Consider required definitions in relation to specific terms. What terms need to be defined? Consider: ☐

    4.1   personal data; ☐

    4.2   data subject; ☐

    4.3   processing; ☐

    4.4   fees, charges; ☐

    4.5   requirements; ☐

    4.6   services. ☐

5 Are there any specific standards of performance? Consider provision ☐

of service in accordance with instructions or requirements. Will the services be provided with reasonable still and care?

6 When will the agreement begin? Review and consider: ☐

6.1 specific date; ☐

6.2 earlier of two dates of occurrence of event; ☐

6.3 deemed commencement date; ☐

6.4 upon satisfaction of conditions; ☐

6.5 following delivery of personal data. ☐

7 For how long will the services be provided? In relation to the term, consider: ☐

7.1 fixed period; ☐

7.2 roll over period; ☐

7.3 open term subject to termination; ☐

7.4 continuous until completion of services; ☐

7.5 term linked to other related agreement (database building, database management). ☐

8 Specify required standards of performance including provision of services: ☐

8.1 in accordance with agreed service levels; ☐

8.2 to specified standards; ☐

8.3 according to industry best practice standards; ☐

8.4 with reasonable skill and care; ☐

8.5 according to timetable as set out within reasonable time; ☐

8.6 with or through specific personnel; ☐

8.7 in accordance with standard operating procedure; ☐

Commercial Contracts Checklists

    8.8   in accordance with written instructions. ☐

9   Consider and specify obligations of the data processor: ☐

    9.1   to provide service in accordance with required or specified standards; ☐

    9.2   not to transfer the personal data outside the European Economic Area; ☐

    9.3   to process relevant data only as authorised in writing; ☐

    9.4   to maintain back-up and disaster recovery procedures at its own cost; ☐

    9.5   to restore any lost, unusable or corrupt data promptly; ☐

    9.6   to provide copy of personal data (in required media or format) to the data controller upon request; ☐

    9.7   to process personal data in accordance with consent provided by data subject; ☐

    9.8   to comply with the data controller's data protection notice and procedure; ☐

    9.9   not to disclose the personal data to unauthorised or unapproved third parties; ☐

    9.10   to permit audit of its processing procedures, documents and facilities; ☐

    9.11   to promptly amend database or personal data following data controller's request; ☐

    9.12   not in any way to modify the data controller's data protection notice; ☐

    9.13   to only collect data in accordance with the specified data protection notice; ☐

    9.14   to immediately notify the data controller of any notice or correspondence from any relevant authority with regard to processing of personal data; ☐

    9.15   to process the personal data in accordance with the terms of agreement and laws of the United Kingdom; ☐

    9.16   to only use properly trained, skilled and data protection experienced personnel for all processing under agreement; ☐

    9.17   provide such assistance as required by data controller including: ☐

        9.17.1   generally; ☐

9.17.2 in respect of provision of information; ☐

9.17.3 for subject access requests from data subjects; ☐

9.17.4 reimbursement of costs incurred on its behalf. ☐

10 Specify the data controller's obligations including: ☐

    10.1 to provide instructions; ☐

    10.2 to provide requested information; ☐

    10.3 to promptly provide assistance; ☐

    10.4 to provide personal data to be processed; ☐

    10.5 to comply with English law in relation to any instructions given ☐

    10.6 to provide copy of the data controller's data protection notice; ☐

    10.7 to inform the data processor of applicable procedures; ☐

    10.8 to undertake to pay fees, charges and agreed or approved expenses. ☐

11 Ascertain legal capacity of data processor and confirm authority to enter into agreement. Will the data processor undertake and warrant its full legal authority to enter into agreement? ☐

12 In relation to fees and charges, consider and specify:

    12.1 obligation to pay; ☐

    12.2 applicable fee or charge; ☐

    12.3 whether charges are exclusive of VAT; ☐

    12.4 date or times of payment; ☐

    12.5 any cap on charges; ☐

    12.6 responsibility in connection with expenses; ☐

Commercial Contracts Checklists

    12.7   applicable invoicing or payment arrangements. ☐

13   Indicate or consider confidentiality obligations and undertakings including: ☐

    13.1   non-disclosure to third parties; ☐

    13.2   definition of confidential information; ☐

    13.3   disclosure for permitted purposes only; ☐

    13.4   notification requirements; ☐

    13.5   liability for third parties; ☐

    13.6   exclusions for matters in the public domain, independently developed information, legally required disclosure etc. ☐

14   What warranties will be given by the data processor? Consider or include warranty: ☐

    14.1   that service will be provided as required and with reasonable skill or care; ☐

    14.2   to carry out service in accordance with relevant laws and regulations; ☐

    14.3   that data processor has required security (appropriate technical and organisational measures) against: ☐

        14.3.1   unauthorised processing; ☐

        14.3.2   unlawful processing; ☐

        14.3.3   accidental loss of personal data, destruction or damage to data; ☐

    14.4   that it has sufficient disaster recovery procedures and back-up mechanisms in place; ☐

    14.5   that it has not relied on any statement. ☐

15   Will each party indemnify the other in respect of costs and expenses, liabilities, actions or losses incurred as a result of breach by the other party? Consider: ☐

    15.1   one way indemnity; ☐

    15.2   limitation of liability; ☐

15.3 exclusion of certain liabilities; ☐

15.4 liability for third party claims; ☐

15.5 liability for Information Commissioner claims; ☐

15.6 what the indemnity should cover; ☐

15.7 liability for loss of business or profits. ☐

16 Ascertain, review and include required acknowledgements in relation to: ☐

    16.1 ownership of any intellectual property rights; ☐

    16.2 any copyright or database right in the personal data created in the course of providing services; ☐

    16.3 requirement for data processor to assign all rights to the data controller; ☐

    16.4 retention of all right, title and interest in the personal data by the data controller; ☐

    16.5 right and ownership of confidential information; ☐

    16.6 specified purpose; ☐

    16.7 the grant of a licence to the data processor to use relevant intellectual property rights; ☐

    16.8 data controller's right to require immediate suspension or resumption of any processing; ☐

    16.9 appointment of sub-contractors or sub-processors; ☐

    16.10 delay not amounting to waiver of rights; ☐

    16.11 no partnership or agency between the parties; ☐

    16.12 restriction on assignment; ☐

    16.13 exclusion of third party right to enforce agreement other than as specified; ☐

    16.14 agreement setting out entire agreement between parties; ☐

Commercial Contracts Checklists

    16.15 non-exclusion of liability for fraud or fraudulent misrepresentations; ☐

    16.16 service of notices and procedures; ☐

    16.17 signature of agreement in two or more counterparts and use of fax copies; ☐

    16.18 governing law and jurisdiction; ☐

    16.19 severance of illegal or unenforceable provisions; ☐

    16.20 irrevocable and unconditional waiver of right to rescind agreement for misrepresentation or claim damages; ☐

    16.21 right of data subject to enforce the agreement directly against the data processor; ☐

    16.22 non-solicitation of employees for specified period without consent; ☐

    16.23 if applicable, force majeure provisions; ☐

    16.24 liability for costs of preparation and negotiation of agreement. ☐

17   In relation to termination of the agreement, consider termination:

    17.1 with or without cause; ☐

    17.2 upon service of written notice upon occurrence of certain events including insolvency or related events; ☐

    17.3 for non-performance; ☐

    17.4 for material breach (not remedied); ☐

    17.5 for material breach not capable of remedy; ☐

    17.6 upon cessation of business by a party; ☐

    17.7 following repeated breaches of duties or obligations by either or one party; ☐

    17.8 upon expiry of period. ☐

18   Specify the consequences of termination together with applicable post-termination obligations. Consider: ☐

Intellectual Property and Media-Related Agreements

18.1 return or destruction of personal data; ☐

18.2 return or destruction of confidential information; ☐

18.3 destruction or deletion of material or information as requested; ☐

18.4 certification of compliance; ☐

18.5 cessation of processing of personal data.. ☐

19 Consider and specify as appropriate in the schedule details of: ☐

19.1 personal data to be processed; ☐

19.2 applicable service levels; ☐

19.3 other services to be provided; ☐

19.4 personnel to be used; ☐

19.5 timetable for service provision; ☐

19.6 any language requirements; ☐

19.7 organisational and technical measures of, or to be adopted by, the data processor; ☐

19.8 information or documents to be provided by the data controller; ☐

19.9 periodic reporting obligations; ☐

19.10 audit procedures; ☐

19.11 required format or media for provision of data after processing; ☐

19.12 data protection notice; ☐

19.13 applicable procedures; ☐

19.14 charges, fees, payment arrangements; ☐

Commercial Contracts Checklists

    19.15 approved expenses, dates and other relevant terms. ☐

20 Ascertain and specify dispute resolution mechanism or procedures if appropriate: ☐

    20.1 initial discussions and attempted resolution; ☐

    20.2 dispute resolution body referral; ☐

    20.3 appointment of independent expert; ☐

    20.4 costs of expert and liability for payment; ☐

    20.5 final and binding notice; ☐

    20.6 right of appeal. ☐

See Precedent 5.3 on accompanying CD.

5.4 Presenter's Agreement

Overview

Description of Agreement/Document

A presenter's agreement is a form of engagement and services contract. Under the contract, the production, radio or television company engages an individual to present a programme, for a specific purpose or series of projects. The agreement sets out the presenter's engagement and services to be provided, presenter's status, parties' obligations, ownership of rights and required warranties.

Practical Guidance/Issues List

The parties will have their respective practical and legal concerns in respect of the arrangement. In essence, the presenter would not wish to be restricted in relation to all his activities, whilst the broadcasting company will seek to ensure that they are getting what they pay for and have relevant rights transferred.

The broadcasting company:
- will need to provide in the contract that the presenter is not employed notwithstanding the form of agreement may indicate an employment relationship;
- can provide for an option to renew the agreement or extend the provision of the services;
- may wish to restrict the presenter's participation in any endorsement or promotional activities without approval;
- should provide for and obtain relevant assignment of all rights to all the presenter's written, spoken or unscripted contributions in connection with the project or programme;
- should ensure the right to use the services of the presenter in future programmes or projects, if continuity is an issue;
- may wish to ensure exclusivity of the presenter's service for a certain period;
- should consider including relevant restrictions in the contract for the company's protection having regard to the nature of the services or medium.

The presenter should consider:
- resisting any blanket indemnities or exclusion of liability;
- whether the services will be exclusive or if the presenter wishes the freedom to participate in other activities;
- ensuring that there is agreement on payment for the presenter's accommodation, living and travel costs or expenses at any required location;
- seek to agree provisions for net profit share in relation to the rights of exploitation of the project or programme;
- requesting additional payments as repeat fees;
- resist any restrictions to present rival programmes or to be involved in similar projects or competing entities unless absolutely necessary and compensated for the loss of opportunity;
- review carefully any restrictions on endorsement or promotional arrangements undertaken by the presenter.

Specific Provisions

Full Fees
The payment specified in the Schedule is in full consideration for the Services and, without limitation, the [Presenter/Commentator] shall not (except as expressly provided in this Agreement) be entitled to receive any overtime, repeat fees, use fees, residuals, royalties or other payments whatsoever and such payment shall constitute full, equitable and adequate remuneration in relation to any rental or other performer's property rights under Part II of the Copyright, Designs and Patents Act 1988.

Copyright
The Commentator with full title guarantee by way of assignment of present and future copyright hereby assigns to the Company the entire worldwide copyright and all other right, title and interest of whatsoever nature whether vested or contingent including but not limited to the right to exploit the project and programme together with the

products of the Services by any and all means and in all media throughout the world to hold the same unto the Company absolutely throughout the universe for the full period of copyright and all renewals and extensions and in perpetuity

CDPA
The Commentator by this Agreement grants to the Company all consents required under the Copyright, Designs and Patents Act 1988 or any statutory re-enactment thereof for the time being in force to enable the Company to make the fullest use of the Commentator's services hereunder.

Use of Image
The Commentator grants to the Company the right at all times to use (and authorise others to use) the Commentator's name, photographs and other reproductions of his or her physical likeness and recordings of his or her voice taken or made in whole or in part in connection with the advertisement, publicity, exhibition and commercial exploitation of the programme or subsequent series and any music, records or books derived from and in association with the advertisement, publicity, commercial exploitation of any merchandising and other commodities.

Moral Rights
The Commentator irrevocably waives his or her moral rights insofar as is permissible by law and, without limitation, the Commentator agrees that the Company has the unlimited right to edit, copy, alter, add or take from, adapt or translate the products of the Services.

Indemnity
The Commentator indemnifies and shall at all times keep the Company fully and effectively indemnified from and against all actions, proceedings, costs (including reasonable legal costs), claims, damages and losses whatsoever suffered or incurred by the Company as a result of any breach or non-performance of any of the agreements or warranties or undertakings of the Commentator under this Agreement.

Further Assurance
The Commentator shall do all such acts and execute all such documents as the Company may require to vest in or further assure to the Company the said copyright and all other rights herein expressed to be granted.

Checklist 5.4 Presenter's Agreement Checklist

In preparing a presenter's agreement or letter, individuals or businesses should consider the following non-exhaustive matters.

Actions/Issues:	Comments:	✎
1 Ascertain and review the terms of the appointment and details of the parties.		☐
2 Is it worth reciting the background and proposal in the introductory paragraphs?		☐
3 What is the proposed form of contract:		☐
3.1 letter of engagement or appointment;		☐
3.2 formal agreement;		☐
3.3 employment agreement.		☐
4 Review basis of engagement and the proposed services or duties of the presenter.		☐
5 Is there a specific programme, event or project to be presented or performed?		☐
6 What is the period of the agreement? Is it for:		☐
6.1 a fixed period;		☐
6.2 a rolling period, extendable or renewable term;		☐
6.3 indefinite period subject to termination by notice.		☐
7 Consider and specify the engagement of the presenter by the producer, broadcaster or company.		☐
8 Specify where the services will be provided. Is the presenter engaged to present the programme, event or project on:		☐
8.1 radio broadcast?		☐
8.2 television broadcast?		☐
8.3 broadcast over the internet?		☐

Commercial Contracts Checklists

      8.4   broadcast in any media? ☐

9   Consider when the services will be provided or the programme presented: ☐

    9.1   specific presentation days; ☐

    9.2   specific periods; ☐

    9.3   during hourly slots or specified terms; ☐

    9.4   on an ad hoc basis. ☐

10   In relation to the presenter and provision of the services, consider and indicate: ☐

    10.1   engagement as a presenter; ☐

    10.2   periods for provision of the services; ☐

    10.3   whether the services are to be exclusive generally or on the specified days/periods; ☐

    10.4   any restrictions on the presenter presenting a similar programme or project with similar content and/or format; ☐

    10.5   obligations of the presenter; ☐

    10.6   presenter's undertaking not to engage in conflicting activities or duties as a presenter of the programme or project; ☐

    10.7   any exclusivity or freedom to perform for third parties; ☐

    10.8   obligation to co-operate with company or broadcaster in relation to specified matters or generally; ☐

    10.9   undertaking of presenter to be available as cover for other unavailable presenters at specified times; ☐

    10.10 any entitlement to holidays or rest periods (and any attendant obligations); ☐

    10.11 any option to use the presenter or their services in future events, programmes or projects; ☐

    10.12 required preparation obligations; ☐

    10.13 undertaking by presenter to promptly and faithfully comply with directors of company, broadcaster or engager; ☐

10.14 compliance with applicable rules and regulations; ☐

10.15 obligation to perform services as a 'first professional class' presenter, diligently and skilfully; ☐

10.16 the place at which the services or presenting will be carried out; ☐

10.17 obligation to participate in publicity events (with or without additional remuneration). ☐

11 What are the payment provisions? Consider and specify:

11.1 consideration for services; ☐

11.2 amount of fee or agreed basis; ☐

11.3 rate of fee; ☐

11.4 whether inclusive or exclusive of VAT; ☐

11.5 authority to deduct sums required by law from fees; ☐

11.6 applicable expenses and responsibility for payment or reimbursement; ☐

11.7 whether payment is in advance or arrears or instrumental; ☐

11.8 fee as full consideration and exclude royalties, overtime, repeat fees, residuals or other payments; ☐

11.9 any procedure for rendering invoices or payment; ☐

11.10 payment date; ☐

11.11 applicable conditions prior to payment; ☐

11.12 requirement to support expenses with appropriate or requested documentation. ☐

12 Will the presenter warrant:

12.1 nationality? ☐

12.2 the he or she is and will remain a 'qualifying person' under the Copyright, Designs and Patents Act 1988? ☐

13 Consider (worldwide) assignment (with full title guarantee) by presenter of: ☐

    13.1   present and future copyright; ☐

    13.2   other right, title or interest in the programme, event or project; ☐

    13.3   the right, title and interest in all the products of the presenter's services under the agreement. ☐

14   In relation to the assignment, specify that the assignment: ☐

    14.1   is to be effective immediately; ☐

    14.2   for the full period of copyright including extensions or renewal; ☐

    14.3   in perpetuity; ☐

    14.4   of future copyright (if not all in existence); ☐

    14.5   is subject to further assurance covenant to execute documents and do things to perfect assignment; ☐

    14.6   is in addition to the grant of the right to use (and allow use) of: ☐

        14.6.1   photographs; ☐

        14.6.2   sound effects of presenter's voice; ☐

        14.6.3   images; ☐

        14.6.4   computer generated likeness; ☐

        14.6.5   reproductions of presenter's image or likeness; ☐

        14.6.6   voice recordings; ☐

        14.6.7   presenter's name; ☐

        14.6.8   presenter's biography. ☐

15   Can all presenter's rights or rights granted be used for: ☐

15.1 advertising, merchandising, commercial exploitation? ☐

15.2 such other matters as required in all forms of media? ☐

16 Specify the required warranties, undertakings and indemnities. ☐
Consider undertakings and warranties:

16.1 as to authority to enter agreement; ☐

16.2 excluding that no employment intended; ☐

16.3 as to good health to enable obtaining of insurance; ☐

16.4 that presenter unauthorised to act as agent; ☐

16.5 not to make press or publicity statements without prior approval or consent; ☐

16.6 to observe rules applicable at location or other premises; ☐

16.7 not to disclose information other than as permitted; ☐

16.8 not to use or permit others to use the name, logo or endorse any product; ☐

16.9 to remain a qualifying person (EC and UK resident); ☐

16.10 dress in accordance with specific requirements of programmes; ☐

16.11 to carry out obligations to presenter's best ability and skill; ☐

16.12 to comply with requirements of production insurance; ☐

16.13 take steps, as required to apply for visas required to tender services; ☐

16.14 to be available for promotional trailers; ☐

16.15 ownership of copyright in relevant work; ☐

16.16 presenter's work not to infringe third party rights; ☐

16.17 presenter's work not to be offensive, illegal or defamatory; ☐

16.18 agreement to comply with specified guidelines, rules and regulations; ☐

16.19 to render the services at specified location; ☐

16.20 to return all documents including scripts at the end of assignment or projects. ☐

17 If applicable, set out indemnity against all action or loss resulting from presenter's breach or non-performance. ☐

18 Consider and indicate (as appropriate): ☐

18.1 exclusion of relationship of employee and employer; ☐

18.2 confirmation that fee amounts to self-employed income with presenter liable for tax or national insurance; ☐

18.3 grant of all consents or licences required under the Copyright, Designs and Patents Act 1988 to enable full use of services; ☐

18.4 waiver of moral rights to the extent permitted by law; ☐

18.5 right to dub into different languages; ☐

18.6 exclusion of liability by engager for: ☐

18.6.1 loss or damage to property; ☐

18.6.2 personal injury or death not caused by negligence of engager; ☐

18.6.3 claim for loss of publicity; ☐

18.6.4 loss of opportunity. ☐

18.7 credits and entitlement; ☐

18.8 right to assign agreement by engager and restriction for presenter to assign; ☐

18.9 delay not to amount to waiver; ☐

18.10 notice provisions; ☐

18.11 entire agreement contained in contract; ☐

Intellectual Property and Media-Related Agreements

18.12 inclusion of liability for fraudulent misrepresentation; ☐

18.13 exclusion of third party rights. ☐

19 What are the termination arrangements? Consider: ☐

19.1 termination by notice (with or without cause); ☐

19.2 breach or material breach; ☐

19.3 failure to perform; ☐

19.4 ill health injury or other reason; ☐

19.5 if programme, event or project in interrupted or delayed for specified period; ☐

19.6 termination for misconduct or prejudicial conduct; ☐

19.7 termination for action which has material adverse effect on programme, event or project; ☐

19.8 payment for termination in certain circumstances; ☐

19.9 effect of termination and consequences of termination; ☐

19.10 Post-termination obligations. ☐

See Precedent 5.4 on accompanying CD.

Commercial Contracts Checklists

5.5 Contributor's Agreement

Overview

Description of Agreement/Document

A contributor's agreement is entered into between a contributor and publisher. A party contributes textual material to a publisher and the publisher agrees to publish such materials on the terms of the agreement. The contract between the parties normally sets out the exact nature, content and extent of the required contribution. In addition the agreement sets out the parties' respective obligations in respect of the work, reservation or assignment of intellectual property rights, together with relevant warranties and indemnities.

Practical Guidance/Issues List

Such arrangements between a publisher and contributor will normally be on the publisher's standard form contract. The contributor should review his requirements and be careful about signing away all his intellectual property rights. It may be useful:
- to reserve any rights not expressly granted to the publisher;
- to limit liability to a specified amount and exclude certain liability;
- to seek to reduce the scope of any proposed indemnity or effective capability;
- to obtain an advance payment or structure the fees in a manner that is advantageous for the contributor;
- to ensure that all further assurance or assistance is at the publisher's sole cost and expense;
- to resist exclusion or waiver of moral rights, if possible;
- to ensure that credit for the contribution is always given to the contributor even after replacement of contributor;
- to include an alternative dispute resolution mechanism under relevant body's procedures;
- to set out the required style and format in relation to the required contribution;

The contributor should be as clear as possible about the exact nature, content or length of the required contribution. Careful consideration should be given to any proposed or required warranties and indemnities.

It is important that the publisher secures warranties that the work is original and obtains an assignment of the relevant copyright. An indemnity may be useful but only effective to the extent that the contributor is able to stand behind it. In effect, practical efforts should be made to ascertain the originality of the work and to avoid infringement of third party rights.

The assignment of copyright should extend to future copyright. Practical measures should be taken to monitor progress of the contributor's work to avoid delays. If possible, the contributor should be offered a bonus as an incentive for delivery of contribution material on time.

Law/Compliance Requirement

The contributor's agreement is a matter of contract law but subject to intellectual property legislation. Copyright law is governed by the Copyright, Designs and Patents Act 1988.

Stamp duty is no longer due on licences and assignments of intellectual property rights following the Finance Act 2000. Stamp duty may be payable on exclusive irrevocable licences for the life of intellectual property.

Some Key Definitions

'Contribution' means the written material to be produced by the Contributor in accordance with the specification set out in the Schedule and delivered in the required format to the Publisher on or before the date specified in the Schedule.

'Rights' means all the Contributor's existing and future rights of copyright together with the Contributor's accrued rights of action in any part of the Territory.

'Charges' means the fees and charges payable by the Publisher to the Contributor in accordance with the terms of this Agreement.

'Work' means the work titled [specify title] and proposed to be published by the Publisher including the contributor's material on or prior to the Publication Date.

'Agent' means the agent appointed by the Contributor for the purpose of [specify purpose] under or in connection with this Agreement whose full details are set out in the Schedule.

Specific Provisions

Contribution
The Contributor has agreed pursuant to the provisions of this Agreement to write, prepare, edit and deliver to the Publisher the Contribution for inclusion in the Work.

Assignment of Rights
To facilitate publication of the Work and protect the Publisher, the Contributor by this Agreement assigns from the date of this Agreement all the Rights to the Publisher throughout the Territory for the full period of copyright in the Contribution (including all renewals and revivals of such period) permissible or arising under applicable laws. Such assignment under this Agreement shall by way of full title guarantee and include present assignment of future copyright.

Ownership
The Contributor warrants that it is the sole owner of the Rights and the sole author of the Contribution having full rights to enter into this Agreement.

Content Delivery
The Contributor shall use his or her *[best/reasonable]* endeavours to deliver the Contribution in the form, content and media required by the Publisher as specified in the Schedule not later than [insert date or period] or the long stop date provided in the Schedule.

Delivery Failure
The Publisher reserves the right to request refund of any advance payment or terminate this Agreement upon service of notice in writing to the Contributor in any event that the Contributor fails to deliver the Contribution on the specified date or otherwise in accordance with the provisions of this Agreement.

Checklist 5.5 Contributor's Agreement Checklist

In preparing a Contributor's Agreement or letter, individuals or businesses should consider the following non-exhaustive matters.

Actions/Issues: **Comments:**

1 Review proposed arrangements for contribution and specify nature or extent of contribution or work.

2 Recite if necessary, relevant publication, extent of contribution or contributor's involvement, involvement of other third party contributors and assignment of rights for fee.

3 Ascertain and indicate parties to the contract. Set out addresses and identification details including registration number and registered address. Will any agent be a party to the contract?

4 Consider contributor's legal status and capacity to contract.

5 Consider relevant terms for definition including (as applicable):

   5.1 intellectual property rights, intellectual property;

   5.2 rights;

   5.3 contribution, work;

   5.4 fee, price, charge;

   5.5 term, territory;

   5.6 agent, contributor, publisher, recipient.

6 Ascertain, consider and set out provisions in relation to:

   6.1 assignment of rights in territory;

   6.2 relevant consideration (fee);

   6.3 further assurance provision to give full effect of benefit;

   6.4 publisher's right to deduct tax liability payments from fee;

Intellectual Property and Media-Related Agreements

    6.5   liability for costs and expenses incurred by publishers in ensuring performance of obligations; ☐

    6.6   payments to be exclusive of VAT; ☐

    6.7   publisher's sole right and discretion to decide details of production and publication of the work; ☐

    6.8   obligations to advertise and liability for costs; ☐

    6.9   waiver by contributor of right to object to derogatory treatment of material or contribution; ☐

    6.10   publisher's discretion to pass on to another contributor incomplete work. ☐

7   What are the obligations in respect of delivery and acceptance of contribution. Consider obligations or undertakings to:

    7.1   complete and deliver material by specified date; ☐

    7.2   consider time of the essence; ☐

    7.3   produce clean, legible copies of work in required or specified format; ☐

    7.4   comply with style and format requested by publishers; ☐

    7.5   keep the publishers informed of progress of preparation of material; ☐

    7.6   deliver material in accordance with specification in complete and final form; ☐

    7.7   retain a copy of the submitted contribution material; ☐

    7.8   amend the material to the form and level requested by the publishers following initial review; ☐

    7.9   procure third party editor to review and amend material in the absence of contributor. ☐

8   Consider and include:

    8.1   obligation on contributor to obtain all required copyright permissions in writing; ☐

    8.2   consequences of failure to deliver the contribution material. Consider:

        8.2.1   right of publisher to terminate; ☐

Commercial Contracts Checklists

  8.2.2 right of publisher to extend time; ☐

  8.2.3 requirement of advance payment to be refunded; ☐

  8.2.4 publisher's right to complete the work without further reference to contributor; ☐

8.3 provisions or conditions for acceptance of the contribution material; ☐

8.4 waiver of moral rights by the contributor under any applicable law or regulation; ☐

8.5 payment dates and related arrangements or structure:

  8.5.1 advance fee; ☐

  8.5.2 payment of part on execution of agreement; ☐

  8.5.3 payment on part or balance of contribution material; ☐

  8.5.4 final payment on approval of contribution material; ☐

8.6 provision for the supply of agreed numbers of free copies of finished work or relevant work incorporating the contribution material; ☐

8.7 details of proposed production and publication; ☐

8.8 proof corrections obligations, undertakings and procedures; ☐

8.9 inclusion of textual or illustrative materials obligations and liability; ☐

8.10 restriction on preparation of other work competitive to the proposed publication or which would prejudice sales; ☐

8.11 obligation to credit/include contributor's name prominently in every copy of work; ☐

8.12 contributor's ability to use the contribution for professional and personal use notwithstanding publication; ☐

8.13 requirement for acknowledgement of the work where used by contributor in personal or professional capacity; ☐

8.14 undertaking not to carry on any activity which may damage sales of the work or prejudice the publication of the work; ☐

8.15 provisions and arrangements for new editions or subsequent updates and issues. ☐

Intellectual Property and Media-Related Agreements

9 Will the Contributor be required to give any warranties? Consider warranties (as appropriate) that: ☐

    9.1 material does not infringe third party rights, copyright or licence; ☐

    9.2 the material is original and not previously published; ☐

    9.3 the contribution does not contain obscene, defamatory or unlawful content; ☐

    9.4 the contributor has full power and authority to contract, due care has been taken and regard had to nature of potential readership in preparation of work; ☐

    9.5 the contributor is the sole owner of the rights and sole author of the contribution; ☐

    9.6 the contributor is and will remain a 'qualifying person' within the meaning of Copyright, Designs and Patents Act 1988. ☐

10 Consider inclusion of an indemnity from the contributor to the publisher in respect of: ☐

    10.1 all losses, claims and costs resulting from breach; ☐

    10.2 legal fees; ☐

    10.3 third party claims; ☐

    10.4 amount paid to compromise or settle claim following legal advice; ☐

    10.5 breach or infringement of third party intellectual property rights. ☐

11 Consider and insert provisions relating to: ☐

    11.1 joint and several liability (where a party comprises more than one person or entity); ☐

    11.2 assignment of agreement with or without consent; ☐

    11.3 agreement containing the entire understanding of the parties; ☐

    11.4 termination of the agreement; ☐

    11.5 consequences of termination, post-termination rights of the publisher in respect of third party agreement, warranties and indemnities together with right to sell works; ☐

    11.6 arbitration or alternative dispute resolution procedure; ☐

11.7 service of notices; ☐

11.8 force majeure (events beyond the control of the parties) occurrence and effect; ☐

11.9 exclusion of third party rights of enforcement; ☐

11.10 reservation by contributor of all rights not specifically or expressly granted to publisher; ☐

11.11 alteration, modification or amendment of the agreement; ☐

11.12 waiver not effect of any delay by either party; ☐

11.13 terms which will survive termination of the agreement; ☐

11.14 partnership and agency exclusion except in relation to the appointed agent for collection and/or receipt of payment; ☐

11.15 rights and remedies available to the parties being cumulative; ☐

11.16 binding effect of agreement on successors, personal representatives and permitted assigns. ☐

12 What confidentiality obligations or undertakings are applicable to the parties? Consider: ☐

12.1 undertaking to keep secret all confidential information; ☐

12.2 what amounts to confidential information; ☐

12.3 mutual undertakings; ☐

12.4 permitted disclosures; ☐

12.5 non-application of undertakings to certain information (including available in public domain). ☐

See Precedent 5.5 on accompanying CD.

5.6 Research and Development Agreement

Overview

Description of Agreement/Document

A research and development agreement normally relates to particular sectors or organisations. These organisations include manufacturing, technology and intellectual property companies, educational, academic and other non-governmental research or charitable entities.

The agreements vary from an engagement to carry out research to joint co-operation or collaboration arrangements between parties. The agreement may also extend to a commission to research and develop a particular product. The relevant agreement contains the usual commercial and legal provisions. Importantly, it details the parties' participation or engagement in relation to the research, funding and publication arrangements, ownership, protection and commercial exploitation of rights or products of the research.

Practical Guidance/Issues List

The party funding the research and development may:
- require ownership or control of all results and rights of the research and/or development;
- require specific warranties from the researcher to protect its position and ensure it gets what it pays for;
- insist on limiting the use of the research by the researcher or developer during and after the agreement;
- impose restrictions on the researcher or developer's other activities in the same field;
- obtain an indemnity for specific breaches;
- require ownership or licence in relation to background and foreground intellectual property.

Where the agreement is mainly an agreement for the provision of services, the service provider (or in certain cases the inventor or researcher) should:
- indicate and have parties acknowledge the experimental nature of the research, if such is the case, and disclaim safety or warranties in relation to accuracy, viability, registrability, infringement or performance;
- expressly agree rights in relation to the publication or intellectual property rights;
- ensure that the proper party enters into the agreement, where the party is a large commercial entity,
- group company or institution;
- provide for force majeure events and consequent exclusion of liability for delays;
- seek to obtain a licence for use for certain specified purposes;
- retain its original intellectual property or rights contributed to the research, development or project;
- seek such protection as may be necessary;
- consider issues in relation to warranties and ensure they are reviewed carefully;
- ensure that time is not of the essence of the contract;
- resist blanket indemnities in favour of the other party;
- expressly agree and insert any relevant funding or fund injection arrangements;
- insert relevant exclusions and limitations of liability as appropriate.

The parties should ensure that the agreement sets out clearly the arrangements in respect of:
- entry into a suitable non-disclosure and non-circumvention agreement;
- restrictions as to permitted use;
- joint ownership of results and rights, if appropriate or where research and development is jointly carried out;
- payment and funding arrangements in relation to type, rates, royalties, options, fixed price and adjustments;
- publication restrictions;
- where relevant, ensure data protection and other legal compliance and reduce potential liability exposure;
- revenue sharing, where appropriate;
- confidentiality arrangements and undertakings where sensitive material;
- who decides the nature and extent of the research project together with any changes or developments;
- protecting the rights arising out of the research and development;
- progress, information, review, updating and reporting obligations;
- how the product is developed and how results or rights arising will be commercially exploited.

Law/Compliance Requirement

Enforceability of restrictions in a research and development agreement will be subject to contract law and the concept of reasonableness in certain circumstances.

In addition, there are certain regulations that apply to agreements of this nature depending on the exact nature of the contract or contractual obligations.

The Competition Act 1998 contains relevant provisions which may need to be complied with.

The Finance Act 2000 and stamp duty compliance issues or concerns may be irrelevant or reduced following its abolition for transfers of intellectual property.

The block exemptions for research and development agreements (Regulation 2659/2000) may apply, where relevant. The other EC block exemptions for vertical agreements (Regulation 2790/1999) and specialisation (Regulation 2658/2000) may also require careful review having regard to any relevant application.

On 1 May 2004, the new Technology Transfer Agreements Block Exemption Regulation (Regulation 772/2004) and its related guidelines came into effect. The block exemptions may be relevant to certain types of research and development obligations or agreements.

Some Key Definitions

'Control' (in the case of any corporation or limited liability company) means direct or indirect ownership of at least 50% of the voting shares or otherwise direct or indirect ownership of at least 50% of the equity power and interest with the power to direct the management of such entity.

'Research' means research and development carried out during the Term relating to [insert project details] as described in [specify document] and excluding [specify applicable exclusions].

'Term' means the period beginning on the Commencement Date and ending on the Expiry Date or on any other date on which this Agreement may be terminated in accordance with its provisions.

Specific Provisions

Research Project
The Researcher agrees to carry out the Research on the terms and subject to the conditions of this Agreement. In the event that the parties agree to any extension of the scope of the Research, they shall use their respective best endeavours to agree a mutually acceptable increase in the relevant fees and expenses to reflect any such expansion and work or costs necessary to achieve the required results.

Management
The parties will discuss the progress report and progress of the Research from time to time and will arrange for their respective representatives to meet regularly at least once every [month] on a mutually convenient time, date or location during the Term of this Agreement.

Representatives
Each party shall appoint a representative acceptable to the other in connection with the Research. The representatives shall consult from time to time on the progress of the Research and be entitled to attend meetings or participate in the management of the Research.

Funding
No payment shall be made by the Company (and the Company shall not be obliged to make any other payments under this Agreement) unless and until it is satisfied with the progress, update and work carried out to the date of the invoice in respect of the Research.
- The Researcher shall take all reasonably practicable measures to secure all Research information and materials. Except with the Company's prior written agreement, the Researcher shall not disclose to any third party any information obtained from any Research document or correspondence marked 'Confidential' or related to the Research.

- The obligation in this clause relating to non-disclosure shall remain in force and shall survive this Agreement for a period of *[five (5)]* years from the date of termination unless overridden by law or contract.

Research Publication Rights
The Company acknowledges and recognises the Researcher's rights (notwithstanding any provision to the contrary) to use and publish papers containing details of results of the Research in professional or academic publications provided that a copy of the proposed publication is first provided to the Company at least *[three (3)]* months prior to publication.

Intellectual Property
All right, title and interest to all patentable inventions (other than Research materials) made by the Researcher pertaining to [insert details of project or field], whether made before the Commencement Date or such as may be made during the Term in the course of performing the Research services (together with all application rights) shall be owned by [specify party].

Exploitation The parties acknowledge and agree that from the Expiry Date until [   ], the [specify party] shall have the right to manufacture, sell or otherwise commercialise any product described set out in [the Schedule or specify relevant document].

Commercial Contracts Checklists

Checklist 5.6 Research and Development Agreement Checklist

In preparing a research and development agreement or letter, individuals or businesses should consider the following non-exhaustive matters.

Actions/Issues:	Comments:	✎

1   What is the nature of the research and development agreement ('R&D')? Consider the relevant organisation involved: ☐

    1.1   educational establishment; ☐

    1.2   technology and intellectual property company; ☐

    1.3   manufacturing comparer; ☐

    1.4   research company and institution. ☐

2   Consider the relevant parties and specify applicable contact details including: ☐

    2.1   name and correct legal status or title; ☐

    2.2   registered address or business address; ☐

    2.3   registration number; ☐

    2.4   other contact details and information required for notices; ☐

    2.5   country or place of registration; ☐

    2.6   legal status; ☐

    2.7   guarantor's detail, if applicable; ☐

    2.8   third party contracting agent. ☐

3   Consider background, research and development project, the parties' roles or expectations and recite in the introductory paragraphs. Set out the subject matter and main obligation (e.g. funding R&D into a product). ☐

4   What is the term of the agreement? Is it a fixed or indefinite term terminable on notice? ☐

5   Consider and specify the R&D project. Ascertain and indicate the relevant research specification. In particular, review and consider: ☐

   5.1   whether the work is to be carried out jointly or by a specific party; ☐

   5.2   relevant services or facilities in connection with the project; ☐

   5.3   where the r&d work will be carried out; ☐

   5.4   period for carrying out the work including the commencement date for the project; ☐

   5.5   any obligation to provide staff, material, equipment or employees; ☐

   5.6   appointment of projects representative by each party; ☐

   5.7   provisions for varying the specification; ☐

   5.8   obligation to carry out the project in good faith using reasonable skill and care; ☐

   5.9   specific employees required; ☐

   5.10 project management arrangements. ☐

6   Consider restrictions in relation to: ☐

   6.1   entry into agreement with third party related to the scope of the project; ☐

   6.2   commercialisation without consent; ☐

   6.3   assignment of any rights; ☐

   6.4   use of a party's intellectual property; ☐

   6.5   carrying out work outside scope of contract including any evaluation; ☐

   6.6   access to intellectual property; ☐

   6.7   carrying out work outside the specification or for its own benefit. ☐

7   How will the project be managed? Consider:

Commercial Contracts Checklists

    7.1   requirement for review; ☐

    7.2   requirement for reports; ☐

    7.3   periodic liaison meetings in relation to project. ☐

8   How is the R&D project to be funded? Who will fund the project and are contributions required? Consider: ☐

    8.1   funding contribution; ☐

    8.2   dates of payment; ☐

    8.3   payment of balance; ☐

    8.4   method of calculation of the funding; ☐

    8.5   reward for funding. ☐

9   What are the payment terms? Consider: ☐

    9.1   how much is payable; ☐

    9.2   whether inclusive of VAT; ☐

    9.3   obligation to invoice and provide information; ☐

    9.4   undertaking to keep payment records; ☐

    9.5   how and where will the payment be made; ☐

    9.6   specify currency of payment; ☐

    9.7   any rights of set off or deduction; ☐

    9.8   whether there are additional costs and expenses (who is liable?); ☐

    9.9   repayment or refund obligations; ☐

    9.10   interest on late payment at the specified date; ☐

9.11 when payments should be made; ☐

9.12 rights of audit of relevant records or accounts. ☐

10 Are there any arrangements for the: ☐

    10.1 sharing of revenue? ☐

    10.2 commercial exploitation of the product? ☐

    10.3 payment of royalties? ☐

    10.4 registration of any intellectual property? ☐

    10.5 withholding of tax? ☐

    10.6 service of notices? ☐

    10.7 mutual indemnity? ☐

    10.8 assistance and/or further assurance? ☐

11 Ascertain importance of confidentiality obligations in relation to the project. Consider applicable provisions and specify: ☐

    11.1 what amounts to confidential information; ☐

    11.2 the extent of information covered; ☐

    11.3 the obligation not to disclose information. ☐

    11.4 whether it must be written information; ☐

    11.5 who is disclosing the information; ☐

    11.6 specific undertakings or obligations of the information or recipient; ☐

    11.7 the position of independently developed confidentiality information; ☐

    11.8 exceptions to non-disclosure obligations including: ☐

Commercial Contracts Checklists

        11.8.1   information disclosed following a court order; ☐

        11.8.2   information in the public domain; ☐

        11.8.3   information received from a third party; ☐

        11.8.4   disclosure to employees (on a need to know basis); ☐

    11.9   obligations and duties of the recipient of the confidential information; ☐

    11.10 information obligations and duties of the discloser information. ☐

12   Specify the terms of termination and consider: ☐

    12.1   material breach; ☐

    12.2   for insolvency event; ☐

    12.3   in the event of circumvention; ☐

    12.4   for conflict of interest; ☐

    12.5   upon occurrence of force majeure event; ☐

    12.6   any other reason. ☐

13   Ascertain and set out the consequences of termination. Consider any post-termination obligations or undertakings. ☐

14   In relation to the intellectual property, consider and indicate: ☐

    14.1   who owns what; ☐

    14.2   who will own improvements; ☐

    14.3   whether any rights will be assigned or licensed to either party; ☐

    14.4   responsibility for costs of maintenance of the intellectual property. ☐

15   Review and specify relevant boilerplate provisions including (as appropriate): ☐

15.1 force majeure occurrence; ☐

15.2 amendment of agreement; ☐

15.3 right to assign agreement with consent; ☐

15.4 service of notices; ☐

15.5 entire agreement; ☐

15.6 that the agreement can not be enforced by third parties. ☐

See Precedent 5.6 on accompanying CD.

6 Corporate Contracts

6.1 Acquisition Due Diligence Questionnaire

6.2 Employment/Service Agreement

6.3 Share/Asset Sale and Purchase Agreements

6.4 Joint Venture/Shareholders Agreement

6.5 Partnership Agreement

Corporate Contracts

6.1 Acquisition Due Diligence Questionnaire

Overview

Description of Agreement/Document

The due diligence questionnaire or shopping list is a checklist of matters in relation to which the buyer requires information in connection with its investigation into the assets and business or company it proposes to purchase. The questionnaire seeks to highlight the main issues relating to the company or its business and assets.

Practical Guidance/Issues List

Documents and information required by the buyer in connection with an acquisition of a company or business and assets will depend on the type of transaction and extent of required due diligence.

The buyer should consider and analyse the responses carefully. The list will not be exhaustive and in many cases there will be a need to send supplemental questions or requests for further information. Separate explanation should be requested in relation to documents from which a full understanding cannot be obtained.

Reference to "the Company" can be deemed to refer to the Company and to any subsidiaries of the Company and all information should be provided in relation to each company to avoid duplication.

The checklist deals with general legal issues and the buyer should ensure due diligence is also carried out in relation to the specific type of business. The questions should be appropriately tailored to the type of business or matters crucial to the business.

The buyer's investigation should also extend to business, financial and accounting matters over and above the legal due diligence.

Where special due diligence needs to be undertaken, the questions are usually more detailed and concentrate on relevant areas. For example, environmental due diligence can be conducted as a specialist matter having regard to its technical nature. A buyer purchasing a technology company which owns several patents will concentrate on the intellectual property, contracts and technology issues of the business or company.

It may be useful and save time to require that the documents and information are provided as they become available rather than waiting to assemble all the information before sending it.

The buyer may wish to require that the seller provide the information for the period since incorporation or such other period as is specified in the questionnaire, where the scope extends to historic as well as current information.

Law/Compliance Requirement

The principle that the buyer should beware (*caveat emptor*) means that the buyer should investigate the proposed acquisition to ensure it gets what it wishes to buy without undisclosed liabilities or defects.

If a buyer purchases a company, it buys it with all its liabilities subject to the parties' agreement. In effect, the target company's non-compliance with legal obligations remains. The company will still be liable for the non-compliance and the buyer will end up with a company in such a state.

Commercial Contracts Checklists

Checklist 6.1 Acquisitions Due Diligence Information Request/Questionnaire Checklist

In preparing a due diligence information request or questionnaire, individuals or businesses should consider the following non-exhaustive matters.

Actions/Issues:	Comments:	✎

1 The buyer or its representatives should consider what documents, information and confirmation should be supplied in respect of the proposed acquisition of the entire [issued share capital/business and assets] of the [Company]. ☐

2 Ascertain and consider extent of due diligence required in relation to: ☐

    2.1   legal due diligence; ☐

    2.2   business and operations due diligence; ☐

    2.3   financial and accounting due diligence; ☐

    2.4   environmental compliance matters; ☐

    2.5   specific matters or special interest including: ☐

        2.5.1   insurance matters; ☐

        2.5.2   property issues; ☐

        2.5.3   contracts and business arrangements; ☐

        2.5.4   health and safety matters; ☐

        2.5.5   pensions issues; ☐

        2.5.6   employment matters; ☐

        2.5.7   litigation and disputes; ☐

        2.5.8   competition law matters; ☐

        2.5.9   data protection compliance; ☐

Corporate Contracts

        2.5.10   intellectual property rights, licences and related matters; ☐

        2.5.11   technology matters; ☐

        2.5.12   assets of the business; ☐

        2.5.13   licences, authorisations, permits and consents; ☐

        2.5.14   organisational, corporate and company structure and related issues; ☐

        2.5.15   environmental matters. ☐

3   Consider information and documents disclosed in connection with due diligence information request in relation to each category of investigation. ☐

4   Request supplemental documents and information resulting from evaluation of supplied due diligence materials. ☐

5   Consider:

    5.1   and identify the assets and business or company being acquired; ☐

    5.2   the type of business, assets or company being acquired; ☐

    5.3   carrying out searches and the results of company or bankruptcy charges; ☐

    5.4   application of the TUPE regulations to the transaction; ☐

    5.5   seller's authority to sell the assets, business or company; ☐

    5.6   establishing a due diligence team and arrange for co-ordination of the exercise; ☐

    5.7   results of due diligence and the responses to questions; ☐

    5.8   if a due diligence report is required for the board or specific group in relation to approval of acquisition. ☐

6   Review and identify any areas of concern including (as appropriate):

    6.1   whether there are any shared assets with third parties; ☐

    6.2   how the intellectual property rights and other consents are held; ☐

6.3 the necessity to assign, terminate, transfer or novate any contracts and licences; ☐

6.4 the potential liability to maintain filings, pay renewal fees and other payments; ☐

6.5 effect of any rights granted to third parties; ☐

6.6 validity of rights granted to the business or company; ☐

6.7 onerous terms in any contracts; ☐

6.8 change of control termination provisions; ☐

6.9 any infringements of third party rights; ☐

6.10 threatened, existing or pending litigation, disputes or arbitration; ☐

6.11 breaches or agreements; ☐

6.12 retention of title difficulties. ☐

7 Review and ensure: ☐

7.1 relevant insurance can be obtained, renewed, assigned or novated as required; ☐

7.2 recovery of outstanding book debts is practicable; ☐

7.3 stock take requirement; ☐

7.4 suitable continuity arrangements can be put in place; ☐

7.5 information technology and computer equipment is up to date and suitable or sufficient for the business requirements; ☐

7.6 ownership and transfer of domain names, web site, URLs and other intellectual property rights; ☐

7.7 lock in of key employees or consultants; ☐

7.8 enforceability of restrictions for the protection of the business or company; ☐

7.9 applicable notices are served; ☐

7.10   regulatory requirements and compliance issues. ☐

8   Ascertain and consider: ☐

    8.1   long standing arrangements or irrevocable grants; ☐

    8.2   non-commercial arrangements in existence; ☐

    8.3   post-completion effect of sale on suppliers, customers, business and third parties; ☐

    8.4   future costs and financial commitments to be adopted; ☐

    8.5   any judgements against the business, assets or company; ☐

    8.6   existence and terms of any charges on shares, company, business or assets ☐

    8.7   terms of any unusual contracts or arrangements; ☐

    8.8   departing employees and any potential liability; ☐

    8.9   any intellectual property of commercial significance which is unregistered; ☐

    8.10 ongoing negotiations which need to be adopted; ☐

    8.11 special ongoing relationships; ☐

    8.12 quality and valuation of stock and/or work in progress; ☐

    8.13 arrangements for disclosure of confidential information. ☐

9   Should: ☐

    9.1   specialist and independent searches be carried out? ☐

    9.2   an independent patent search be commissioned? ☐

    9.3   environmental due diligence and report be required? ☐

    9.4   unregistered intellectual property rights capable of registration be registered? ☐

Commercial Contracts Checklists

9.5 pensions specialists be consulted? ☐

See Precedent 6.1 on accompanying CD.

6.2 Employment/Service Agreement

Overview

Description of Agreement/Document

The employment or service agreement governs the relationship of the employer and employee. The agreement sets out the statutory particulars required under employment legislation in addition to specific agreed terms. At the basic level, the contract details the employee's position, job description, pay, employment benefits, holiday and other entitlements as well as mutual termination rights.

Practical Guidance/Issues List

The employment terms can easily be set out in a less formal way, e.g. they can be detailed in a letter.

Employers find it useful to have a standard form contract prepared in respect of each level of employee. In addition, it may be useful to set out an employment manual or handbook with the comprehensive provisions.

Enforceability of any restrictions will still need to be considered having regard to reasonableness.

The parties should aim for an agreement that provides adequate protection for both the employer and employee.

The employer should ensure it provides a set of employment terms for the employee.

Law/Compliance Requirement

The Employment Rights Act 1996 requires certain particulars to be set out for the employee. The employer also needs to comply with its requirements in terms of timing and other matters.

Company law may also impose certain requirements in relation to directors and directors' service agreements. The relevant Finance Act and the Taxes Act 1988 will also apply. The employer company will in the normal way be liable to deduct and make payments in respect of income tax.

Some Key Definitions

'Board' means the board of directors of the Company from time to time.

'Customer' means any person, firm or company who is contracted or in the process of contracting with the Company or any Group Company at any time during [specify period] for the supply of any Restricted [Matters/Products/[Services].

'Restricted Area' means the United Kingdom of Great Britain and Northern Ireland and any country in which the Company carries on business or is able to demonstrate that it has substantive and developed plans to commence doing business.

'Restricted Matters' means all and any services or goods of a kind which are provided, manufactured or supplied by the Company or any Group Company in the ordinary course of the Company's business from time to time.

'Technical Information' means in relation to the Company's products and services, all and any trade secrets, secret formulae, processes, inventions, designs, know-how discoveries, technical specifications and other technical information.

'Term' means the period of the appointment starting on and from the Commencement Date and continuing in full force and effect until the Termination Date but the term of this Agreement shall not in any event extend beyond the [Executive/Employee]'s 65th birthday.

Specific Provisions

Hours
You are entitled to terminate your agreement with the Company that the working hours limit under the Working Time Regulations 1988 ('the Regulations') does not apply to you by giving not less than three months' written notice to the Company. The Company will comply with the Regulations.

Following the successful completion of your Probationary Period your employment will continue until it is terminated by either you or the Company giving notice to the other in accordance with the notice provisions set out in paragraph [ ] below.

Holidays
On termination of your employment for any reason any outstanding holiday must be taken during the notice period and no further holiday entitlement shall accrue during the notice period.

Maternity/Paternity
The Company shall comply with its obligations under current legislation. You may obtain further details from the [Managing Director].

Rights
You also irrevocably and unconditionally, so far as is permitted by law, waive any and all moral rights in relation to any works you create and agree that the work can be used in the future, without further reference to you in any jurisdiction.

Termination
The Company reserves the right, at its absolute discretion, to terminate your employment by making a payment of basic salary in lieu of notice.

Internet
You shall not at any time place any item, article, message, web page or document of whatever nature on the internet (or any other media) concerning the Company or any of our customers, partners, directors, representatives, employees or suppliers.

Data
The Company maintains a data protection notification under the Data Protection Act 1998 and the Employee must familiarise himself with the Company's Data Protection and Privacy Policy (a copy of which is on the Company's website or available from the [Board]).

Third Party Information
You recognise that the Company has received and in the future will receive from third parties their confidential or proprietary information subject to a duty on the Company's part to maintain the confidentiality of such information and to use it only for certain limited purposes.

Deductions
The Company reserves the right in its absolute discretion to deduct from your salary or other benefits payable to you or require payment from you any money which you directly or indirectly owe to the Company.

Freedom
You represent and warrant to the Company that you are not under any restriction or obligation which prevents you from freely entering into this Agreement.

Rules
The disciplinary rules applicable to your employment are set out in the Company's disciplinary procedure, as amended from time to time. During any investigation of a disciplinary offence by you, the Company may suspend you on full pay. [The disciplinary rules and grievance procedures of the Company are of a policy nature and do not form part of your contract of employment.]

Corporate Contracts

Checklist 6.2 Employment/Service Agreement Checklist

In preparing an employment/service agreement or letter, individuals or businesses should consider the following non-exhaustive matters.

	Actions/Issues:	Comments:	☐
1	Review nature and proposed arrangements for employment of employee.		☐
2	Consider and ensure particulars of employment or details required by legislation will be included.		☐
3	Ascertain and indicate:		☐
	3.1 employers name and address;		☐
	3.2 employee's name and address;		☐
	3.3 job description;		☐
	3.4 employee's job title;		☐
	3.5 applicable probationary period.		☐
4	Specify:		☐
	4.1 date employment commenced;		☐
	4.2 any previous employment/period of continuous employment, where applicable;		☐
	4.3 length and period of employment;		☐
	4.4 specific duties of employee in addition to general job description;		☐
	4.5 any requirement to work for other group or associated companies.		☐
5	Ascertain, consider and indicate in relation to term of employment:		☐
	5.1 whether fixed term contract;		☐
	5.2 whether for an indefinite period;		☐

Commercial Contracts Checklists

    5.3   whether terminable by notice; ☐

    5.4   applicable employer notice period to terminate; ☐

    5.5   applicable employee notice period; ☐

    5.6   whether employment is permanent; ☐

    5.7   relevant contracting out of statutory claims in respect of fixed term contract, where applicable; ☐

    5.8   flexi-time scheme; ☐

    5.9   shift working arrangements and rota system, if applicable; ☐

    5.10   clocking in procedures; ☐

    5.11   any continuance following expiry of fixed term. ☐

6   Consider and specify: ☐

    6.1   employee's principal place of work; ☐

    6.2   flexibility required in relation to place of work; ☐

    6.3   entitlement to relocate the employee; ☐

    6.4   entitlement to any relocation expenses; ☐

    6.5   whether employee required to work at different locations; ☐

    6.6   extent of any geographical mobility provision; ☐

    6.7   required employee consent to specified overseas relocation; ☐

    6.8   any restrictions on ability to relocate from present place of work. ☐

7   In relation to employee's working hours, indicate: ☐

    7.1   normal working hours; ☐

7.2 any other working hours, such as such time required for proper performance of duties; ☐

7.3 full time or part time; ☐

7.4 time to be devoted to business of employer; ☐

7.5 requirement to work overtime. ☐

8 Payment details and remuneration should be set out including: ☐

    8.1 basic salary; ☐

    8.2 rate and payment intervals; ☐

    8.3 frequency of payments; ☐

    8.4 dates of periodic review of remuneration; ☐

    8.5 discretionary and/or contractual bonuses; ☐

    8.6 commission entitlement, method of calculation, drawings on account and terms of payment; ☐

    8.7 any other benefits; ☐

    8.8 right to withdraw discretionary benefits; ☐

    8.9 over time payment rates; ☐

    8.10 any directors fees; ☐

    8.11 automatic cost of living increases in relevant periods. ☐

9 What additional benefits will the employee be entitled to? Ascertain and specify as appropriate: ☐

    9.1 pension provision including: ☐

        9.1.1 whether company scheme or private pension scheme applicable; ☐

        9.1.2 membership of pension scheme; ☐

9.1.3 contribution by employer to scheme; ☐

9.2 company car including: ☐

    9.2.1 maximum value of car to be provided; ☐

    9.2.2 liability for tax and maintenance; ☐

    9.2.3 required care by employee; ☐

    9.2.4 use of own car; ☐

    9.2.5 responsibility for insurance; ☐

    9.2.6 use of vehicle; ☐

    9.2.7 responsibility for running costs; ☐

    9.2.8 maintenance of driving licence condition; ☐

    9.2.9 compliance with company car policy; ☐

    9.2.10 position in relation to private use and cost of consumed fuel; ☐

    9.2.11 replacement vehicle; ☐

    9.2.12 mileage allowance; ☐

    9.2.13 options to purchase vehicle; ☐

    9.2.14 arrangements to return car on termination; ☐

9.3 mobile telephones; ☐

9.4 private medical insurance for employee and family; ☐

9.5 permanent health insurance scheme. ☐

10 Ascertain and set out details of: ☐

10.1 required travel in respect of employment; ☐

10.2 payment of expenses and required supporting documentation; ☐

10.3 sick pay arrangements and entitlements; ☐

10.4 person to whom employee reports; ☐

10.5 employees duties and responsibilities; ☐

10.6 holiday entitlement, accrued holidays arrangements; ☐

10.7 provisions relating to inventions, copyrights and new processes; ☐

10.8 right to make payment in lieu of notice; ☐

10.9 provisions for incapacity for work as a result of injury or sickness. ☐

11 What is the employee's holiday entitlement? Indicate relevant details, including: ☐

11.1 number of days holiday/annual entitlement; ☐

11.2 the employer's holiday year; ☐

11.3 when holidays can be taken (any time or as agreed with board/manager; ☐

11.4 any unpaid holiday entitlement; ☐

11.5 whether holidays must be taken in a holiday year; ☐

11.6 whether holidays can be carried forward; ☐

11.7 whether a day's holiday is equivalent to a day's basic pay; ☐

11.8 any restrictions on consecutive holiday days; ☐

11.9 procedure for accrued holidays; ☐

11.10 arrangements for overdrawn holidays; ☐

Commercial Contracts Checklists

      11.11 entitlement to accrued pay for holidays at end of employment; ☐

      11.12 obligation to retain and take holidays over specific or seasonal periods. ☐

12   Consider and provide:

      12.1 confidentiality undertakings restricting disclosure of company information; ☐

      12.2 restriction on acceptance of gifts; ☐

      12.3 right to make deductions from salary; ☐

      12.4 right to vary employment terms; ☐

      12.5 statement as to whether any collective agreement applies; ☐

      12.6 restrictions on outside working or on agreed terms; ☐

      12.7 retirement age; ☐

      12.8 employer's entitlement to make joint appointment or subsequent appointment of an employee to jointly hold position; ☐

      12.9 total or partial restriction during employment on involvement with other businesses; ☐

      12.10 whether any other contract will subsist during the employment term; ☐

      12.11 procedure for ensuring employer's ownership of all inventions by employee; ☐

      12.12 specific restrictive covenants or undertakings; ☐

      12.13 right to impose garden leave. ☐

13   Require compliance with terms contained in employment manual or other documents including: ☐

      13.1 employee handbook; ☐

      13.2 data protection policy; ☐

      13.3 health and safety policy; ☐

13.4 confidentiality rules; ☐

13.5 employer rules and regulations; ☐

13.6 disciplinary and grievance policy; ☐

13.7 equal opportunities policy; ☐

13.8 car policy; ☐

13.9 internet and e-mail rules. ☐

14 Illness and sick pay arrangements should be considered and specified. Review and provide (as appropriate) for:

    14.1 requirement to notify of absence due to illness; ☐

    14.2 provision of medical certificates or other evidence of incapacity; ☐

    14.3 self-certification for short absences; ☐

    14.4 right to require medical examination of employee; ☐

    14.5 employee's entitlement to proportion of salary for specified period; ☐

    14.6 employer's right to terminate after certain continuous or total period of absence in each holiday year; ☐

    14.7 entitlement to statutory sick pay only; ☐

    14.8 qualifying days for statutory sick pay. ☐

15 For disciplinary and grievance procedures, detail:

    15.1 relevant grievance procedure; ☐

    15.2 person or body to whom grievances should be addressed; ☐

    15.3 any adopted grievance codes; ☐

    15.4 disciplinary procedures; ☐

15.5 list of non-exhaustive of disciplinary offences; ☐

15.6 disciplinary appeals procedures. ☐

16 Termination of employment provisions should be specified including termination: ☐

    16.1 by service of written notice; ☐

    16.2 for breach of contract; ☐

    16.3 automatically on retirement age; ☐

    16.4 by either party on specified grounds; ☐

    16.5 by employer on incapacity; ☐

    16.6 for misconduct; ☐

    16.7 if prohibited from being a director; ☐

    16.8 by resignation from office; ☐

    16.9 following suspension; ☐

    16.10 for bringing employer into serious disrepute; ☐

    16.11 upon employee being convicted of a criminal offence; ☐

    16.12 for employee's acts of dishonesty; ☐

    16.13 following employee's bankruptcy; ☐

    16.14 on change of control or reorganisation; ☐

    16.15 on any other grounds. ☐

17 Ascertain, consider applicable post-termination obligations for required period and specify: ☐

    17.1 restrictions on non-solicitation of staff; ☐

17.2 restrictions against dealing with suppliers and customers of the business; ☐

17.3 non-competing obligations or involvement in similar business within specified location; ☐

17.4 return of employer's property, documents, materials and equipment; ☐

17.5 exclusion, if applicable, of redundancy pay for relevant fixed term contracts; ☐

17.6 resignation as director or other specified office; ☐

18 Review and indicate whether: ☐

18.1 all excludable rights have been excluded; ☐

18.2 agreement amounts to the entire agreement between the employer and employee; ☐

18.3 reasonableness of restrictions; ☐

18.4 inclusion of required statutory particulars and all requirements of employment statute; ☐

18.5 there are any residence requirements; ☐

18.6 notices will be required to be given in a particular manner; ☐

18.7 English law and jurisdiction apply. ☐

See Precedent 6.2 on accompanying CD.

6.3 Share/Asset Sale and Purchase Agreements

Overview

Description of Agreement/Document

The agreement for sale sets out the terms of acquisition of shares or assets from a seller. It details the price payable, applicable conditions together with any warranties and vendor protection provisions. The agreement may also contain indemnities and guarantees in respect of specified matters.

Practical Guidance/Issues List

Care should be taken in defining relevant terms in the agreement as important provisions may be interpreted by reference to the defined terms.

It is important that the proper parties and their respective capacities are set out in the agreement. Corporate parties should be identified by registration numbers as names may be changed in the future.

Consider the value of any warranties and whether an alternative arrangement would be more effective (for example, retention of part of the purchase price).

Relevant third parties, if any, who should be entitled to enforce the agreement under the Contracts (Rights of Third Parties) Act 1999 should be considered.

In general, the parties may wish to consider:
- whether any obligations should be guaranteed;
- any notices that need to be given to third parties;
- any third party rights which may be subsisting;
- sending due diligence information request to the seller and review responses;
- whether all of the conditions can be satisfied without reliance on any third party or event;
- whether separate transfers of assets or shares are required and ensure they are dealt with;
- planning permissions;
- required assignments or novations;
- application of Transfer of Undertakings (Protection of Employment) Regulations 1981 (TUPE) and deal with in accordance with requirements.

Practical arrangements should be made and if relevant, the parties should provide for the following:
- method and arrangements to value stock and work in progress;
- how trade debtors and future receipts will be treated in an asset sale;
- insurance matters including commencement or cancellation of policies;
- reviewing contracts for any onerous, unusual or special terms;
- checking to ensure that no charges are subsisting;
- arrangements to change name, reprint stationery;
- existing agreements and any termination as a result of change of control;
- notifying authorities of transaction in order to deal with administrative matters including accounts or membership transfer and/or reissue of certificates;
- stamp duty and VAT and any possible steps to minimise such tax;
- ability to satisfy conditions by the specified date and time;
- any actual or pending litigation or arbitration.

The terms of any disclosure letter or vendor protection provisions should be reviewed carefully by each party.

The parties should consider any unlawful financial assistance by the company in connection with the acquisition of shares. Relevant approval should also be obtained in respect of related parties.

The buyer should seek comprehensive warranties to force disclosures by the seller as well as provide for relevant protection including compensation in the event of a breach.

Specific warranties or relevant indemnity should be sought by the buyer in relation to matters discovered from the due diligence exercise. If necessary, the buyer should insist that the replies or specific replies are warranted by the seller.

The buyer in a share purchase should consider an acquisition of the assets in the event that the seller is not able or willing to provide extensive or sensible warranties.

The buyer may also wish to expressly exclude the limitation period under the Limitation Act 1980 in relation to claims under the tax indemnity which can be made at any time up to seven years.

The buyer may wish to obtain indemnities in respect of:
- specifically disclosed liabilities;
- missing documents;
- litigation outcome;
- liability for tax.

The meanings of full or limited title guarantee should be understood or considered. The seller should be aware of the benefits of covenants conferred by law (Law of Property (Miscellaneous Provisions) Act 1994) on the buyer by use of the relevant phrase ('full title guarantee').

Law/Compliance Requirement

Legal and compliance issues to bear in mind may include matters or requirements under the relevant legislation including:
- Companies Act 1985
- general contract law;
- Transfer of Undertakings (Protection of Employment) Regulations 1981 (TUPE);
- Competition Act 1998 and EC Competition rules;
- Income and Corporation Tax Act 1988 and Taxation of Chargeable Gains Act 1992;
- Finance Act 2003 (new stamp duty land tax provisions) as updated or amended from time to time;
- VAT (Special Provisions) Order 1995 in respect of VAT and transfers of going concerns.

In relation to share sale, stamp duty will be payable on the value of the purchase price at the 0.5% rate.

Some Key Definitions

'Business Day' means a day other than Saturday, Sunday or a day on which banks are authorised to close in London.

'Consideration' means the sum specified in clause [ ] to be paid to the Seller at Completion by the Purchaser.

'Shares' means [ ] Ordinary Shares of £1 each in the capital of the Company further details of which are set out in the Schedule.

'Assets' means the assets owned by the Vendor and used in the Business at the Effective Date, being the assets to be sold and purchased under clause [ ] of this Agreement but excluding [   ];

'Business' means the business of the [   ] and related business;

'Contracts' means any contracts entered into in the ordinary course of business prior to the Effective Date by the Vendor for the supply of goods and/or services to the Business which, as at the Effective Date, remain to be performed (in whole or in part) and contracts and orders in relation to the sale of goods which have been entered into by or on behalf of the Vendor for the supply by the Vendor of goods in relation to the Business and entered into by the Vendor in connection with the Business.

'Charge' means the fixed and floating charge with the [   ] over the property and assets of the Vendor.

'Customer Deposits' means the amounts received by the Vendor on or prior to the Effective Date and continuing to be held by them on such date, in respect of deposits previously placed by customers or potential customers of the business or any part of it for goods not yet delivered.

'Debtors' means all book debts and other debts payable to the Vendor as at Completion in connection with the carrying on of the Business up to Completion (whether or not yet due and payable and including, without limitation, those debts relating to the sale of goods by the Vendor prior to Completion).

'Excluded Items' means any assets or rights or any obligations and liabilities consisting of or comprised in the following:
(a) cash at the bank;
(b) any claim for repayment of tax to the Vendor or any liability for tax in relation to the Business payable by the Vendor arising in the period prior to the Effective Date;
(c) the benefit or the burden of all inter-company balances between the Vendor and any Group Company.

'Goodwill' means the goodwill of the Business and the exclusive right of the Purchaser to represent itself as carrying on the Business in succession to the Vendor.

'Group Company' means [   ] and any company which is its subsidiary. The words 'holding company' and 'subsidiary' shall have the meanings ascribed to them by section 736 of the Companies Act 1985.

'Intellectual Property' means all trade marks, database rights, names, logos, designs, copyrights, confidential information, customer databases, know-how, software, confidential information, trade or business secrets and any similar rights used or licensed by or to the Vendor;.

'Liabilities' means the liabilities of the Vendor arising in the ordinary course in connection with the Business outstanding at the Effective Date but for the avoidance of doubt excluding all tax liabilities, all amounts owed to Group Companies and any liabilities arising through current litigation.

'Records' means all books, accounts, sales and stock records, lists of customers and suppliers and all records relating to the employees (if any) and other records and documents relating to the Business and the Assets;

Specific Provisions

Sale and Purchase
Subject to the terms and conditions of this agreement, [the Seller[s] shall sell with [full/limited] title guarantee and the Buyer shall buy the [Shares/Assets] free from any and all Encumbrances together with all accrued benefits and rights attaching or accruing to the [Shares/Assets].

Consideration
The consideration for the sale and purchase of the [Shares/Assets] shall be the sum of [   ] pounds (£[   ]) [(subject to any adjustment pursuant to clause [ ])], which shall be satisfied in accordance with the provisions of this clause [ ].

Conditions Precedent
Completion of the sale and purchase of the [Shares/Assets] is conditional upon:
(i) the resolution of the shareholders/board of the Buyer approving the proposed acquisition;
(ii) legal, financial, commercial and property due diligence into the affairs of the [Company/Assets] having been carried out to the [reasonable] satisfaction of the Buyer;
(iii) all required approvals, licences, authorisations and consents required for [   ] obtaining or in respect of [   ].

Pending Completion
Pending Completion, the Seller shall carry on the Business in the ordinary and normal course having due regard to the interests of the Buyer under this agreement.

The Seller undertakes to consult with the Buyer in relation to any matters which may have a material effect upon the [Assets/Shares] or [any other matter relevant to the acquisition under this agreement].

The Seller undertakes not to sell, transfer or otherwise dispose of any of the Intellectual Property Rights or agree to do so; or otherwise create or sell any of its assets at any time pending completion of this agreement.

Joint and Several
Each agreement, undertaking, covenant, warranty and representation made or given in this agreement and any agreement or document entered into pursuant to this agreement by any of the Sellers shall be deemed for all purposes to be made or given [jointly and severally/severally] by each of the Sellers.

Indemnity
The Seller agrees to indemnify and keep effectively indemnified the Buyer from and against all losses, actions, proceedings, claims, liabilities, costs and expenses which the Buyer may suffer or incur as a result of the Seller's breach of the terms or its obligations under this agreement.

Release
The Seller undertakes to the Buyer that following Completion and prior to [   ], it shall use its [reasonable/best] endeavours to procure or obtain the release of [   ] from any guarantees and, pending such release, the Buyer shall be indemnified by the Seller in respect of all amounts paid by it to any third party pursuant to any such guarantees.

Warranties
The Seller warrants, represents and covenants to the Buyer that subject to the provisions of the Disclosure Letter, each of the Warranties set out in Schedule [ ] is true and accurate as at the date of this agreement.

The rights and remedies of the Buyer in respect of any breach of the Warranties shall not be affected by or any investigation made by or on behalf of the Buyer into the [Assets/affairs of the company]].

Liability
Under no circumstances shall the total liability of the Seller under the Warranties exceed the total consideration actually paid to the Seller pursuant to clause [ ].

The Seller shall not be liable in respect of any claim for breach of any of the Warranties unless the aggregate amount of the liability of the Seller exceeds the threshold of [£   ] in respect of all claims under the Warranties.

Appendix 6.3 Share/Asset Sale and Purchase Agreement Checklist

In preparing a share/asset sales and purchase agreement, individuals or businesses should consider the following non-exhaustive matters.

Actions/Issues:		Comments:	☐
1	What is the nature of the proposed transaction?		☐
2	Consider and review the proposed arrangements for acquisition or disposal of shares or assets.		☐
3	Who are the parties to agreement? Consider identity of vendor, purchase and company.		☐
4	Review and initial regard should be had to the following:		☐
4.1	list, extent or description of relevant assets or shares;		☐
4.2	terms of any heads of agreement, confidentiality undertaking or memorandum of understanding/letter of intent;		☐
4.3	applicable exclusivity and lock out periods;		☐
4.4	related property transaction;		☐
4.5	relevant employment, tax and pensions issues;		☐
4.6	whether conditional contract;		☐
4.7	whether exchange and completion will be separate;		☐
4.8	extent of due diligence carried out or required;		☐
4.9	answers from seller to buyer's relevant information request;		☐
4.10	memorandum and articles of association of relevant entities and terms of any shareholders agreement;		☐
4.11	any required consents, authorisations, board approval or restrictions;		☐
4.12	proposed completion date.		☐

5 Review and consider reciting preliminary matters, background, purpose of agreement, existing agreements, type of business, capacity and legal status of parties and proposed arrangements in the introductory paragraphs. ☐

6 Are there any other required documents other than the share or asset sale agreement? ☐

7 Consider definitions of specific terms: ☐

    7.1 assets, business, business day; ☐

    7.2 commencement date, agreed form; ☐

    7.3 accounts, accounts date, completion accounts; ☐

    7.4 conditions, transfer date; ☐

    7.5 disclosed, disclosure letter; ☐

    7.6 encumbrance; ☐

    7.7 group, subsidiary, holding company; ☐

    7.8 book debts, creditors, fixtures and fittings; ☐

    7.9 intellectual property rights, goodwill, contracts; ☐

    7.10 excluded liabilities, excluded assets. ☐

8 Indicate the basic agreement between the parties and set out: ☐

    8.1 the agreement for sale and purchase of the shares or assets; ☐

    8.2 whether the sale is by full or limited title guarantee; ☐

    8.3 the sale to include the rights attaching to the shares or assets; ☐

    8.4 if shares, a waiver of pre-emption rights by the sellers; ☐

    8.5 expressly that sale of the assets or shares is to be free from all encumbrances. ☐

Commercial Contracts Checklists

9   If asset sale, specify as applicable: ☐

    9.1   sale of business as going concern; ☐

    9.2   the assets to be sold including: ☐

        9.2.1   goodwill; ☐

        9.2.2   property; ☐

        9.2.3   fixed assets; ☐

        9.2.4   stocks; ☐

        9.2.5   benefit of contracts; ☐

        9.2.6   intellectual property rights; ☐

    9.3   excluding the specified Excluded Assets. ☐

10   What is the purchase consideration? Consider and set out, as relevant: ☐

    10.1   the amount payable; ☐

    10.2   how the price will be paid; ☐

    10.3   whether any non-cash consideration (including issue of consideration shares); ☐

    10.4   any adjustments to the price; ☐

    10.5   any retention and operation of escrow or joint account; ☐

    10.6   any earn out provisions; ☐

    10.7   mechanism for ascertaining the purchase price or completion accounts requirements. ☐

11   Will any conditions need to be satisfied prior to completion? ☐

12   In relation to conditions, consider: ☐

    12.1   buyer's satisfaction with due diligence; ☐

Corporate Contracts

    12.2   buyer's shareholder or board resolution approving acquisition; ☐

    12.3   entry into certain contracts; ☐

    12.4   tax clearances; ☐

    12.5   key employees' new employment agreement; ☐

    12.6   non-alteration or termination of specified key contracts; ☐

    12.7   third party consents or clearances; ☐

    12.8   no occurrence of material adverse change; ☐

    12.9   specify a long stop date after which either party can walk away if conditions not satisfied. ☐

13   What are the arrangements for completion of the acquisition and disposal? Review or set out: ☐

    13.1   when completion will take place; ☐

    13.2   where completion will take place; ☐

    13.3   transactions to be carried out at completion; ☐

    13.4 parties' respective completion obligations; ☐

    13.5   requirement to deliver the assets or shares and deeds together with relevant signed transfers and other documents; ☐

    13.6   discharge of specified contractual undertakings or release of security ☐

    13.7   required resignations and appointments of company officers and auditors, in a company share sale; ☐

    13.8   requirement for board meeting and minutes; ☐

    13.9   payment of consideration for the shares or assets by required method. ☐

14   For assets sales and disposals, consider making appropriate provision for: ☐

    14.1   valuation and payment for stocks and cash float; ☐

14.2 debtors and collection of book debts; ☐

14.3 settlement or discharge of the creditors and liabilities; ☐

14.4 changes to or retention of the business name; ☐

14.5 trading contracts; ☐

14.6 employees; ☐

14.7 insurance. ☐

15 Insert provision that seller is deemed to have made reasonable enquiry in respect of warranties qualified by knowledge, information or belief. ☐

16 Review required acknowledgements and indicate: ☐

16.1 requirement for the seller to disclose events inconsistent with warranties which arise; ☐

16.2 that rights of the buyer not affected by investigation carried out; ☐

16.3 exclusion of representation or guarantee of accuracy in relation to supplied information; ☐

16.4 that entry into the agreement is not based on any inducement; ☐

16.5 any agreed restrictive agreement in relation to non-competition or non-solicitation of business and employees; ☐

16.6 applicable seller protection provisions; ☐

16.7 that agreement will bind successors, assigns and personal representatives; ☐

16.8 liability for costs; ☐

16.9 whether time shall be of the essence of the agreement; ☐

16.10 arrangement for service of notices; ☐

16.11 confidentiality undertaking and restrictions on announcement; ☐

16.12 restrictions on assignment; ☐

16.13 further assurance obligations; ☐

16.14 costs contribution or liability; ☐

16.15 entire agreement provision; ☐

16.16 terms which will survive termination; ☐

16.17 severance of unenforceable provisions; ☐

16.18 variation and waiver. ☐

17 What warranties will be included in the agreement. Will the seller be required to warrant: ☐

    17.1 that it has full capacity, power and authority to enter into agreement? ☐

    17.2 ownership of assets, sufficiency of assets and condition of assets? ☐

    17.3 the trading, business and financial position? ☐

    17.4 arrangements concerning the business? ☐

    17.5 nature of contracts and any defaults? ☐

    17.6 all title documents have been stamped? ☐

    17.7 non-existence of litigation, disputes or arbitration? ☐

    17.8 no encumbrance affecting the shares or assets? ☐

    17.9 liability will be on a joint and several basis? ☐

    17.10 the accuracy and truth of the information provided? ☐

    17.11 the contents of the disclosure letter? ☐

    17.12 compliance with Data Protection Act obligations? ☐

    17.13 the warranties set out in the schedule are true and accurate? ☐

Commercial Contracts Checklists

18 Ascertain, consider and indicate required general warranties to be set out in the schedule of warranties. Detail warranties (as appropriate) in respect of: ☐

    18.1 the preparation and fair portrayal of the accounts together with matters set out in it; ☐

    18.2 budgets and forecasts provided; ☐

    18.3 keeping of accurate and proper books and records; ☐

    18.4 information technology matters and equipment; ☐

    18.5 ownership of intellectual property rights and related licensing issues; ☐

    18.6 employment matters ☐

    18.7 corporate matters including in relation to directors, subsidiaries, options over capital, branches, constitutional documents, filing of documents, keeping statutory books and correctness of information given to buyer; ☐

    18.8 taxation and related matters; ☐

    18.9 finance matters, bank borrowings and facilities; ☐

    18.10 trading matters including effect of sale, conduct of business, compliance with statutes, subsisting contracts, licences and consents, guarantees and indemnities; ☐

    18.11 employees, terms of employment and applicable arrangements; ☐

    18.12 assets, ownership of assets and the absence of any encumbrance; ☐

    18.13 environmental matters and compliance; ☐

    18.14 property, planning and related matters ☐

    18.15 insurance. ☐

19 Consider whether indemnities are required in relation to certain matters. ☐

20 In relation to the tax affairs of the company set out relevant tax warranties and tax indemnity for all taxation. ☐

21   Will the seller be required to provide a sweeper up warranty that there are no facts or circumstances or other material information in relation to the business or assets or company which have not been disclosed in writing and which if disclosed might be expected to affect the buyer's decision to enter into the agreement? ☐

22   Consider vendor protection provisions and include: ☐

    22.1   total liability; ☐

    22.2   time limits for claims; ☐

    22.3   financial thresholds; ☐

    22.4   rights of set off. ☐

See Precedent 6.3 on accompanying CD.

Commercial Contracts Checklists

6.4 Joint Venture/Shareholders Agreement

Overview

Description of Agreement/Document

A joint venture or shareholders arrangement documented by the relevant agreement is simply a mechanism for individuals, investors or entities to come together in the pursuit of a commercial goal. The agreement may reflect the investment in a new limited liability company which is used to achieve the relevant commercial objective. The basic agreement details the commercial objective, the parties' participation in the corporate entity as well as its organisation and management. The relevant agreement also sets out the regulation of rights including provisions relating to deadlock, pre-emption, board representation, minority protection, dispute resolution decision making and funding the entity or project. The agreement is usually drafted alongside the relevant entity's articles of association.

Practical Guidance/Issues List

The parties to such an agreement need to decide whether there are any restrictions or obligations which require the company to be a party to the agreement. It is desirable for the company to enter into the agreement as it allows for direct enforcement.

Certain obligations and provisions are contained in the articles and others in the agreement. The position needs to be reviewed to ensure that the relevant obligations and provisions are considered in relation to the relevant remedies available for breach of the document. It may be that relevant provisions are inserted in both the articles and the agreement. The different remedies for breach should be noted.

The capacity of each party should be considered and if necessary relevant searches undertaken in respect of each party including company and bankruptcy searches.

It is useful to provide in the agreement that the parties are under an obligation to procure certain matters or compliance by the company or third party entities under its control.

If the joint venture vehicle is a corporate entity, it may be better that it is a newly incorporated entity with no liabilities. If not, the parties would need to consider what relevant trading assurances or warranties are required for comfort.

In agreeing relevant percentages of shareholdings, parties should have regard to the legal effect and control effected by their holding. A holding of more than 25% entitles the holder to block the passing of a special resolution (which requires 75%) and more than 50% gives the holder control as they are able to pass ordinary resolutions.

Serious consideration should be given to the decision making process and management of the joint venture company in the agreement. Matters which require a percentage majority vote and those which require unanimity should be carefully considered and detailed.

Other minority protection provisions should be considered having regard to the minority shareholders' concerns and the nature of the business.

If non-competition is an important issue, the parties should agree and insert a relevant restriction in the agreement. Such restriction needs to be reasonable to be enforceable.

Where the parties would benefit, consideration may be given to the use of an existing company with relevant tax losses or where such company owns the relevant assets for use by the joint venture.

Alternatively, the parties should ensure the immediate transfer of the relevant assets to the newly incorporated entity subject to tax advice in respect of such business transfer.

Valuation of any non-cash assets contributed in payment for the shares should be dealt with appropriately, in accordance with the law and properly recorded.

Additional practical issues should be considered and relevant provisions inserted in relation to:
- right to appoint and remove directors;
- an obligation of good faith;
- offers to sell shares or be bought out at a certain price in certain cases;
- liquidation of the company;
- intra-group transfers;
- resolution of a deadlock;
- provision of additional funding;
- whether the chairman has a casting vote;
- the required quorum and obligation on each party to ensure meetings are quorate.
- dispute resolution mechanism or procedures and terms of reference;
- liability for legal costs and expenses;
- resolution of conflict between the articles and the joint venture/shareholders agreement;
- the full extent of matters reserved for the shareholders.

Each party should ensure they have access to all information and records to the company from time to time.

Law/Compliance Requirement

The Companies Act 1985 governs the joint venture company. The parties' obligations and enforcement of the agreement will be a matter of general contract law. Relevant legal compliance issues may include provisions of the Data Protection Act 1998, tax legislation, the Competition Act 1998 and relevant EU directives.

Some Key Definitions

'Auditors' means the auditors for the time being and from time to time of the Company.

'Board' means the board of directors of the Company as constituted from time to time.

'Budget' means, in respect of each successive financial year of the Company, the detailed operating and capital budget and cash flow forecast (including sales and marketing budgets), if any, in respect of the next financial year, the first Budget being attached to this Agreement as Annexure [A] (or agreed as soon as reasonably practicable).

'Business' means the business of sale, distribution and exploitation of [   ] and related services together with such other business as the parties may agree in writing to be carried on by the Company and its subsidiaries.

'Business Plan' means in respect of each successive financial year of the Company, the business plan of the Company for that financial year (if any) and the initial Business Plan being attached to this Agreement as Annexure [B] (or agreed as soon as reasonably practicable).

'Director' means a director of the Company, (including where applicable an alternate director) and references to a Shareholder's 'Director(s)' shall be construed accordingly.

'Equity Share Capital' has the same meaning as section 744 of the Companies Act 1985 and means the equity share capital in the Company.

'New Articles' means the new articles of association of the Company to be adopted at or prior to Completion in the agreed form or any other articles of association of the Company for the time being and references to an 'Article' or 'the Articles' shall be construed accordingly.

'Relevant Proportion' means in relation to a party, that proportion which the nominal value of the Shares in the Company beneficially owned by that party bears to the aggregate nominal value of the entire issued share capital of the Company.

'Shares' means the ordinary shares of £[ ] each in the capital of the Company (together forming the share capital of the Company) and having the rights and being subject to the restrictions set out in the New Articles.

'Territory' means the United Kingdom and any country in which the Company carries on business or is able to demonstrate that it has substantive and developed plans to commence doing business and for the avoidance of doubt it shall include the following territories [set out territories].

Specific Provisions

Businesses
The primary object of the Company is to carry on the Business and related activities and to do such acts and matters as may be consistent with, necessary for or incidental to the attainment of the foregoing objects.

Tax Efficiency
The Shareholders will (using their respective reasonable endeavours) procure (insofar as they are able) that the Company shall structure tax efficient mechanisms for making payments or returns to Shareholders.

Co-operation
[Neither Shareholder may cause or create any difference or dispute with the other by voting against or failing to agree or co-operate with any act, matter or thing which is properly required to attain the objects of the Business whether or not under the terms of this Agreement.]

The Board, Management and Related Matters
All the business of the Company (other than day to day business) shall be carried on by the Board. Unless the Shareholders otherwise agree in writing Board meetings will be held in the United Kingdom at least once every month.

Appointment of Directors
[Party A] (or the holders for the time being of his Shares) shall have the right to appoint and maintain in office [one (1)] Person to be a Director and to remove any Director so appointed and appoint another Person to be a Director in his place (such appointments and removals to be effected by notice in writing served on the Company signed by [Party A] (or the holders for the time being of his Shares) which shall take effect on delivery at the registered office of the Company or at any meeting of the Board.

Matters Requiring Consent of all Shareholders
The Shareholders undertake to each other and shall exercise all voting rights and powers of control available to them in relation to the Company so as to procure (insofar as they are able to do so) by the exercise of those rights and powers) that without the prior written consent of all the Shareholders, neither the Company nor any of its subsidiaries shall engage in any of the activities or determine any of the matters or take any of the actions referred to in Schedule [ ].

Company's Affairs
The Shareholders shall ensure or procure that during the term of this Agreement the Shareholders are given full opportunity to examine the books, records and accounts kept by the Company. All shareholders will be supplied with all information, including monthly management accounts and operating statistics and such other trading and financial information in such form as they shall reasonably require to keep each of them properly informed about the Business and generally to protect their interests.

The Business Plan, the Budget and Accounts
The Shareholders shall procure that the Business Plan shall be updated at least once annually, or (if earlier) following any significant increases or developments in the Business.

The Company shall prepare management accounts containing trading and profit and loss accounts, with comparisons to budgets, balance sheets, cash flow statements and forecasts every calendar month and shall make them available to the Shareholders within 10 days after the end of each calendar month.

The books and records of the Company will be maintained at the principal offices of that company. The books and records of the Company shall at all times be maintained in accordance with generally accepted accounting principles in effect from time to time and in accordance with the applicable laws of England.

Disposal, Charging or Transfer of Shares
None of the Shareholders shall mortgage, charge, pledge, hypothecate, assign or transfer as security or otherwise

encumber or dispose of the whole or any part of the Shares held by them without the prior written approval of the other Shareholders.

Indemnity of Tax
Each Shareholder hereby agrees with and undertakes to the others to indemnify the other Shareholders and to keep them indemnified at all times against all losses, demands, damages, costs, claims, charges, actions, expenses and other liabilities of whatsoever nature suffered or incurred by such other Shareholder arising out of the failure to pay any tax to HM Inland Revenue or HM Customs and Excise (as appropriate) properly attributable to the other Shareholder as a direct or indirect result of this Agreement.

No Fetter on the Company
The Company shall not be bound by any provision of this Agreement to the extent that it would constitute an unlawful fetter on any statutory power of the Company but this shall not affect the validity of the relevant provision as between the other parties to this Agreement or the respective obligations of such other parties as agreed between themselves.

Ambiguity or Conflict
In the event of any ambiguity or conflict arising between the terms of this Agreement and those of the Company's Memorandum and Articles, the terms of this Agreement shall prevail. In such event the parties shall procure (to the extent permissible by law) such modification to the Memorandum and Articles of the Company as shall be necessary.

Further Assurance
Each of the parties agree to take any other such action and do all other things as are [reasonably] required of them (including without limitation amending the Articles of Association) at any time to give full force and effect to the provisions of this agreement.

Each Shareholder agrees to exercise their respective powers and votes (including such powers and votes as may be vested in any nominee) to ensure that the terms of this Agreement and the Articles of Association are complied with in full.

Accrued Liability
Except as agreed between the Shareholders in writing or provided by clause [ ], or in respect of any relevant accrued liability or obligations expressed to survive any termination of this Agreement, any Shareholder who ceases to hold Shares or ceases to be the beneficial owner of Shares in the Company shall also cease to have the benefit of this Agreement or liability or obligations under this Agreement.

Adherence
No person who is not a party to this Agreement shall be registered as a shareholder unless and until he enters into a deed of adherence in substantially the form set out in Schedule [ ]

Appendix 6.4 Joint Venture/Shareholders Agreement Checklist

In preparing a share/asset sales and purchase agreement, individuals or businesses should consider the following non-exhaustive matters.

Actions/Issues:	Comments:	✎

1. Review nature and proposed arrangements for joint venture or between the shareholders as parties to the agreement. ☐

2. What is the appropriate vehicle? Consider whether the arrangements should be through: ☐

    2.1 a company; ☐

    2.2 a partnership; ☐

    2.3 a contractual relationship between the parties. ☐

3. Review and consider reciting preliminary matters, background, purpose of agreement, existing agreements, UK or offshore residence of joint venture company, type of business and proposed arrangements in the introductory paragraphs. ☐

4. Are there any other required documents other than the joint venture or shareholders agreement, such as heads of agreement, articles of association, directors or employment contracts to be considered? ☐

5. Details to be set out including: ☐

    5.1 names and addresses of all shareholders/joint venture parties including registration details if corporate or incorporated partner; ☐

    5.2 capacity and legal status of shareholders; ☐

    5.3 business of the company; ☐

    5.4 project, agreement and/or business commencement date; ☐

    5.5 commercial objectives; ☐

    5.6 any consents or authorisations required; ☐

    5.7 any conditions precedent to the agreement; ☐

5.8 of any pre-existing company, shareholdings and arrangements to transfer or issue shares; ☐

5.9 ratification of any pre-incorporation contracts; ☐

5.10 intended premises and location(s) of the business. ☐

6 Are there any specific terms that need to be defined. Consider: ☐

    6.1 business, business day; ☐

    6.2 commencement date; ☐

    6.3 board; ☐

    6.4 equity share capital; ☐

    6.5 budget, business plan; ☐

    6.6 new articles; ☐

    6.7 subsidiary, holding company, group; ☐

    6.8 directors; ☐

    6.9 territory; ☐

    6.10 shareholders, parties. ☐

7 Indicate the parties' respective shareholdings and whether any separate classes of shares with applicable rights or restrictions. ☐

8 Ascertain, consider and indicate arrangements in respect of investment, funding and finance. Detail: ☐

    8.1 whether budgets and forecasts have been prepared and how much funding is required; ☐

    8.2 how funds will be injected by way of capital or loans; ☐

    8.3 the agreed capital structure; ☐

    8.4 whether additional finance is to be provided by the parties and arrangements in the event of failure to make additional finance available; ☐

Commercial Contracts Checklists

8.5 the relevant proportions of contributions and terms of any investment; ☐

8.6 any loans to be made or guarantees given by the shareholders, on what terms and security; ☐

8.7 if non-financial contributions are required; ☐

8.8 whether any contribution will be made by way of access to intellectual property rights, permission to use premises or secondment of employees; ☐

8.9 requirement for additional investment; ☐

8.10 any loans that are required from third parties, other entities and on what terms; ☐

8.11 any security for finance or loan required; ☐

8.12 whether joint venture losses will be available to members and on what terms; ☐

8.13 parties' different interests and whether they will be reflected in separate classes of shares or right to preferential dividends; ☐

8.14 bank facilities that are required and arrangements for its operation or guarantee. ☐

9 Set out details in respect of the:

9.1 company's objectives, business and activities; ☐

9.2 conduct of the business in the best interests of the company; ☐

9.3 shareholders furthering the objects of the company using their respective best endeavours; ☐

9.4 treatment of the company as a UK resident tax company and the structure of tax efficient mechanisms for each shareholder; ☐

9.5 exercise of the company's management and control in the UK; ☐

9.6 subscription, issue or transfer at completion of shares to relevant shareholders and payment by shareholders; ☐

9.7 adoption at completion of new articles of association, if necessary; ☐

9.8 completion of the agreement and execution of related agreements. ☐

10 In relation to the board, management and administration matters, review and set out as appropriate: ☐

   10.1   responsibility of the board for day to day matters; ☐

   10.2   board meetings, arrangement notices and attendance; ☐

   10.3   appointment of directors and managing directors of the company; ☐

   10.4   exercise of voting powers and rights to give effect to agreement; ☐

   10.5   implementation of business plan and budgets; ☐

   10.6   entitlement to vote at meetings and any casting or second vote in the event of equality of votes; ☐

   10.7   required quorum. ☐

11 As to the appointment of directors, consider as required and provide for: ☐

   11.1   appointment and removal of director rights for each shareholder; ☐

   11.2   number of directors; ☐

   11.3   manner of appointment and removal of directors; ☐

   11.4   entitlement to appoint alternate director; ☐

   11.5   the maximum number of directors; ☐

   11.6   directors' voting arrangements. ☐

12 Consider and detail matters requiring 75% majority or unanimous resolution of all shareholders before company can do certain things. Consider: ☐

   12.1   alteration of articles and memorandum; ☐

   12.2   alteration of share capital or attached rights; ☐

   12.3   issue or creation of new shares; ☐

   12.4   acquisition of property or disposal of undertakings; ☐

Commercial Contracts Checklists

    12.5   cease business or wind up company; ☐

    12.6   petition for administration order; ☐

    12.7   capitalise reserves; ☐

    12.8   vary certain material contracts; ☐

    12.9   change its business; ☐

    12.10 borrow monies generally or over agreed limits; ☐

    12.11 give any guarantee or indemnity; ☐

    12.12 incur capital expenditure over agreed limit; ☐

    12.13 dispose of company asset; ☐

    12.14 engage or dismiss any employee; ☐

    12.15 enter into or conduct litigation or arbitration; ☐

    12.16 mortgage or charge any company asset; ☐

    12.17 give loan or credit; ☐

    12.18 issue debenture or other charge; ☐

    12.19 do anything outside ordinary course of business; ☐

    12.20 make distribution or pay dividend; ☐

    12.21 remove or appoint auditors or other third party; ☐

    12.22 depart from agreed budgets and plans. ☐

13   Require the shareholders to exercise all rights and powers to procure proper progress and conduct of company's business. ☐

14   Consider and set out that during the term of the agreement the following will be maintained unless parties otherwise agree: ☐

Corporate Contracts

14.1 board to determine general policy; ☐

14.2 board to reserve all major matters and unusual decisions to itself; ☐

14.3 no change to registered office; ☐

14.4 no change to bankers; ☐

14.5 company complies with articles; ☐

14.6 shareholders allowed access to records and accounts; ☐

14.7 supply of information to shareholders as requested; ☐

14.8 no change to business of company; ☐

14.9 telephonic meetings permitted; ☐

14.10 cheques require two signatories; ☐

14.11 specified quorum; ☐

14.12 parties to co-operate with each other; ☐

14.13 parties to keep information confidential; ☐

14.14 each party to do such things as necessary to implement agreement. ☐

15 Ascertain, consider and set out provisions relating to: ☐

15.1 non-competition restrictions and enforceability; ☐

15.2 non-solicitation restrictions; ☐

15.3 confidentiality undertakings; ☐

15.4 duration of agreement; ☐

15.5 termination rights and provisions; ☐

15.6 service of notices under the agreement; ☐

15.7 responsibility for payment of legal costs or any contribution; ☐

15.8 restrictions or transferring any rights or obligations without consent; ☐

15.9 severance of unenforceable clauses; ☐

15.10 exclusion of rights of third parties to enforce the agreement. ☐

16 Set out governing law and jurisdiction selection. ☐

17 Provide for signature as a deed if required. ☐

See Precedent 6.4 on accompanying CD.

6.5 Partnership Agreement

Overview

Description of Agreement/Document

A partnership agreement is a contract between parties to carry on business in common with a view to profit. The agreement or partnership deed normally details the relationship between the partners setting out the agreement in relation to contribution and administration of capital, sharing of profits and losses, management of a partnership, admission of new partners, outgoing partners and dissolution of a partnership.

The form of agreement or deed is not as important as the substantive terms agreed by the parties. It is important that the parties consider how they wish to deal with relevant matters or particular issues or concerns.

Practical Guidance/Issues List

Arrangements in respect of 'sleeping' partners should be documented.

Goodwill should be dealt with and agreement reached on how it will be valued or shared by the parties. This will be relevant when a partner leaves the partnership.

The partnership should reserve tax in respect of the partners and make the relevant payments to the Inland Revenue.

Insurance in relation to public liability, professional indemnity, medical expenses, and death in service benefit should be considered and arranged.

Practical procedures and arrangements should be put in place in relation to both incoming and outgoing partners.

Partners can agree and specify precisely what would give rise to expulsion (such as failure to maintain professional qualifications or non-compliance with applicable rules and regulations).

The Compliance with Business Names Act 1985 puts in place obligations in respect of display of a list of partners names on relevant stationery and premises.

The parties should ensure a specific duration for the partnership to avoid a partner simply terminating the partnership upon notice under the Partnership Act 1890.

Care should be taken to ensure that any pre-existing business or assets are properly valued and transferred to the partnership upon formation.

Any assets not intended to be partnership property should be specifically excluded.

Consider allocation of profits and losses on the basis of a points system rather than percentages if frequent changes are likely in the profit sharing percentages.

If practical, a management or executive committee may be formed in addition to the managing partner's day to day management responsibilities.

Banking arrangements need to be attended to including signatories, identification and client account requirement for client monies if a professional partnership.

Arrangements for drawings and any specific level can be agreed from time to time rather than set out in the deed.

Administrative arrangements and provisions should be made in relation to an expelled or retiring partner. In addition, female partners' maternity (and for men paternity) leave should be provided for as appropriate.

It is preferable that the retirement of partners is set at the end of a relevant accounting period or specific accounting date of the partnership.

Commercial Contracts Checklists

The proposed partners may wish to consider the financial position of the partners prior to partnership formation. They can carry out relevant bankruptcy searches.

Review and consider whether the deeds will require registration or stamping.

Goodwill needs to be considered and a decision made as to whether or not goodwill will be written out of the agreement. This will reduce or limit disputes with parties in respect of valuation and sharing.

Law/Compliance Requirement

The partnership arrangements between parties can be formed under the Partnership Act 1890. That Act contains provisions applicable to partnership agreements. Other legislation may also apply. The Business Names Act 1985 must be complied with in respect of a partnership name.

The normal rules will apply to validity, reasonableness and enforceability of any restrictions against a partner in a partnership deed. The Companies Act 1985 contains a provision (section 716) prohibiting the formation of partnership consisting of more than 20 persons unless registered as a company or formed under another Act. The restriction does not apply to certain professional partnerships.

The Limited Liability Partnership Act 2000 applies to certain types of partnership.

The tax position, whether in respect of income tax, capital and gains, stamp duty or inheritance tax, will be subject to applicable tax legislation.

Some Key Definitions

'Accountants' means [   ] of [   ] or such other firm of chartered accountants appointed from time to time by the Partners or Partnership.

'Continuing Partners' means the Partners who remain Partners after an Outgoing Partner shall have ceased to be a Partner, on the Succession Date.

'Partnership' means the partnership carried on by the Partners as constituted by this Deed.

'Partners' means the parties to this Deed (and any other person who is admitted to the Partnership and agrees to be bound by this Deed) and the survivors or survivor of them or the person or persons who shall from time to time and for the time being be partners in the Partnership and 'Partner' shall mean any one of the Partners.

'Net Profits' means the profits of the Partnership shown by the accounts prepared by the Accountants in relation to an Accounting Period after charging all expenses [(including any payment of interest on capital and undrawn profits payable in accordance with the provisions of this Deed)].

'Outgoing Partner' means a Partner who for any reason ceases to be a Partner.

'Succession Date' means the date on which the Outgoing Partner ceases or is deemed to have ceased to be a Partner under this Agreement.

'Taxation' means any income tax, corporation tax, capital gains tax, value added tax, national insurance contributions (whether employer's, employee's or self-employed) and all interest or other penalties levied or leviable thereon as well as all other governmental levies or imposts in the nature of taxation and all interests and penalties therein in every case where leviable on the Partners by reference to the Partnership in respect of the Partnership business.

Specific Provisions

Establishment of the Partnership and Business
The Partners shall become and be Partners with effect from the Commencement Date in carrying on the Business.

Partnership Name and Place of Business
The Partnership Business shall be carried on by the Partners under the name and style of the Partnership Name or such other name or names as may be agreed by the Partners.

Each of the Partners acknowledges that all proprietary and other rights in the Partnership Name are vested exclusively in the Partnership.

Capital
The Partnership Capital shall be contributed by and belong to the Partners in the proportions in which they are or would have been entitled to share in the Net Profits of the Partnership.

Any profits or losses or liabilities of a capital nature shall belong to or be borne by the Partners in the proportions in which they are or would have been entitled to share in the Net Profits of the Partnership.

Advances and Drawing
If in any Accounting Period or other relevant financial period the total amount of advances received by any Partner (together with all other sums debited to its capital account for that year or other period) shall on approval of the accounts be found to be in excess of its share as shown by such accounts, then that Partner shall immediately upon the adoption of the accounts refund to the Partnership the excess so advanced without interest.

Management and Meetings
Unless otherwise provided in this Deed or agreed by the Parties, all matters which may arise during the continuance of the Partnership relating to or affecting the management or conduct of the affairs of the Partnership shall be decided by a [majority of votes] of the Partners with each Partner having one vote per percentage of profits that he is entitled to from time to time.

Outgoing Partner
During the period of [twelve (12)] months following the date on which the Outgoing Partner ceases to be a Partner the Outgoing Partner or its professional advisers shall be permitted upon reasonable advance notice in writing to inspect the books of account, records, letters and other documents of the Partnership during normal business hours so far as they relate to any period preceding the Succession Date on which the Outgoing Partner ceases to be a partner provided that all information so obtained shall be kept strictly confidential by the Outgoing Partner or its duly authorised agent.

Appointment of Attorney
Each partner irrevocably appoints every other Partner and the person deriving title under the last surviving or continuing Partner to be its attorney in the event of the Partnership being dissolved, only for the purposes of getting any assets and completing payment of any debts of the Partnership and of giving notice to any clients or suppliers of the Partnership and for these purposes, and the attorney may make or execute any relevant deed or instrument.

Commercial Contracts Checklists

Appendix 6.5 Partnership Agreement Checklist

In preparing a partnership agreement or letter, individuals or businesses should consider the following non-exhaustive matters.

Actions/Issues:	Comments:	✎

1 Review nature and proposed arrangements for partnership between the parties to the agreement. ☐

2 Recite background, parties' vision, existing agreements, type of business, any transfer of pre-existing business and proposed arrangements in the introductory paragraphs. ☐

3 Consider in general the proposed partnership and partners' details including: ☐

    3.1   names and addresses of all parties including registration details if corporate or incorporated partner; ☐

    3.2   capacity and legal status of partners; ☐

    3.3   type of partnership; ☐

    3.4   partnership agreement and/or business commencement date; ☐

    3.5   partnership name; ☐

    3.6   trading style; ☐

    3.7   partnership business; ☐

    3.8   whether any pre-existing business and arrangements to transfer to partnership; ☐

    3.9   ratification of any pre-partnership contracts; ☐

    3.10   intended partnership premises and location(s) of the business. ☐

4 Are there any specific terms that need to be defined. Consider: ☐

    4.1   Business, the succession date; ☐

    4.2   partners, partnership, continuing partners, outgoing partners; ☐

    4.3   managing partner, senior partner; ☐

4.4 partnership assets, partnership premises; ☐

4.5 net profits, profit share, profits; ☐

4.6 taxation, accounting year, accounting date; ☐

4.7 special majority, firm name; ☐

4.8 partnership bankers, partnership accountants. ☐

5 Ascertain, consider and indicate arrangements in respect of capital and finance. Detail or review (as appropriate): ☐

    5.1 whether capital is to be provided by the partners; ☐

    5.2 relevant proportions of contributions; ☐

    5.3 if non-financial contributions are required; ☐

    5.4 the agreed procedure for the recording, measurement, valuation and management of non-monetary contributions; ☐

    5.5 requirement for additional capital; ☐

    5.6 withdrawal restrictions and controls; ☐

    5.7 whether capital accounts are applicable; ☐

    5.8 if interest on capital is due and agreed rates and dates; ☐

    5.9 whether new partners will be required to make payment and related procedures; ☐

    5.10 provision for payments to third parties on behalf of partners and whether it will be treated as drawings; ☐

    5.11 whether any loans are required from the partners or other entity and on what terms; ☐

    5.12 whether any security for finance or loan is required; ☐

    5.13 whether repayments of capital will be made, when and on what terms; ☐

    5.14 whether provision is to be made for tax reserves; ☐

Commercial Contracts Checklists

    5.15   whether current account balances are paid out at the end of the accounting year, remain as next year's opening balance or are transferred to partners' capital accounts. ☐

6   Will the partnership profits and losses be shared equally or in specified proportions? Indicate (as appropriate): ☐

    6.1   how profits of the firm will be shared; ☐

    6.2   how the partners will share losses; ☐

    6.3   any entitlement to salary or drawings prior to share of balance; ☐

    6.4   entitlement to profits in specified circumstances such as incapacity, maternity leave or partner's ill health; ☐

    6.5   procedure and arrangements for variation of profit and loss sharing proportions; ☐

    6.6   partners' year of joining and departure entitlements; ☐

    6.7   arrangements relating to drawings in general; ☐

    6.8   whether charges on profit will include interest on capital; ☐

    6.9   precedence arrangements in relation to payments to or on behalf of partners; ☐

    6.10   applicable measure or points system in relation to proportions. ☐

7   Accounts and accounting arrangements should be set out including (as appropriate): ☐

    7.1   partnership accounting year and date; ☐

    7.2   partnership accountants, auditors and tax advisers; ☐

    7.3   provision and preparation of management accounts; ☐

    7.4   whether unanimity or majority required for approval of accounts; ☐

    7.5   whether accounts will expressly exclude goodwill; ☐

    7.6   partners' ability to inspect partnership books or records and any applicable restrictions; ☐

    7.7   location and keeping of partnership accounts and books; ☐

7.8 agreed accounting system and taxation arrangements; ☐

7.9 treatment of goodwill and other intangibles; ☐

7.10 how work in progress will be treated; ☐

7.11 who signs the accounts and alternative arrangements; ☐

7.12 general approval of accounts procedure and arrangements. ☐

8 Review and specify rights and duties of the partners. In relation to partners' rights or obligations, consider and indicate as relevant: ☐

8.1 confidentiality restrictions; ☐

8.2 restrictions on competitive activity; ☐

8.3 restrictions on involvement with any other business; ☐

8.4 requirement of spending whole time and attention on partnership business; ☐

8.5 right to holidays and agreed procedures; ☐

8.6 arrangements in relation to illness and incapacity; ☐

8.7 entitlement to pension contribution or applicable arrangements; ☐

8.8 insurance cover for partners in relation to sickness, death in service or incapacity; ☐

8.9 right to assign or bequeath partnership share or agreed arrangements upon death; ☐

8.10 entitlement to salary, drawings, reimbursement or recovery of expenses, credit cards and other financial arrangements; ☐

8.11 restrictions on charging partnership share; ☐

8.12 provision in respect of holding or acceptance of external office or official positions by partners; ☐

8.13 position on conflicts of interest; ☐

8.14 applicable professional qualifications or standards to be attained, held or maintained; ☐

Commercial Contracts Checklists

    8.15   compliance with required professional obligations; ☐

    8.16   arrangements in respect of non-active investor type partners; ☐

    8.17   management responsibilities, meetings and administrative obligations; ☐

    8.18   right to information, access and inspection of books and records; ☐

    8.19   entitlement to cars and arrangements in respect of general insurance and professional indemnity insurance; ☐

    8.20   good faith, declaration of interests, secret profits and conduct provisions; ☐

    8.21   matters requiring consent of partnership or managing partner; ☐

    8.22   general and specific limitations on individual partners' authority; ☐

    8.23   entitlement to indemnity for certain matters or in certain circumstances; ☐

    8.24   applicable arrangements in relation to firm name where there is a 'name' partner; ☐

    8.25   post-departure obligations, rights and restrictions. ☐

9   Ascertain and specify arrangements and procedures for incoming and outgoing partners. Review and consider procedure or arrangements for: ☐

    9.1   admitting new members to the partnership on required majority or unanimous consent; ☐

    9.2   determining level and profit share entitlement of new partner; ☐

    9.3   expelling members and partners; ☐

    9.4   retirement of partners on specified age or notice; ☐

    9.5   outgoing partner's partnership share; ☐

    9.6   for documenting incoming and outgoing partners together with any required elections, tax procedures or arrangements; ☐

    9.7   dissolution of partnership or exclusion of right to dissolution; ☐

    9.8   forced retirement upon ill health, mental or other incapacity; ☐

9.9   partners' expulsion or admission committees; ☐

9.10   grounds for compulsory expulsion or upon professional disqualification; ☐

9.11   garden leave or other restrictions on partner during notice period; ☐

9.12   valuation of outgoing partner's undrawn profits and capital, valuation of work in progress and acceleration of outstanding instalments in the event of arrears; ☐

9.13   periodic and geographic extent of any post-departure obligations; ☐

9.14   restrictions on non-solicitation of employees, business and clients; ☐

9.15   restrictions on competitive activities; ☐

9.16   return of partnership property; ☐

9.17   third party notification procedures following date of retirement, expulsion or departure; ☐

9.18   optional or automatic acquisition of outgoing partner's share by other partners; ☐

9.19   payments to deceased partner's family; ☐

9.20   instalment repayment arrangements in respect of capital; ☐

9.21   indemnifying the outgoing partner. ☐

10   Management responsibilities, administration procedures and obligations should be detailed. Consider and specify:

10.1   majority required for specific matters; ☐

10.2   any power of veto or casting vote in the event of deadlock; ☐

10.3   management or senior partner positions, appointment, tenure, functions and duties; ☐

10.4   normal venue, notice and frequency in relation to partners' meetings; ☐

10.5   convening and attending meetings; ☐

10.6   whether all partners will be entitled to attend all meetings; ☐

10.7 any management or other committee, appointment or election, duties and procedures; ☐

10.8 agreed minutes and agenda procedures; ☐

10.9 use of written signed resolutions; ☐

10.10 quorums and chairmanship of meetings; ☐

10.11 decision making at meetings, unanimity and required majority; ☐

10.12 delegation of decision making to special partners or committees; ☐

10.13 any other relevant or applicable matters in respect of the management and administration of the partnership. ☐

11 Ascertain, consider and detail provisions relating to: ☐

11.1 professional status and qualifications of parties and partners; ☐

11.2 deemed commencement arrangements; ☐

11.3 previous arrangements which need to be superseded; ☐

11.4 duration of the partnership (whether indefinite, until occurrence of an event, completion of project or specific business, fixed period, during the lives of partners); ☐

11.5 express termination events or events excluded from giving rise to termination; ☐

11.6 effect of death and bankruptcy of a partner; ☐

11.7 third party businesses with same or similar name; ☐

11.8 obtaining required registration or consents; ☐

11.9 type of partnership (limited, general or limited liability partnership); ☐

11.10 compliance with applicable laws; ☐

11.11 property ownership, type, any trust arrangements in relation to the property or rental arrangements; ☐

11.12 what amounts to partnership property; ☐

11.13 partnership bank, banking arrangements, permitted signatories, restrictions, instructions and mandates; ☐

11.14 maternity or paternity leave entitlement and arrangements for partners; ☐

11.15 valuation of any property or business to be transferred to the partnership; ☐

11.16 arrangements in respect of partners' holidays and sabbaticals; ☐

11.17 repayment of over-drawings; ☐

11.18 payment by partnership of partners' income tax and National Insurance contributions; ☐

11.19 arrangements for payment of drawings, amounts, timing and frequency; ☐

11.20 holding positions in voluntary and charitable organisations; ☐

11.21 apportionment of accounts or preparation of retirement accounts on departure of a partner; ☐

11.22 partners' existing obligations to a former partnership, business or firm; ☐

11.23 insurance cover and profits share arrangements in relation to unwell or incapacitated partner; ☐

11.24 assets revaluation policy. ☐

12 Detail provisions:

12.1 for notices and manner of service; ☐

12.2 appointing other partners as attorney for each partner; ☐

12.3 in relation to dissolution of the partnership; ☐

12.4 for suspending a partner, applicable disciplinary procedures and voluntary retirement; ☐

12.5 compliance with applicable regulations and laws; ☐

12.6 for amending the agreement; ☐

12.7 for consent or inclusion and display of names on stationery; ☐

12.8 resolution of disputes by alternative dispute resolution procedures (mediation, expert determination etc.), arbitration or the courts; ☐

12.9 for procuring partners' release from specified obligations or contracts; ☐

12.10 relating to non-disclosure of information and confidentiality undertakings; ☐

12.11 acknowledging ownership of partners' 'book of business' or clients; ☐

12.12 excluding third party enforcement rights under legislation except as specified with regard to personal representatives upon a partner's death; ☐

12.13 relating to record keeping. ☐

13 Consider and indicate: ☐

13.1 governing law; ☐

13.2 exclusivity or non-exclusivity of jurisdiction; ☐

13.3 acknowledgement of forum and undertaking not to object; ☐

13.4 appointment of agent for service, if necessary; ☐

13.5 signature of partnership agreement or execution as a deed. ☐

See Precedent 6.5 on accompanying CD.

7 Internet and E-Commerce Contracts

7.1 Web Development/Hosting

7.2 Website Materials

7.3 Advertising Terms and Conditions/Agreement

7.4 Affiliate Program Services Agreement

7.5 Promotion Agreement

7.1 Web Development/Hosting Agreement

Overview

Description of Agreement/Document

The agreement for the provision of website development and hosting services relates to the development and design of the website for a client together with its hosting (storage of a website and its content on a service provider's server). The agreement may document both services or detail the services in separate contracts.

In whatever form, the agreement details the parties' requirements, respective obligations and sets out the position with regard to ownership of intellectual property rights in connection with the design, development or other services. It is most likely that companies or entities seeking web hosting services will be presented with a standard web hosting contract favourable to the hosting company. A client can negotiate relevant provisions of such a hosting agreement and individual clients may be protected from any unfair terms by relevant regulations. Hosting services are typically provided by an Internet Services Provider (ISP) as part of a wide range of internet related services, but in some cases service providers offer stand-alone hosting services.

Practical Guidance/Issues List

Depending on the size of the project, the services may extend to overall management of the client website and include ongoing maintenance and general support. It is important from the client's perspective that there are adequate warranties and relevant indemnities in relation to the services being provided by the designer and further that there is the opportunity to conduct acceptance testing. This ensures that the finished product accords with the client's specified standards and requirements.

Care should be taken in agreeing the scope of the services. The client should ensure that there is provision for a detailed specification. This is important from the client's perspective as it allows the client to specify with sufficient detail its particular requirements for the website and measure these against the performance of the actual services provided by the designer.

A specific time frame should be put in place requiring the designer to meet specific timelines and, in relation to the services and performance, on target and within budget.

The designer should request a relevant provision for the acknowledgement of the designer's contribution. The parties should agree the precise nature and level of recognition to be given including relevant wording or required prominence.

The client should ensure that the payment obligations will be tied to specific milestones. This allows the client to withhold payment in the event that milestones are not completed in accordance with the acceptance testing and delivery obligations of the agreement.

The ownership of intellectual property in the website is often subject to extensive negotiation between the parties. The parties may wish to agree a distinction between pre-existing intellectual property and intellectual property created in the course of the services. The client should ensure it is not restricted by the designer in making use of the material produced for the website.

Depending on the circumstances of the project the client may require that specific personnel work on the project. It may be in the designer's interest to impose non-poaching or non-solicitation obligations on the client in respect of its staff engaged in the project.

The delivery, testing and acceptance provisions are very important from the client's perspective. It is important that there be certain minimum levels imposed on the designer with respect to the provision of the services. Importantly there should be an obligation on the designer to warrant that it does not infringe the intellectual property rights of a third party during the course of providing the services. In addition, the client should ensure that the agreement makes provision that the services are to be performed using all diligence and skill and in accordance with the agreement and specification.

The client may wish to resist any mutual indemnity provision in the agreement where broadly drafted. In addition, the client should make certain that the termination provisions contain the usual provisions. Such provisions should give the client the right to terminate in the event of breach, insolvency or in the event that the designer fails to meet timelines as set out in the plan.

Availability of the website is crucial in relation to any online business. Availability is generally on a 24 hours a day, seven days a week, 365 days a year basis (or 24/7/365) or a target percentage of say 99 per cent.

Standard limitation of liability clauses which seek to reduce the liability of the hosting service provider in respect of the services should be provided. It will be enforceable subject to applicable legal restrictions.

Should it be necessary for the hosting provider to utilise any third party software in providing hosting services, the client should ensure that the responsibility to obtain the necessary permissions is set out in the agreement.

Whilst the hosting provider is to provide the servers, data room and other equipment necessary for the provision of hosting services, it is the client's responsibility to ensure that the client provides and has access to the basic equipment allowing access to these hosting services.

It is not unusual for an online conduct policy or acceptable use policy to be in use and incorporated into the agreement.

The extent of any warranties given by the parties will depend on the significance and value of the agreement and the parties' respective bargaining positions. Generally, the hosting provider will seek to minimise the extent of any warranties given. The client should seek to resist this position and insist on reasonable warranties.

The service provider should provide for matters beyond its control. Such a clause should specifically include power shortage and access to the internet as force majeure events.

Some Key Definitions

'Additional Services' means any other services other than the Services agreed to be provided by the Service Provider to the Client on agreed terms and set out as such in the Services Sheet.

'Charges' means the Service Provider's charges [as set out on the Charges Sheet or the Conditions and] from time to time for the provision of the Services unless otherwise expressly agreed with the Client and specified in the Contract.

'Web Space' means the agreed amount of space including an allocation of storage space on a web server together with applicable bandwidth allocation.

'Documents' includes, in addition to a document in writing, any map, plan, graph, drawing or photograph, any film, negative, tape or other device embodying visual images, and any disc, tape or other device (electronic or otherwise) embodying any other data.

'Client Material' means any Documents or other materials, and any data or other information, provided by the Client relating to the Services;

'Services' means the [web design/development] [Hosting] [and maintenance] services to be provided by [the Service Provider] for the Client and set out in the Services Sheet (and the 'Services' shall include the Additional Services where the context admits).

'Term' means the period from the start date to the end date (being and including the minimum or initial period) for the provision of the Services as set out in the Contract and continuing thereafter in full force and effect unless terminated in accordance with the provisions of these Conditions.

'Plan' means the plan set out in Annex [ ] specifying the function and timetable for the delivery of the Services and includes any updates on a regular basis by mutual agreement between the parties.

'Intellectual Property' means all intellectual property rights anywhere in the world (including present and future intellectual property rights) relating to any Confidential Information, business names and logos, copyright, database rights, patents, trade or service marks, designs, software, computer data, generic rights, software programs and source code and all variations, modifications or enhancements to each of them together with any application or right to apply for registration or protection of those rights.

'Internet' means the global computer network comprising of interconnected networks using a standard set of rules that regulate the manner of transmission of data.

Specific Provisions

Pre-existing Rights
Any pre-existing or other Intellectual Property rights owned by either party and required for the performance by the other party of its obligations under this Agreement or the use of the Website by the Client shall be licensed to that other party on a non-exclusive, irrevocable, royalty-free basis for the period during which the use of those rights by that party pursuant to this Agreement is required.

Services
The Client pursuant to the Contract engages the Service Provider to provide the Services to the Client and the Service Provider agrees to provide the Services for the Term upon the terms and subject to the conditions of the Contract.

Provision of Materials
Unless otherwise agreed by the parties in writing, the Client shall at its own expense supply the Service Provider with all necessary Documents or other materials, and all necessary data or other information relating to the Services, within sufficient time to enable the Service Provider to provide the Services in accordance with the Contract. The Client shall ensure the accuracy of all Client Material and clarity of any instructions.

Third Party Suppliers
The Service Provider does not warrant, guarantee or undertake on behalf of any third party supplier or service provider that access to any facilities or any products or services will be uninterrupted or of any particular level of availability or quality.

Charges
The Service Provider Charges are due and payable in advance on the [first business working day of each month]. The web pages are deemed to be delivered once the templates are completed and activated upon the Service Provider server for population with data, copy and imagery. Advertising the pages to web search engines and updating occur only after the site has been populated and the first payment is made.

Independent Contractor
The Client is engaging the Service Provider as an independent contractor for the specific project of developing and/or improving a world wide website to be installed on the Client's web space on a Service Provider's hosting computer. The Client hereby authorises the Service Provider to access the Client's current web hosting account and authorises the web hosting service to provide the Service Provider with access and '*write permission*' for the Client's web page directory and any other directories or programs which need to be accessed for this project.

Timing
In the absence of a timetable agreed by both the Service Provider and the Client and attached to the Contract, if the Client does not supply the Service Provider with complete text and graphic content for all web pages contracted for within the specified time and in any event no later than [six] weeks after the date the Contract was signed, the monthly lease amounts set out in the Contract remain due and payable. If the Client has not submitted or entered complete text and graphic content within [   ] months of the signing of this Contract, the term of this Contract will be extended by one month for each and every subsequent month that passes.]

Liability
The Service Provider shall have no liability to the Client for any loss, damage, costs, expenses or other claims for compensation arising from any Client Material or instructions supplied by the Client which are incomplete, incorrect, inaccurate, illegible, out of sequence or in the wrong form, or arising from their late arrival or non-arrival, or any other fault of the Client.

Indemnity
Each party ('the first party') indemnifies and undertakes to keep indemnified the other party, its officers, employees and agents ('the second party') against any loss, damage, liability, costs or expenses (including the cost of any settlement) arising out of any claim, action, proceeding or demand that may be brought, made or prosecuted against the second party by any person or arising out of or as a consequence of an unlawful or negligent act or omission of the first party, its officers, employees or agents in any way connected with this Agreement whether arising from any failure by the first party to comply with the terms of this Agreement, infringement of any Intellectual Property rights or otherwise.

Data Protection
The Service Provider agrees and warrants to the Client that it will at all times comply with the provisions and obligations imposed by the Data Protection Act 1998 including the storing and processing of personal data and all personal data acquired by it. The Designer agrees to indemnify the Client in respect of any loss, damage, liability, costs or expenses incurred by the Client by reason of the unauthorised disclosure of personal data or any breach of the Data Protection Act 1998.

Appendix 7.1 Web Development/Hosting Agreement Checklist

In preparing a web development/hosting agreement, individuals or businesses should consider the following non-exhaustive matters.

Actions/Issues: **Comments:**

1 Ascertain and review the nature and proposed arrangements for the website development and hosting between the parties to the agreement.

2 Recite background, parties' service requirements, existing agreements and relevant proposed arrangements in the introductory paragraphs.

3 Consider in general the proposed parties' details, setting out the names and addresses of all parties including registration details if corporate or incorporated party.

4 Set out and define relevant terms. Consider:

   4.1 confidential information;

   4.2 consultant, designer;

   4.3 design services, hosting services, services;

   4.4 intellectual property, materials;

   4.5 server, client content, excusable downtime;

   4.6 web page, website, web space.

5 Ascertain, consider and indicate arrangements in respect of the services to be provided. Detail:

   5.1 nature of services to be provided;

   5.2 whether design only or design and hosting;

   5.3 whether changes to the services can be made unilaterally or agreed in writing by the designer or service provider;

   5.4 whether time will be of the essence in the performance of the service provider's obligations;

   5.5 relevant duration of the services;

Commercial Contracts Checklists

    5.6   applicable service specification; ☐

    5.7   relevant equipment or server specification or requirements; ☐

    5.8   agreed timetable; ☐

    5.9   responsibility for providing specification. ☐

6   The applicable charges and fees should be considered and specified including: ☐

    6.1   required deposit payment; ☐

    6.2   initial pre-payment fees; ☐

    6.3   invoicing arrangements and frequency; ☐

    6.4   fees as exclusive of VAT; ☐

    6.5   right to default interest rate at specified rate for late payments; ☐

    6.6   any sum to be reserved pending release after warranty or retention period; ☐

    6.7   any rights of set off, deduction or withholding; ☐

    6.8   changes in fees; ☐

    6.9   instalmental or milestone payments; ☐

    6.10   payment currency ☐

    6.11   right to exercise lien over client's materials, data and documents for non-payment; ☐

    6.12   liability for additional sums; ☐

    6.13   liability and reimbursement of expenses or service related disbursements; ☐

    6.14   terms of payment. ☐

7   Detail the client's obligations under the agreement: ☐

Internet and E-Commerce Contracts

7.1   provide written specification; ☐

7.2   indemnify the consultant/service provider against liability as a result of the client's breach; ☐

7.3   include specified acknowledgement on website; ☐

7.4   grant of licence to publicly display site for specified period; ☐

7.5   to obtain and maintain appropriate insurance; ☐

7.6   supply required materials and data; ☐

7.7   ensure accuracy of all programs or information supplied; ☐

7.8   retain duplicate copies of materials; ☐

7.9   insure against loss or damage; ☐

7.10 afford the service provider access to its information records; ☐

7.11 responsibility for its web content and compliance with law; ☐

7.12 obtaining and maintaining all permissions and consents for its works; ☐

7.13 responsible for backing up its own files ☐

7.14 provide up to date address, contact and service details; ☐

7.15 acknowledge no warranty of response rate or download time; ☐

7.16 acknowledge the nature and risks of the internet ☐

7.17 display of warnings to inappropriate material; ☐

7.18 provide requested information and respond to communications promptly; ☐

7.19 provide clear instructions to the service provider in relation to its requirements from time to time; ☐

7.20 co-operate and liaise with service provider and its representatives; ☐

391

Commercial Contracts Checklists

    7.21   pay fees and/or any default interest promptly. ☐

8   As to the service provider's rights and obligations, consider: ☐

    8.1   right to make changes to the design or other service; ☐

    8.2   compliance with legislation; ☐

    8.3   right to make amendments or prepare derivative works; ☐

    8.4   right to decide number or which employees provide the services; ☐

    8.5   ownership of copyright to assembled work; ☐

    8.6   ability to alter services for safety, security or legal compliance; ☐

    8.7   acknowledgement of independent contractor status; ☐

    8.8   quality of deliverable; ☐

    8.9   right to remove client's website from server in relation to complaints or allegations of offending material; ☐

    8.10   use reasonable endeavours to perform the development, design or hosting services; ☐

    8.11   no warranty that access to server or website will be uninterrupted or error free; ☐

    8.12   provide client with password and identification without liability; ☐

    8.13   right to suspend access or move site in certain circumstances; ☐

    8.14   ability to vary or increase charges for specified reasons; ☐

    8.15   right to amend standard service provision terms. ☐

9   Ascertain and set out the duration of the contract. Consider and indicate: ☐

    9.1   any minimum periods of the contract; ☐

    9.2   whether terminable by notice. ☐

10 Will any warranties be given? Consider and set out warranties as applicable:

    10.1 right to enter into agreement; ☐

    10.2 that all consents and authorisations have been obtained; ☐

    10.3 that services will be provided with reasonable skill and care; ☐

    10.4 ownership of domain names; ☐

    10.5 ownership of materials and data supplied ☐

    10.6 compliance with specification; ☐

    10.7 availability of the service provider's equipment and server; ☐

    10.8 that the website is virus free; ☐

    10.9 no third party rights infringement; ☐

    10.10 fitness for purpose; ☐

    10.11 level of security; ☐

    10.12 functionality of equipment. ☐

11 Review and provide for: ☐

    11.1 authorisation to use materials or data provided; ☐

    11.2 indemnity for non-compliance with obligations; ☐

    11.3 maintenance requirements or obligations and applicable hourly rate; ☐

    11.4 additional charges; ☐

    11.5 completion date and acceptance of final product; ☐

    11.6 applicable timetable; ☐

14.5   in the event of a conflict of interest; ☐

14.6   in the event of occurrence of insolvency related matters; ☐

14.7   upon occurrence of material adverse event; ☐

14.8   in the event of prejudicial conduct. ☐

15 Set out provisions: ☐

15.1   relating to liability and payment of liquidated damages; ☐

15.2   specified percentages of uptime for hosting services; ☐

15.3   back ups and security; ☐

15.4   for non-disclosure of confidential information; ☐

15.5   transfer of website to a new, different or updated server; ☐

15.6   service of notices under the agreement; ☐

15.7   arrangements for consultancy or additional services; ☐

15.8   maintenance and support of the website or server ☐

15.9   monitoring or recordings for training or quality control; ☐

15.10 severance of unenforceable provisions; ☐

15.11 provisions relating to any additional services; ☐

15.12 data protection notification and compliance; ☐

15.13 use of sub-contractors; ☐

15.14 project management obligations or arrangements; ☐

15.15 identification or use of key personnel; ☐

15.16 reporting and record keeping requirements; ☐

15.17 contract being the entire agreement between the parties; ☐

15.18 interpretation position in the event of conflict or ambiguity between provisions; ☐

15.19 non-waiver of rights by delay; ☐

15.20 exclusion of partnership or agency relationship between the parties; ☐

15.21 non-assignment of rights under contract; ☐

15.22 requirement for consent prior to undertaking certain matters; ☐

15.23 testing and acceptance; ☐

15.24 change control procedures; ☐

15.25 exclusion of third party rights to enforce agreement; ☐

15.26 applicable jurisdiction and governing law. ☐

See Precedent 7.1 on accompanying CD.

Commercial Contracts Checklists

7.2 Website Materials

Overview

Description of Agreement/Document

The agreements and documents forming the website materials will differ depending on the nature of the website. However, apart form a specifically tailored set of user terms, most websites should contain basic website materials for the protection of the website operator. The website terms set out the ownership rights of the website operator, grants a limited licence to users, sets out applicable restrictions and disclaims liability for certain content.

The basic website materials include copyright notice, contents disclaimer, privacy policy, data protection and security policies. In addition, where applicable a site should set out its policy on linking (as the law is unclear on the subject), a forums user participation and a conduct policy.

Practical Guidance/Issues List

The website operator should seek advice in respect of compliance with relevant legislation.

In addition, it may be that there are registrable trade marks which can be registered by the operator.

Apart from the registration of the relevant domain name, other intellectual property protection should be investigated.

The website materials need to be properly incorporated into any contract between the website operator and the site user. In effect, the site user should have the relevant materials brought to their attention prior to use. A prominent link on the home page may assist in bringing the material to the user's attention. Relevant incorporation is easier to achieve where there is a registration element to the site.

The operator's provision of a data protection or security policy is a legal requirement in relation to compliance with the Data Protection Act 1998. Such practice goes towards compliance with the legislation and requires the operator to take relevant action including maintenance of registration and data protection security measures.

Law/Compliance Requirement

E-commerce and the internet are heavily regulated. Operators need to comply with several statutes and regulations. In addition, there are various laws that impact upon the relevant activities. An operator may need to comply with the Data Protection Act 1998, various EU and National E-Commerce Regulations, advertising legislation and codes, the Consumer Protection (Distance Selling) Regulations 2000 and applicable European directives.

Specific Provisions

Copyright Notice
Unless otherwise expressly stated, copyright, database right or similar rights in all material presented on this Site (including graphical images, text, video clips, reprographics, sounds, demos, patches and other files) is owned, controlled or licensed by the Operator or its affiliates and is protected or covered by copyright, trade mark, intellectual property law and other proprietary rights.

You have limited permission to display, print or download extracts from these pages for your personal non-commercial and non-profit use only and you shall not be entitled to commercialise any such material in any way.

Disclaimer
We will not be liable for any damages (including, without limitation, damages for any consequential loss or loss of business opportunities or projects, or loss of profits) howsoever arising and whether in contract, tort or

otherwise from the use of or inability to use the Site, or any of its contents and materials, or from any action or omission taken as a result of using the Site or any such contents. In any event our liability for all damages and losses (including negligence) shall not in any circumstances exceed the amount paid by you, if any, for accessing this Site.

We make no warranty that the contents of the Site are free from infection by viruses or anything else which has contaminating or destructive properties and shall have no liability in respect thereof. You should note that certain links on the Site lead to resources located on servers maintained by third parties over whom we have no control and accordingly we accept no responsibility or liability for any of the material contained on those servers.

Forum User Rules
You are fully and solely responsible for your postings, messages, comments or discussions and accept liability for any resulting actions. The comments, postings and messages are opinions of the respective contributors or authors and do not necessarily reflect our opinions. We accept no responsibility for and make no representations relating to any messages, postings, comments and discussions. We do not confirm or represent the legitimacy, accuracy, reliability, correctness or currency of any data or postings entered by a user.

Data Security Policy
We control physical security in relation to the information and personal data that is contained at our facilities and restrict access to the site, buildings, computer rooms, office desk, technology areas, equipment and other facilities where unauthorised access by people could compromise our security.

Privacy Policy and Data Protection Statement
We may provide the data collected from you to members of our group companies [or other third party including our agents and contractors in connection with the service]. We will inform you prior to disclosing your information to any third party. If you can be identified from the information that is disclosed, then we will not disclose such information without prior notification to you and having obtained your permission to do so. You may inform us at any time not to pass on or share your personal information with any third parties.

Appendix 7.2 Website Materials Checklist

In preparing website materials, individuals or businesses should consider the following non-exhaustive matters.

	Actions/Issues:	**Comments:**	✎
1	Ascertain and review nature and proposed arrangements for the website.		☐
2	What is the proposed web business or practice?		☐
3	Are there any special compliance or regulatory issues that must be dealt with?		☐
4	Consider and upload the basic website materials having regard to whether standard information or transactional website.		☐
5	In relation to general or standard website materials, consider the following:		☐
	5.1 copyright notice;		☐
	5.2 contents disclaimer		☐
	5.3 user terms;		☐
	5.4 linking terms and conditions;		☐
	5.5 privacy and data protection policy;		☐
	5.6 security policy;		☐
	5.7 forums policy.		☐
6	In relation to the copyright notice, detail:		☐
	6.1 ownership of all copyright in all material on site;		☐
	6.2 limited permission for users to download pages;		☐
	6.3 any restrictions on use;		☐
	6.4 termination of permission;		☐

	6.5	that no other rights are granted.	☐
7	In relation to the contents disclaimer, provide that:	☐
	7.1	site contents are for general information;	☐
	7.2	no performance warranties given;	☐
	7.3	no responsibility for inaccuracy of materials;	☐
	7.4	no guarantee of freedom from viruses;	☐
	7.5	third party materials liability is excluded;	☐
	7.6	site terms may be updated or changed;	☐
	7.7	site is provided 'as is';	☐
	7.8	English law and jurisdiction apply.	☐
8	With regard to the user terms, specify as appropriate:	☐
	8.1	the use of the site;	☐
	8.2	access to parts of site;	☐
	8.3	compliance with policies;	☐
	8.4	exclusion and limitation of liability;	☐
	8.5	ownership of site contents and intellectual property rights;	☐
	8.6	right to terminate access to and use of site;	☐
	8.7	reference and link to all applicable policies;	☐
	8.8	contractual incorporation;	☐
	8.9	additional relevant provisions if e-commerce transactional site;	☐

Commercial Contracts Checklists

    8.10   governing law and jurisdiction.

9   As to the linking terms and conditions, consider and set out:

    9.1   grant of right to link to site;

    9.2   right to change linking terms;

    9.3   acceptance of terms by linking;

    9.4   ownership of all rights and restrictions on use;

    9.5   right to terminate licence to link;

    9.6   undertakings and obligations;

    9.7   acknowledgement that no proprietary right is granted;

    9.8   consent required for deep linking or framing;

    9.9   no liability for site owner;

    9.10   governing law and submission to jurisdiction.

10   Privacy and data protection policy should include provisions regarding:

    10.1   consent to collect information;

    10.2   what the information collected is used for;

    10.3   the information collected;

    10.4   whether the information is shared;

    10.5   details of entity with whom information is shared;

    10.6   right to opt out;

    10.7   right to request access to information or subject access;

10.8   measures taken to protect information; ☐

10.9   whether the policy creates contractual rights; ☐

10.10   use of cookies, information and explanation of meaning and workings of cookies; ☐

10.11   right to require correction of incorrect data; ☐

10.12   exclusion of liability; ☐

10.13   right to change and amend policy. ☐

11   The security policy can detail: ☐

    11.1   corporate commitment to data protection; ☐

    11.2   compliance with legislation; ☐

    11.3   appointment of compliance officer; ☐

    11.4   employee briefing on data protection importance and staff training; ☐

    11.5   physical security measures; ☐

    11.6   electronic protection methods; ☐

    11.7   control of access to personal data; ☐

    11.8   maintenance of continuity plans; ☐

    11.9   monitoring, detection and investigation of breaches; ☐

    11.10   no guarantee of security notwithstanding technical and organisational protective measures. ☐

12   A web forums policy applicable to the site should contain: ☐

    12.1   facility for discussion and email exchange; ☐

    12.2   indication that it forms part of the terms of site use; ☐

Commercial Contracts Checklists

    12.3   restriction on objectionable materials; ☐

    12.4   provision that user is solely responsible for postings and any legal liability; ☐

    12.5   availability of identification and email addresses; ☐

    12.6   exclusion of commercial use; ☐

    12.7   acknowledgement of inability to monitor all messages; ☐

    12.8   site owner's exclusion of liability; ☐

    12.9   owner's right to remove materials from site; ☐

    12.10 grant of licence to owner to use materials; ☐

    12.11 restrictions on spamming, impersonation and inaccuracy of postings; ☐

    12.12 indemnity in favour of site owner against loss or claim arising out of forum participation. ☐

13   Ascertain and note:

    13.1   ownership of domain name; ☐

    13.2   authorship or developer of website; ☐

    13.3   copyright content; ☐

    13.4   third party content, rights, trade marks or links; ☐

    13.5   trade mark registration; ☐

    13.6   use of meta-tags (key words embedded in a website's software); ☐

    13.7   database rights; ☐

    13.8   web design and development; ☐

    13.9   ownership of software; ☐

13.10 access to the internet; ☐

13.11 liability issues. ☐

See Precedent 7.2 on accompanying CD.

Commercial Contracts Checklists

7.3 Advertising Terms and Conditions/Agreement

Overview

Description of Agreement/Document

The agreement sets out the detailed arrangements between a company and its client for the provision of web advertising services. The contract may be in short form and refer to standard advertising terms and conditions. Whatever the form of agreement, it sets out the parties' rights, obligations and undertakings in connection with the required advertising services. The agreement sets out what services are to be provided, ownership rights and liability of the parties.

Practical Guidance/Issues List

Many contracts relating to advertising are informal arrangements simply documented by correspondence. To avoid or limit disputes, the arrangements between the parties should be set out clearly in a written contract.

The parties should ensure that ownership of any rights is expressly set out. This is particularly important in relation to intellectual property rights.

The codes of the Committee of Advertising Practice are a good starting point for ensuring compliance.

Ensure that any advertising or media agents enter into the contract as principal in relation to the legal arrangements.

The client should make provision for approving copy and layouts.

A fixed fee and payment structure can be negotiated for the client's benefit.

The client should resist any attempt at blanket exclusions of liability. In addition, any attempts to deprive the client of its intellectual property right entitlement should be resisted.

Law/Compliance Requirement

Web advertising is subject to significant legislation and local or international self-regulation codes. Certain advertisements are regulated and will require compliance with relevant legislation.

Some Key Definitions

'Advertising' means any advertising material or promotional material supplied by the Customer for transmission by the Internet from the Manager's Site (including without limitation advertising banners being electronic advertising whose dimensions and delivery format are agreed) that are placed on pages of the Manager's Site, customised links and sponsorship logo display.

'Fees' means the fees and charges payable by the Customer as set out in Schedule [1] or specified by the Manager from time to time.

'Internet' means the global computer network comprising interconnected networks using a standard set of rules that regulate the manner in which data is transmitted between computers.

'Manager Site' means [URL] or other website operated and maintained by or on behalf of the Manager.

'Promotion' means any promotion or promotional material supplied by a Customer for transmission on or by the Internet from the Manager's Site.

'Schedule' means the Schedule or Schedules (if any) to the Agreement in whatever form setting out the Fees, Required Format, Commencement Date, Services, Term and Notice Period (as the case may be).

'Services' means the services in respect of the Advertising, and any related services agreed to be provided by the Manager to the Customer pursuant to the Agreement, further details of which are set out in Schedule [2].

'Term' means the period from the Commencement Date for the agreed period (as specified in Schedule [1] or otherwise expressly by the Manager) for which the Advertising is to be placed until terminated in accordance with the Agreement.

Specific Provisions

Acceptance
The Manager may, without derogation from the warranties and obligations set out in clause [ ] above refuse or require to be amended any artwork, materials or copy for or relating to an Advertising so as to comply with the legal or moral obligations placed upon the Manager or the Customer or to avoid infringing a third party's rights or any statutory or regulatory requirements.

Services
In consideration of the payment of the Fees the Manager agrees to perform the Services in accordance with Schedule [2]. The Agreement shall apply to the provision of the Services to the exclusion of all other agreements and the Customer agrees that uploading of the Advertising on to the Manager's Site shall be deemed acceptance of the Agreement.

The Manager shall bear any and all costs of supplying, updating, owning and operating the Manager's Site. The Manager shall use reasonable commercial efforts to maintain the availability of the Manager's Site twenty four (24) hours per day, seven (7) days per week.

Payment Provisions
All sums due in respect of the Fees are exclusive of Value Added Tax or other applicable sales tax, for which the Customer shall be additionally liable. All sums due from the Customer which are not paid on the due date (without prejudice to the Manager's other rights under this Agreement) shall bear interest at the annual rate of [3%] over the prevailing base rate of [   ] Bank. Such interest shall accrue from the due date until payment is made in full.

Customer Responsibility
For the purpose and duration of the Advertising the Customer grants to the Manager a royalty-free, non-exclusive licence to use, publish and reproduce the Customer's name, logo, trade marks and brands to the extent necessary to enable the Manager to comply with its obligations under the Agreement.

Liability
The Manager accepts no responsibility for any mistakes or errors whatsoever that arise during the course of publication of any Advertising and will not be liable for any loss of copy, artwork, photographs, data or other materials which the Customer supplies to it and the Customer shall be responsible for retaining in its possession sufficient quality and quantity of such materials for whatsoever purposes it may require.

Indemnity
The Customer undertakes to the Manager that the Customer will, without prejudice to any other right of action which the Manager may have, at all times keep the Manager fully and effectively indemnified against any liability (which liability shall include, without limitation, all losses, costs, claims, demands, actions, damages, legal and other professional fees and expenses on a full indemnity basis) which the Manager may suffer or incur as a result of any Advertising, the infringement of any intellectual property rights of any third party, or by reason of any breach or non-fulfilment of any of the Customer's obligations in respect of the Agreement.

Commercial Contracts Checklists

Appendix 7.3 Advertising Terms and Conditions/Agreement Checklist

In preparing advertising terms and conditions/agreement, individuals or businesses should consider the following non-exhaustive matters.

Actions/Issues:		Comments:	☑
1	What is the nature of the proposed arrangements?		☐
2	Indicate parties' names and addresses including registered offices and numbers.		☐
3	Recite relevant information in the introduction including, as appropriate:		☐
	3.1 nature of client/customer's business;		☐
	3.2 details of the manager/service or content provider providing advertising space on its site;		☐
	3.3 precise nature of the client's requirement;		☐
	3.4 agreement to provide the services on the terms but subject to the conditions of the agreement.		☐
4	What needs to be defined? Consider relevant terms having regard to the nature of the service provision and:		☐
	4.1 advertising, advertiser;		☐
	4.2 client, customer, manager, buyer;		☐
	4.3 advertising materials, intellectual property;		☐
	4.4 affiliates, group;		☐
	4.5 internet, website;		☐
	4.6 promotion, promoter;		☐
	4.7 services, required format;		☐
	4.8 term, commencement date;		☐
	4.9 objectionable material, consequential loss;		☐

	4.10	publication, display.	☐
5	Payment provisions should be set out. Specify:		☐
	5.1	relevant amount of fees;	☐
	5.2	agreed rates or set charges;	☐
	5.3	payment structure;	☐
	5.4	payment dates;	☐
	5.5	commission arrangements;	☐
	5.6	additional fees;	☐
	5.7	invoicing arrangements;	☐
	5.8	VAT payment and liability;	☐
	5.9	default interest liability provisions for late payments.	☐
6	In relation to the services, specify:		☐
	6.1	provision of the services in consideration of fees;	☐
	6.2	exclusion of all other agreements;	☐
	6.3	acceptance of agreement by uploading advert.	☐
7	Consider obligations and undertakings from the client. Include as appropriate, warranties:		☐
	7.1	that advert complies with relevant legislation;	☐
	7.2	that contract is entered into as principal;	☐
	7.3	that materials comply with applicable codes;	☐
	7.4	that all required authority or consents have been obtained;	☐

Commercial Contracts Checklists

    7.5   as to completeness or accuracy of information supplied; ☐

    7.6   of non-infringement of third party rights; ☐

    7.7   relating to decency and honesty of advert; ☐

    7.8   as to non-inclusion of offensive or objectionable material; ☐

    7.9   that written approval has been for regulated advertisements from relevant authority; ☐

    7.10   of authority to enter into agreement. ☐

8   Parties obligations should include: ☐

    8.1   customer's provision of information in required format; ☐

    8.2   maintenance of site; ☐

    8.3   liability for relevant costs; ☐

    8.4   service provider's right to make necessary changes; ☐

    8.5   indemnity against third party claims; ☐

    8.6   checking accuracy of adverts; ☐

    8.7   grant of licence to use client's logo, copyrights, database and trade marks. ☐

9   Arrangements for acceptance of the advertising and performance of the services. Indicate service provider's right to:

    9.1   remove advertising from the site for breach or illegality; ☐

    9.2   refuse advert; ☐

    9.3   require amendment of materials; ☐

    9.4   decline to publish; ☐

    9.5   restrict access in or from territories where material may be unlawful; ☐

9.6 change prominence or positioning of advert. ☐

10 For the avoidance of doubt, set out intellectual property ownership provisions. Consider: ☐

    10.1 who retains right in content of relevant sites; ☐

    10.2 who retains all other intellectual property rights; ☐

    10.3 customer's right to the advertising and attendant rights; ☐

    10.4 rights and ideas developed during provision of services; ☐

    10.5 indemnities for third party infringement claims or other loss. ☐

11 Duration of the arrangements and term of the agreement should be specified. Who can terminate, when and for what? Consider: ☐

    11.1 term of the agreement; ☐

    11.2 termination:

        11.2.1 by service provider for failure to pay on due date; ☐

        11.2.2 by service provider for failure to perform by client; ☐

        11.2.3 for inaccuracy of warranties or representations; ☐

        11.2.4 for breach of applicable law; ☐

        11.2.5 for prejudicial conduct or conflicts of interest; ☐

        11.2.6 for false representations or warranties; ☐

        11.2.7 for material breach; ☐

        11.2.8 on insolvency or related events by either party. ☐

12 As to liability, consider: ☐

    12.1 non-exclusion for personal injury or death; ☐

Commercial Contracts Checklists

12.2 liability for misrepresentation; ☐

12.3 non-exclusion of liability for fraudulent misrepresentation; ☐

12.4 limiting total liability of service provider to fixed sum; ☐

12.5 mutual exclusion of liability for consequential loss; ☐

12.6 liability for publication mistakes and errors; ☐

12.7 loss of copy or other materials. ☐

13 Indemnity provisions where applicable should be included for specific breach or issues. Consider infringement of third party rights, claims and non-performance of obligations under the agreement. ☐

14 Will the service provider require force majeure provisions protection for delays? Will it include notification obligations and right to terminate? ☐

15 Consider and insert provisions relating to: ☐

15.1 confidentiality undertakings and non-disclosure; ☐

15.2 data protection compliance; ☐

15.3 third party enforcement rights exclusion; ☐

15.4 assignment of the agreement; ☐

15.5 governing law and jurisdiction; ☐

15.6 alternative dispute resolution procedure; ☐

15.7 severance of unlawful or unenforceable provisions; ☐

15.8 non-waiver by delay; ☐

15.9 entire agreement between the parties; ☐

15.10 cancellation rights; ☐

15.11 acknowledgements that no guarantees as to usage statistics; ☐

15.12 fact of no partnership or agency between parties; ☐

15.13 time being of the essence; ☐

15.14 further assurance. ☐

See Precedent 7.3 on accompanying CD.

Commercial Contracts Checklists

7.4 Affiliate Program Services Agreement

Overview

Description of Agreement/Document

The affiliate program services agreement details the contractual arrangements between a service provider/site operator and a member.

The contract grants membership to the member of the program and indicates the obligation to establish relevant links to the operator's web site for the agreed purpose. Such a purpose normally relates to the sale of goods and services with reference to the links provided. The arrangements include the payment of commission based on the net sales of relevant products.

The agreement also details the parties' respective obligations, relevant undertakings, grant of licence and ownership of rights.

Practical Guidance/Issues List

The member should ensure that the contract adequately sets out the agreement.

The right to terminate the contract should arise in the event of any unacceptable changes to the terms and conditions.

The member should also resist any wide indemnity provisions in favour of the site operator.

Any rights to use intellectual property granted to either party should terminate on breach or termination of the contract.

Care needs to be taken in agreeing relevant restrictions. Such restrictions may be unenforceable or enforceable only to the extent considered reasonable by the courts. In certain cases, the restrictions will be subject to scrutiny under competition law.

The agreement can be set out informally or in letter form. Where there is no consideration, the contract should be executed as a deed.

Some Key Definitions

'Affiliate(s)' means all members of the Program from time to time.

'Net Sales' means the total amount of money actually charged and paid to and received by the Operator in respect of the Operator Products bought directly from the Operator Site by New Customers only, less any shipping, handling and similar charges, discounts, mark downs, sales tax, value added tax or similar taxes, duties (including, without limitation, import and export duties), bad debt and credit card fraud, and credits for returns.

'Operator Products' means any product or service that is available for purchase through the Operator Site from time to time.

'Links' means the graphic and/or textual links provided by Operator to the Member from time to time pursuant to the Contract.

'New Customers' means customers who (i) are first redirected to the Operator Site via a Link displayed on the Member's Site; and (ii) register their details in order to open an Operator account through the Operator Site pursuant to such redirection; and (iii) are not Existing Customers at the date of such registration.

'Existing Customers' means Customers who have made one or more purchases (including, without limitation, by means of the Operator Site or Operator catalogues, in Operator stores or in any other way whatsoever) of any products or services generally sold by the Operator.

'Losses' means all losses resulting from any and all claims, actions, demands, liabilities, losses, damages, judgements, settlements, costs and expenses (including legal fees and costs).

'Licensed Materials' means the Operator's Links, logos, trade names, trademarks and similar identifying material supplied by Operator;

Specific Provisions

Program
This Contract is entered into between the parties for the grant to the Member of a [renewable] licence and membership by the Operator in respect of participation by the Member in the Operator's Affiliate Program ('the Program') and the establishment of links to the Operator Internet web site located at URL [www.   .co.uk] ('the Operator Site') from the Member's Internet web site ('the Member's Site') as detailed [overleaf/below] in the Contract Schedule subject to the provisions of the terms and conditions ('the Conditions').

Contract
The Operator and the Member agree to be bound by the Conditions and this Contract in respect of the membership and participation of the Member in the Program and the supply of the graphic and/or textual links by the Operator to the Member which together with any other documents (signed and attached hereto by the parties) as listed below shall form part of this Contract.

Links
The Operator will make available to the Member a variety of Links which, subject to these Conditions, may be displayed as often and in as many areas of the Member's Site as the Member desires, provided that the Links are displayed prominently in relevant sections of the Member's Site.

Commission
The Operator agrees to pay the Member the Commission as set out in the Contract Schedule provided always that such Commission shall only be payable on Net Sales to New Customers generated initially via the Links, provided further that no Commission will be payable in respect of any Net Sales attributable to any New Customer after the expiry of a period of [twelve (12)] months from the date on which such New Customer first registered its details with Operator through the Operator Site.

Operator's Obligations
The Operator shall have the sole right and responsibility for processing every order for Operator Products, for tracking the volume and amount of sales of Operator Products generated by the Member's Site, and for providing sales statements and reports.

Licences
The Operator hereby grants to the Member a non-exclusive, non-transferable, revocable right to use (i) the Links and (ii) Operator logos, trade names, trademarks and similar identifying material supplied by Operator (but only in the form(s) that they are provided by Operator and solely in connection with the Links) (collectively, the 'Licensed Materials'), for the sole purpose of marketing the Operator Site through the Member's Site and solely in accordance with these conditions.

Representations and Warranties
The Operator makes no express or implied warranties or representations whatsoever to the Member with respect to the Program, the Operator Web Site, the amount of Commission that may be received or any of the Operator Products. Operator will not be liable for the consequences of any interruptions or errors in respect of the Operator Site.

Appendix 7.4 Affiliate Program Services Agreement Checklist

In preparing an affiliate program services agreement or letter, individuals or businesses should consider the following non-exhaustive matters.

Actions/Issues:	Comments:	✍

1 Review the nature and proposed arrangements for affiliate program services between the parties to the agreement. ☐

2 In the introductory paragraphs, consider reciting background, parties' intentions, establishment of links to web sites, type of business and proposed arrangements. ☐

3 Consider in general the proposed affiliate services, program membership and parties' details. ☐

4 Set out parties' details including: ☐

    4.1 names and addresses of all parties; ☐

    4.2 corporate registration details (if corporate or incorporated party); ☐

    4.3 contact person's details; ☐

    4.4 parties' other contact details (telephone, email, web site address and fax numbers); ☐

    4.5 parties' capacity and legal status; ☐

    4.6 invoicing and administration address; ☐

    4.7 agreement, membership and/or services commencement date; ☐

    4.8 affiliate services program name; ☐

    4.9 Parties' trading style. ☐

5 Consider short form contract with attached terms and conditions. ☐

6 The contract schedule or sheet should: ☐

    6.1 incorporate the terms and conditions; ☐

    6.2 grant licence or membership to member on contract terms; ☐

6.3 give details of member's site; ☐

6.4 state location of member's server; ☐

6.5 specify commission percentage; ☐

6.6 specify payment date, method and arrangements; ☐

6.7 contain postal and e-mail address for service of notices,; ☐

6.8 state duration of contract (contract commencement and expiry date); ☐

6.9 contain provisions for contract renewal by agreement and execution of contract schedule. ☐

7 Consider terms that require definition for ease of reference including: ☐

7.1 affiliate; ☐

7.2 commission; ☐

7.3 net sales; ☐

7.4 products; ☐

7.5 links; ☐

7.6 customers; existing customers; new customers; ☐

7.7 profit. ☐

8 As to the terms and conditions, consider and set out provisions relating to: ☐

8.1 interpretation and understanding of the conditions; ☐

8.2 the affiliate program and services; ☐

8.3 commission arrangements; ☐

8.4 site owner's obligations; ☐

Commercial Contracts Checklists

    8.5   member's undertakings and obligations; ☐

    8.6   parties' acknowledgements in respect of the program and services; ☐

    8.7   grant of relevant licences; ☐

    8.8   duration and termination of the services and agreement; ☐

    8.9   parties' representations and warranties; ☐

    8.10   Confidentiality and non-disclosure undertakings; ☐

    8.11   exclusion or limitation of liability arrangements; ☐

    8.12   indemnity provisions; ☐

    8.13   boilerplate clauses. ☐

9   With respect to the program, set out relevant details as appropriate including:

    9.1   grant of membership to member subject to terms; ☐

    9.2   agreement to pay commission; ☐

    9.3   restriction on sales of products; ☐

    9.4   restriction as to competitive promotion of products; ☐

    9.5   obligation to provide agreed prominent links to sites; ☐

    9.6   right to substitute links; ☐

    9.7   provision of sales information on periodic basis. ☐

10   What are the commission arrangements, set out:

    10.1   relevant percentage; ☐

    10.2   basis of calculation; ☐

10.3 exclusion of commission in respect of certain sales; ☐

10.4 invoicing and payment date or arrangements; ☐

10.5 VAT liability; ☐

10.6 default interest provision; ☐

10.7 adjustment of commission arrangements; ☐

10.8 rights of audit; ☐

10.9 rights of set off or withholding. ☐

11 Will site owner's obligations include: ☐

11.1 provision of required links to the relevant site? ☐

11.2 exclusion of uninterrupted access warranty? ☐

11.3 responsibility for processing orders and tracking volumes? ☐

11.4 provision of information and reports? ☐

11.5 customer services? ☐

11.6 ownership or sharing of customer database? ☐

11.7 compliance with law and applicable regulations? ☐

11.8 maintenance of data protection registration? ☐

11.9 compliance with and maintenance of data protection policies? ☐

11.10 provision of indemnity or other comfort for member? ☐

12 In relation to the member's obligations, consider undertaking to: ☐

12.1 maintain data protection policies; ☐

Commercial Contracts Checklists

    12.2   comply with applicable legislation; ☐

    12.3   notify Information Commissioner of uses of personal data; ☐

    12.4   allow access to its site for monitoring purposes; ☐

    12.5   not engage in prejudicial conduct; ☐

    12.6   act in good faith; ☐

    12.7   not use or interfere with site owner's sites; ☐

    12.8   not generate false memberships or sales; ☐

    12.9   not frame or use similar mechanisms or systems in relation to the owner's website; ☐

    12.10   be responsible for development and maintenance of its site. ☐

13   What licences are required, consider the grant of: ☐

    13.1   non-exclusive rights to use; ☐

    13.2   the right to use site owner's logos and marks for specified purpose; ☐

    13.3   right to use in specified format; ☐

    13.4   right with relevant restrictions and right to terminate; ☐

    13.5   right by member for use of its logos, copyright material and trade marks. ☐

14   Are there any applicable warranties and representations? Review and indicate relevant provisions: ☐

    14.1   as to ownership of relevant intellectual property rights; ☐

    14.2   warranties as to web site; ☐

    14.3   warranties in relation to affiliate program; ☐

    14.4   authority to enter into agreement; ☐

    14.5   right to grant licences under the contract. ☐

Internet and E-Commerce Contracts

  14.6 exclusion of specific warranties; ☐

  14.7 no liability for consequences of interruptions and errors on site. ☐

 15 Set out confidentiality undertakings including: ☐

  15.1 definition of what amounts to confidential information; ☐

  15.2 non-disclosure obligations; ☐

  15.3 maintenance of security obligations; ☐

  15.4 exclusions from confidentiality obligations; ☐

  15.5 provisions to survive termination. ☐

 16 As to liability, consider applicable exclusion and/or limitation of liability provisions. Review providing for: ☐

  16.1 non-exclusion of death and personal injury liability; ☐

  16.2 exclusion of consequential loss; ☐

  16.3 define what amounts to consequential loss including indirect or special damages; ☐

  16.4 liability cap by reference to commission paid. ☐

 17 Indemnity provisions should be considered: ☐

  17.1 will either party be required to indemnify the other: ☐

  17.2 what will the party be indemnified for? ☐

  17.3 extent of party and persons indemnified; ☐

  17.4 indemnity for liability incurred from third party claims; ☐

  17.5 indemnity for loss suffered as a result of breach. ☐

 18 How will the contract be terminated? Consider and set out: ☐

Commercial Contracts Checklists

    18.1   term of contract; ☐

    18.2   earlier termination rights; ☐

    18.3   termination by single or either party; ☐

    18.4   grounds for termination generally; ☐

    18.5   termination upon notice; ☐

    18.6   termination immediately following occurrence of certain events; ☐

    18.7   termination for insolvency, prejudicial conduct or conflicts of interest; ☐

    18.8   termination for non-payment of sums due; ☐

    18.9   termination for false warranties and representations. ☐

19   Consider and review general acknowledgements and provisions in relation to the services. ☐

20   Set out, as applicable provisions requiring:

    20.1   compliance with applicable regulations and laws; ☐

    20.2   procedure for amending the agreement; ☐

    20.3   resolution of disputes by alternative dispute resolution procedures (mediation, expert determination etc), arbitration); ☐

    20.4   relating to record keeping; ☐

    20.5   exclusion of partnership or agency; ☐

    20.6   third party rights enforcement to be excluded; ☐

    20.7   assignment to be with prior consent; ☐

    20.8   severance of unenforceable provisions; ☐

    20.9   contract and specified documents as the entire agreement between the parties. ☐

21 Consider and indicate: ☐

    21.1 governing law; ☐

    21.2 exclusivity or non-exclusivity of jurisdiction; ☐

    21.3 acknowledgement of forum and undertaking not to object; ☐

    21.4 appointment of agent for service, if necessary; ☐

22 Signature of affiliate services agreement or execution as a deed. ☐

See Precedent 7.4 on accompanying CD.

7.5 Promotion Agreement

Overview

Description of Agreement/Document

The promotion services agreement sets out the product, business or services promotion arrangements between a company and its client. The promotion can be through any medium including the internet by the provision of web promotion and advertising services. Such a promotion services contract comes in various forms. The parties may either have a short form agreement or a detailed written promotion relationship agreement. In any form, a properly prepared contract for the promotion of a business, service or product will detail the parties' rights, obligations and undertakings in connection with the required promotion services. The agreement will also set out provisions relating to the liability of the parties.

Practical Guidance/Issues List

The parties should consider the terms of any contract carefully, ensuring that obligations are set out clearly in relation to the service to be provided.

In addition, the parties should consider:
- standards requiring compliance;
- payment provisions tied to performance or milestones;
- prior approval in relation to certain matters;
- contribution to funding obligations;
- arrangements for promotion being funded out of commission, if applicable;
- inclusion of promotion in or by certain specified media;
- costs of promotional and marketing materials;
- responsibility for compliance with legislation and applicable promotion and sales codes;
- use of alternative dispute resolution mechanism or procedures;
- arrangements for return of materials at the end of promotion or termination of contract;
- agreeing the quality criteria for relevant materials;
- intellectual property rights ownership, restrictions and compliance issues.

The client whose product, service or business is being promoted may specifically consider restricting the promoter's rights or including standard exclusions of liability. In addition, the client should consider resisting:
- any attempts to deprive it of any of its intellectual property right entitlement;
- progress without approval of copy and layouts;
- blanket rates arrangement and agree a fixed fee;
- unreasonable payment structures;
- informal promotion and marketing arrangements to limit disputes;
- any non-binding arrangements between the parties and insist on terms being set out clearly in a written contract;
- entry into the contract as an agent by any advertising or media agents and insist they enter into the contract as principal in relation to the legal arrangements.

Law/Compliance Requirement

Web promotion and advertising is subject to significant legislation and local or international self regulation codes. The form and content of promotions and other marketing materials in the United Kingdom remains regulated by statute and the common law. In addition, promotions, advertising and marketing in the United Kingdom is subject to European Union regulation including EC directives.

A comprehensive system of regulation and self-regulation applies to marketing and promotions requiring compliance with various codes. Certain codes contain statutory obligations and others are purely voluntary. Promotions must comply with the British Codes of Advertising and Sales Promotion.

The Control of Misleading Advertisements (Amendment) Regulations 2000 may apply to relevant promotions and marketing. The following bodies also oversee promotions and marketing:
- Committee of Advertising Practice;
- Advertising Standards Authority;
- European Advertising Standards Alliance.

The regulation of a relevant promotion or marketing activity may depend on the sector or product. For example, financial services, tobacco and alcohol are all subject to specific regulations. Certain advertisements are regulated and will require compliance with relevant legislation or approval from an authority.

Some Key Definitions

'Business' means business-to-business infrastructure, know-how and services for the promotion and distribution of [insert details of business/product/service].

'Promotion' means any promotional material supplied by the Customer for transmission by the internet from the Promoter's Site (including without limitation promotional banners in specified electronic delivery format).

'Fees' means the fees and charges payable by the Customer as set out in the Schedule or specified by the Promoter from time to time.

'Internet' means that portion of the publicly available computer network or networks that is referred to in common parlance as the internet and/or the 'world wide web' (comprising interconnected networks using a standard set of rules that regulate the manner in which data is transmitted between computers) together with applicable extensions of the internet through proprietary networks such as mobile telephone networks and digital television networks.

'Permitted Use' means use by the Promoter in trade advertisements, announcements, communications and press releases, in each case in relation to the Promoter, whether in English or in local European languages provided always that such trade advertisements, announcements, communications and press releases have the prior written approval of the Customer (such approval to be given promptly within [ ] Business Days after written request by the Promoter.

'Services' means the services in respect of the Promotion, and any related services agreed to be provided by the Promoter to the Customer pursuant to the Agreement, further details of which are set out in Schedule [ ].

'Term' means the period from the Commencement Date for the agreed period (as specified in the Schedule or otherwise expressly stated by the Promoter) for which the Promotion is to be placed until terminated in accordance with the Agreement.

Specific Provisions

Promotion
The Promoter agrees to use its best commercial efforts to promote, market and advertise [the Products or Services] in the Territory and in particular will advertise and promote the Products and Services in the Territory in the [newspapers, magazines, radio, television, directories, pamphlets and other media it considers appropriate].

Brand Guidelines
In connection with the promotion of the [Products or Services] and use of the Customer's logos, trade marks and other intellectual property rights, the Promoter agrees to comply at all times with the Customer's Brand Guidelines as set out in [the Schedule].

Co-operation
The Customer undertakes to provide such assistance as may be reasonably required from time to time by the Promoter in connection with the promotion of the [Products or Services] and in particular agrees to co-operate with Promoter and its representatives in any promotions and marketing campaign, other special activity specified or engaged in by the Promoter as notified to the Customer from time to time.

Quality of Promotional Materials
All promotional, advertising and marketing materials used by or proposed to be used in connection with the promotion of [the Products or Services] shall at all times comply with all legal requirements in the Territory and [Party X] shall use its reasonable endeavours to ensure that such materials are not defamatory or otherwise unlawful.

Acceptance
The Promoter may, without derogation from the warranties and obligations set out in clause [10] above refuse or require to be amended any artwork, materials or copy for or relating to a Promotion so as to comply with the legal or moral obligations placed upon the Promoter or the Customer or to avoid infringing a third party's rights or any statutory or regulatory requirements.

Services
The Promoter shall bear any and all costs of supplying, updating, owning and operating the Promoter's Site. The Promoter shall use reasonable commercial efforts to maintain the availability of the Promoter's Site twenty-four (24) hours per day, seven (7) days per week.

Customer Responsibility
For the purpose and duration of the Promotion, the Customer grants to the Promoter a royalty-free non-exclusive licence to use, publish and reproduce the Customer's name, logo, trade marks and brands to the extent necessary to enable the Promoter to comply with its obligations under the Agreement.

Liability
The Promoter accepts no responsibility for any mistakes or errors whatsoever that arise during the course of publication of any Promotion and will not be liable for any loss of copy, artwork, photographs, data or other materials which the Customer supplies to it and the Customer shall be responsible for retaining in its possession sufficient quality and quantity of such materials for whatsoever purposes it may require.

Appendix 7.5 Promotions Agreement Checklist

In preparing promotions agreements, individuals or businesses should consider the following non-exhaustive matters.

	Actions/Issues:	Comments:	☐

1 What is the nature of the proposed arrangements? ☐

2 Indicate parties' names and addresses including registered offices and numbers. ☐

3 Recite relevant information in the introduction including, as appropriate: ☐

   3.1 nature of client/customer's business; ☐

   3.2 details of the Promoter/service or content provider providing promotion and marketing space on its site; ☐

   3.3 precise nature of the client's requirement; ☐

   3.4 agreement to provide the services on the terms but subject to the conditions of the agreement. ☐

4 What needs to be defined? Consider relevant terms having regard to the nature of the service provision and: ☐

   4.1 Client, customer, promoter, buyer; ☐

   4.2 promotional materials, intellectual property, intellectual property rights; ☐

   4.3 affiliates, group; ☐

   4.4 internet, web site; ☐

   4.5 promotion, promoter; ☐

   4.6 services, required format; ☐

   4.7 term, commencement date; ☐

   4.8 unlawful material, consequential loss; ☐

   4.9 publication, display. ☐

5   Payment provisions should be set out. Specify: ☐

    5.1   relevant amount of fees; ☐

    5.2   agreed rates or set charges; ☐

    5.3   payment structure; ☐

    5.4   payment dates; ☐

    5.5   commission arrangements; ☐

    5.6   additional fees; ☐

    5.7   invoicing arrangements; ☐

    5.8   VAT payment and liability; ☐

    5.9   default interest liability provisions for late payments. ☐

6   In relation to the services, specify: ☐

    6.1   provision of the services in consideration of the fees; ☐

    6.2   exclusion of all other agreements; ☐

    6.3   acceptance of agreement by uploading advert. ☐

7   Consider obligations and undertakings from the client. Include, as appropriate, warranties: ☐

    7.1   that advert complies with relevant legislation; ☐

    7.2   that the contract is entered into as principal; ☐

    7.3   that materials comply with applicable codes; ☐

    7.4   that all required authority or consents have been obtained; ☐

    7.5   as to completeness or accuracy of information supplied; ☐

7.6 of non-infringement of third party rights; ☐

7.7 relating to decency and honesty of advert; ☐

7.8 as to non-inclusion of offensive or objectionable material; ☐

7.9 that written approval has been for regulated advertisements from relevant authority; ☐

7.10 of authority to enter into agreement. ☐

8 Parties obligations should include: ☐

8.1 customer's provision of information in required format; ☐

8.2 maintenance of site; ☐

8.3 liability for relevant costs; ☐

8.4 service provider's right to make necessary changes; ☐

8.5 indemnity against third party claims; ☐

8.6 checking accuracy of adverts; ☐

8.7 grant of licence to use client's logo, copyrights, database and trade marks. ☐

9 Arrangements for acceptance of the promotion and marketing and performance of the services. Indicate service provider's right to: ☐

9.1 remove promotion and marketing from the site for breach or illegality; ☐

9.2 refuse advert; ☐

9.3 require amendment of materials; ☐

9.4 decline to publish; ☐

9.5 restrict access in or from territories where material may be unlawful; ☐

9.6 change prominence or positioning of advert. ☐

Commercial Contracts Checklists

10 For the avoidance of doubt, set out intellectual property ownership provisions. Consider: ☐

    10.1 who retains right in content of relevant sites; ☐

    10.2 who retains all other intellectual property rights; ☐

    10.3 customer's right to the promotion and marketing and attendant rights; ☐

    10.4 rights and ideas developed during the provision of the services; ☐

    10.5 indemnities for third party infringement claims or other loss. ☐

11 Duration of the arrangements and term of the agreement should be specified. Who can terminate, when and for what? Consider: ☐

    11.1 term of the agreement; ☐

    11.2 termination: ☐

        11.2.1 by service provider for failure to pay on due date; ☐

        11.2.2 by service provider failure to perform by client; ☐

        11.2.3 for inaccuracy of warranties or representations; ☐

        11.2.4 for breach of applicable law; ☐

        11.2.5 for prejudicial conduct or conflicts of interest; ☐

        11.2.6 for false representations or warranties; ☐

        11.2.7 for material breach; ☐

        11.2.8 for insolvency or related events by either party. ☐

12 As to liability, consider: ☐

    12.1 non-exclusion for personal injury or death; ☐

    12.2 liability for misrepresentation; ☐

12.3 non-exclusion of liability for fraudulent misrepresentation; ☐

12.4 limiting total liability of service provider to a fixed sum; ☐

12.5 mutual exclusion of liability for consequential loss; ☐

12.6 liability for publication mistakes and errors; ☐

12.7 loss of copy or other materials. ☐

13 Indemnity provisions where applicable should be included for specific breaches or events. Consider infringement of third party rights, claims and non-performance of obligations under the agreement. ☐

14 Will the service provider require force majeure provisions protection for delays? Will such provisions include notification obligations and right to terminate? ☐

15 Consider and insert provisions relating to:

15.1 confidentiality undertakings and non-disclosure; ☐

15.2 data protection compliance; ☐

15.3 third party enforcement rights exclusion; ☐

15.4 assignment of the agreement; ☐

15.5 governing law and jurisdiction; ☐

15.6 alternative dispute resolution procedure; ☐

15.7 severance of unlawful or unenforceable provisions; ☐

15.8 non-waiver by delay; ☐

15.9 entire agreement between the parties; ☐

15.10 cancellation rights; ☐

15.11 acknowledgements that no guarantees as to usage statistics; ☐

Commercial Contracts Checklists

15.12 fact of no partnership or agency between parties; ☐

15.13 time being of the essence; ☐

15.14 further assurance. ☐

See Precedent 7.5 on accompanying CD.